WHERE TO FIND FED
EVIDENCE IN TH

MW00451818

(continued on back endpaper)

EVIDENCE
HOW AND WHEN TO USE
THE RULES TO WIN CASES

Also by Edward T. Wright
How To Use Courtroom Drama To Win Cases (1987)

EVIDENCE

HOW AND WHEN TO USE THE RULES TO WIN CASES

Edward T. Wright, Esquire

PRENTICE HALL
Englewood Cliffs, New Jersey 07632

Prentice-Hall International (UK) Limited, *London*
Prentice-Hall of Australia Pty. Limited, *Sydney*
Prentice-Hall Canada, Inc., *Toronto*
Prentice-Hall Hispanoamericana, S.A., *Mexico*
Prentice-Hall of India Private Limited, *New Delhi*
Prentice-Hall of Japan, Inc., *Tokyo*
Simon & Schuster Asia Pte. Ltd., *Singapore*
Editora Prentice-Hall do Brasil, Ltda., *Rio de Janeiro*

© 1990 *by*
PRENTICE-HALL, Inc.
Englewood Cliffs, NJ

10 9 8 7 6 5 4 3 2 1

Library of Congress Cataloging-in-Publication Data

Wright, Edward T.
    Evidence : how and when to use the rules to win cases / Edward T. Wright.
      p. cm.
   ISBN 0-13-298852-6
    1. Evidence (Law)—United States. 2. Trial practice—United
States. I. Title.
  KF8935.W7 1990
347.73'6—dc20
[347.3076]   89-71118
                                      CIP

Printed in the United States of America

ISBN 0-13-298852-6

PRENTICE HALL
BUSINESS & PROFESSIONAL DIVISION
A division of Simon & Schuster
Englewood Cliffs, New Jersey 07632

This Book Is Dedicated To

My Parents
Denver M. and Mellie Mae Wright

My Wife
Susan R. Wright

My Children
Carol, Ed, Joan, Dory and Jeff

My Grandchildren
Jason, Rachel, June, Henry, Mellie Mae,
Missy, Joseph, Nathan, Willie, David,
Ashley, Sam, Julie and Becky

ABOUT THE AUTHOR

EDWARD T. WRIGHT has been a trial lawyer for forty years, involved in nearly every kind of criminal and civil litigation. He has devoted many years to the study and application of the law of evidence.

He now practices in Clearwater, Florida; formerly practiced in St. Louis County, Missouri; and is a member of the Illinois, as well as the Florida and the Missouri bar associations. Soon after graduating from law school at Mercer University, in Macon, Georgia, he was elected a municipal judge, becoming the youngest judge in Missouri.

He is author of several books, and his speeches and articles have appeared in more than forty journals and reviews. He was one of three judges appointed to draft rules of procedure for municipal courts.

His book, *How To Use Courtroom Drama To Win Cases,* Prentice-Hall, 1987, is used by trial lawyers throughout the world, and has been praised by leading trial lawyers. He is a popular lecturer among trial lawyers.

WHAT THIS BOOK CAN DO FOR YOU

Finally! A book that enables you, as a busy trial lawyer, to master the law of evidence by:

1. Learning thoroughly the Rules of Evidence and the law interpreting those rules;

2. Applying those rules to courtroom situations;

3. Acquiring the art of "speaking the language" and "instantly recalling" this area of law that constitutes a fascinating tool of the trial lawyer;

4. Extending this mastery of the rules from the federal courts into the courts of each state; and

5. Doing all this with a *"trial strategy"* that wins cases.

Learning rules is made easy by setting priorities. You cannot know every case interpreting every rule, but in this one book, you will find what you really need to know.

You can master the rules while learning them, and this is extremely important, since there is no time during trial for research. Some rules must be cited verbatim, and you must be familiar with all rules and know how to find them quickly.

In mastering the rules, you will learn to "speak the language." Certain phrases and certain concepts form the basis of the rules, and being able to use them with ease, tells the court you are prepared and are able to use the trial lawyer's most basic tools.

Memorizing every rule would accomplish little. It is the ability to apply each rule to a given set of facts that makes them useful. This book is full of examples and helpful hints that bring life to the rules.

In applying the rules, the use of trial strategy is imperative. Every rule can be applied one way or another. Every piece of evidence can either help or hurt your lawsuit. It is your duty to develop a talent for using the rules to your advantage.

TRIAL STRATEGY is highlighted throughout this book, because the author knows it is the basis for trying a lawsuit. It is the key to WINNING! Knowing the rules and the law interpreting the rules is important; applying the rules is important, but only for one reason. They enable you to develop a trial strategy.

The final chapter of this book brings together the state and federal law and the entire concept of the law of evidence as it has evolved during recent years. Through use of this book the busy trial lawyer can master the law and master the strategy that will win.

CONTENTS

> *See Federal Rules of Evidence*
> *Article One: General Provisions*

> **See Federal Rules of Evidence**
> **Article Two: Judicial Notice**

> **See Federal Rules of Evidence**
> **Article Three: Presumptions in Civil Actions and Proceedings**

> **See Federal Rules of Evidence**
> **Article Four: Relevancy and Its Limits**

CHAPTER 5   *Privilege Is A Right—Use It* 75

See Federal Rules of Evidence
Article Five: Privileges

CHAPTER 6   *Challenging Competency of Witnesses And Evidence* 85

See Federal Rules of Evidence
Article Six: Witnesses

CHAPTER 7   *How Lay And Expert Witnesses Can Help You* 99

See Federal Rules of Evidence
Article Seven: Opinions and Expert Testimony

> **See Federal Rules of Evidence**
> **Article Nine: Authentication and Identification**

> **See Federal Rules of Evidence**
> **Article Ten: Contents of Writings, Recordings and Photographs**

> **See Federal Rules of Evidence**
> **Article Eleven: Miscellaneous Rules**

1

GENERAL PROVISIONS

PROTECT YOUR APPEAL

KNOW THE RULES AND CITE THEM WITH AUTHORITY

SOLVING EVIDENCE PROBLEMS BEFORE TRIAL

SUBSTITUTES FOR EVIDENCE AND HOW TO USE THEM

See Federal Rules of Evidence:
Article One: General Provisions

KNOW THE RULES AND CITE THEM WITH AUTHORITY

SOLVING EVIDENCE PROBLEMS BEFORE TRIAL

SUBSTITUTES FOR EVIDENCE AND HOW TO USE THEM

GENERAL PROVISIONS

Sec. 1.01 General Provisions   Section 1.01 of the Federal Rules of Evidence provides that the rules apply in the U.S. District Courts, Bankruptcy Courts and before Magistrates. Sec. 1.02 provides that the rules should be construed "to secure fairness in administration, elimination of unjustifiable expense and delay, and promote the growth and development of the law of evidence to the end that the truth may be ascertained and proceedings justly determined."

The purpose and construction may be important to you as a trial lawyer. You should remind a trial judge that all rules must be construed with this purpose in mind.

TRIAL STRATEGY

In Arguing Construction of Any Rule, Argue

1. "Fairness."
2. "Unjustifiable expense and delay."
3. "Growth and development of the law of evidence."
4. "That the truth may be ascertained."
5. "Proceedings justly determined."

PROTECT YOUR APPEAL

Sec. 1.02 Make a TIMELY Objection   Rule 103(a) provides that "*error may not be predicated* upon a ruling which admits or excludes evidence unless *a substantial right of the party is affected, and . . .*"

(1) ". . . a timely objection or motion to strike appears of record, stating the specific ground of objection, if the specific ground was not apparent from the context; or

(2) . . . the substance of the evidence was made known to the court by offer or was apparent from the context within which questions were asked."

Rule 103(b) provides that the court may add statements showing the character of the evidence, the form in which offered, the objection and ruling, and "*it may direct the making of an offer in question and answer form.*"

You must make the objection "at the earliest possible opportunity" (*Saville v. U.S.,* 400 F.2d 397 [1st Cir. 1968]). Where the question was asked, "What did the doctor say to you?", hearsay was obviously called for, so the counsel waives any objection, if he or she does not object to the question.

TRIAL STRATEGY

Both "Objection" and "Motion to Strike" Must Be Timely

1. OBJECT to improper question.
    EXAMPLE: "What did he tell you?"
    "I object, your Honor, the question calls for hearsay."
2. MOVE TO STRIKE improper answer.
    EXAMPLE: "Did you see the car?"
    "No, but John told me it was demolished."
    "I move to strike the answer on grounds of hearsay."

The first opportunity to object was upon hearing the question. The first opportunity to move to strike is upon hearing the answer. NOT SEVERAL QUESTIONS LATER!

The court will not let you speculate as to answer; wait and hear it, then object if you don't like the answer. A lawyer tried that tactic the same year Lindbergh tried flying the Atlantic (*Lambert v. U.S.*, 26 F.2d 773 [9th Cir. 1928]). Lindbergh succeeded!

TRIAL STRATEGY

Before Trial—Make Certain Objections

1. Motions to Suppress.
    See Rule 12(b) and (f), Federal Rules of Criminal Procedure.
2. Motion re tainted out-of-court identification (*Wade v. U.S.*, 388 U.S. 218 [1967]).
3. Motion In Limine—to avoid prejudicial effect and unnecessary proof on rebuttal.
4. Objection to deposition; see Rule 32(c), Federal Rules of Civil Procedure.
5. Other matters that can be stipulated to or otherwise covered at pretrial.

RENEW OBJECTION AT TRIAL OR RISK LOSS OF POINT ON APPEAL (*Collins v. Wayne Corp.*, 621 F.2d 777 [5th Cir. 1980]). (*Contra: Sheeney v. Southern Pacific Transportation Co.*, 631 F.2d 649 [9th Cir. 1980]). ALSO: Judge may give more consideration to objection at trial, and evidence may change court's position, so renew offer or objection.

DON'T DEPEND ON APPEAL! The trial judge has much discretion, and winning at the trial level is imperative. You will not obtain a reversal if highly probable no substantial rights have been affected (*U.S. v. Bagley,* 772 F.2d 482 [9th Cir. 1985]).

OBJECTING TO "WHOLE LINE OF QUESTIONING":

(1)   NOT TIMELY, when made after several questions have been asked, and

(2)   NOT EFFECTIVE if objection not renewed when questions change (*Powell v. Burns,* 763 F.2d 671 [5th Cir. 1985]).

If you want a limiting instruction you must make a timely request (*U.S. v. Enstam,* 622 F.2d 857 [5th Cir. 1980]). Motion to strike must also be timely (*U.S. v. Marquardt,* 695 F.2d 1300 [11th Cir. 1983]). Failure to object to presence of F.B.I. agent, marshall, and law clerk in jury room during deliberations not fatal (*U.S. v. Freeman,* 634 F.2d 1267 [10th Cir. 1980]), BUT OBJECT IMMEDIATELY if sequester rule is being violated.

Sec. 1.03 State a Specific Ground   Rule 103(a) states specifically that you must declare:
"THE SPECIFIC GROUND OF OBJECTION."
Making the objection in time is about three-fourths of the "timely" and "specifically" requirements of Rule 103(a). This is because courts do not forgive tardiness as much as they do vagueness. Vagueness can be clarified, but tardiness means your objection is gone forever.

Though Rule 103(a) requires that the "specific ground" be stated, in real life it does not always work that way. Where counsel said, "I object," and court said, "Sustained," there was no error because judge immediately sustained and specific ground was apparent (*U.S. v. Commiskey,* 728 F.2d 200 [3rd Cir. 1983]).

TRIAL STRATEGY

1.   Object immediately.
2.   Be specific.
3.   Be ready to explain.

You must give the trial judge an opportunity to correct any error, but do not sit back in hope of getting a new trial (*Collins v. Wayne Corp.,* 621 F.2d 777 [5th Cir. 1980]). How specific must you be? Specific enough so the judge can correct any error he would otherwise make.

TRIAL STRATEGY

Narrow Toward Specificity

1. Specify major area of objection.
   EXAMPLE: Opinion.
2. Specify which part of that area of law is the basis of objection.
   EXAMPLE: "This witness is not qualified to give an opinion."
3. Explain why.
   EXAMPLE: "He is a doctor, but has no expertise in this field."

OBJECTING FOR THE WRONG REASON IS EQUIVALENT TO NOT OBJECTING AT ALL! *Common Mistakes:* Objecting on the grounds of relevancy in a *403 situation* is not a proper objection since Rule 403 begins, "Although relevant. . . ." Where counsel claims evidence is not offered to prove the truth of the matter asserted, your hearsay objection probably should have been a relevancy objection.

CITE RULES BY NUMBER! It is the trial judge's duty to know the rules by number, and it is certainly easier to refer to a "403 situation" than the "probative value of the evidence is substantially outweighed by the danger of unfair prejudice, confusion of the issues, or misleading the jury. . . ."

Include All Bases for Objection!

Example ―――――――――――――――――――――――――――――――――――――

"Did the janitor tell you why a similar furnace exploded?" This question is *leading, calls for hearsay, improper opinion,* and *"irrelevant."*

Be Specific as to Which Part of Question Is Objectionable!

Example ―――――――――――――――――――――――――――――――――――――

"Will you tell the jury how many times defendant violated the rule from January to July of this year?" "Objection, your Honor. Under the contract, Defendant is only responsible for violations after notice, and Plaintiff has admitted notice was given on April 1st, so any violation before April 1st would not be relevant."

"Relevancy" is an exception to the need for specificity, since it is the proponent who has the burden of showing why the evidence is relevant. It is, in fact, the only objection that survives the old meaningless, "irrelevant, incompetent and immaterial" kind of general objection. However, "irrelevant" is not sufficient where specificity is required (*U.S. v. Sandini,* 803 F.2d 123 [3rd Cir. 1986]).

It has been held that objection need be specific enough only to be "clear" (*U.S. v. Caputo,* 758 F.2d 944 [3rd Cir. 1985]). *Reason* on appeal must be same as *reason* at trial (*Reese v. Mercury Marine Div.,* 793 F.2d 1416 [5th Cir. 1986]). General objection, plus refusal to accept court offer of limiting instruction, waives objection (*Johnson v. Colt Industries Operating Corp.*, 797 F.2d 1530 [10th Cir. 1986]).

Counsel can rely upon co-party's objection to court ruling on evidence but not as to jury instructions (*Kenny v. Lewis Revel's Rare Coins Inc.*, 741 F.2d 378 [11th Cir. 1984]). Court can supplement record by explaining record, and can even explain what witness would have said had he or she been permitted (*Fidelity Savings & Loan Assoc. v. Aetna Life & Casualty Co.*, 647 F.2d 933 [9th Cir. 1981]).

Sec. 1.04 If Your Evidence Is Excluded, Make an Offer of Proof   Rule 103(a)(2) provides that:

> "In case the ruling is one excluding evidence, *the substance of the evidence was made known to the court by offer,* or was apparent from the context within which questions were asked."

TRIAL STRATEGY

Make Your Offer of Proof By

1. Requesting to make offer outside hearing of jury.
2. State what the witness would testify to.
3. Explain why the evidence should be admitted, including its relevancy.
4. Be ready to explain the law as it pertains to admissibility.
5. Be ready to read the offer into evidence.
   A. in narrative form or
   B. in question and answer form if
      (1) judge requests it
      (2) dramatic considerations or clarity suggests it
6. Make the offer.
7. Mark your "notes for appeal" file.

Appellate courts usually refuse even to hear argument re exclusion of evidence if proponent did not make an offer of proof (sometimes called a "proffer") (*U.S. v. Winkle*, 587 F.2d 705 [5th Cir. 1979]). However, failure to make offer was not fatal where trial court was "aware of general nature of evidence to be offered" (*Charter v. Chleboard*, 551 F.2d 2416 [8th Cir. 1977]).

Proponent must show *specifically* what the evidence will be (even where co-defendant raised it) (*U.S. v. Pugliese*, 712 F.2d 574 [2nd Cir. 1983]). Must cite *specific* rule under which evidence would be admissible (*Huff v. White Motor Corp.*, 609 F.2d 286 [7th Cir. 1979]). One court was divided over whether record was protected where not clear if report offered by Department of Transportation would show actual stopping distances at 60 MPH or merely inference from disputed skidmarks; majority holding relevancy point made, though none too succinctly (*Robbins v. Whelan,* 653 F.2d 47 [1st Cir. 1981]).

Make the offer in good faith, because court can require you to produce the writings and testimony (*Scotland County v. Hill,* 112 U.S. 183 [1884]). State every purpose, since a purpose not stated cannot be considered on appeal (*Foster v. Ford Motor Co.,* 621 F.2d 715 [5th Cir. 1980]).

MAKE YOUR RECORD Every part of the process of making an offer of proof should be made on the record. REMEMBER: You are, in effect, talking to the appellate court, not the trial court, and appellate courts hear only through the record.

The court has much discretion in handling a proffer and can even require that it be in writing (such as an expert opinion) (*Fidelity Savings & Loan Assoc. v. Aetna Life & Casualty Co.,* 647 F.2d 933 [9th Cir. 1981]). Prepare for appeal, but make the best offer possible to the trial judge who, for practical reasons, will probably be your last forum.

Sec. 1.05 Ask to Exclude Jury When Appropriate   Rule 103(c) provides that "to the extent practicable," proceedings shall be conducted as

> *"to prevent inadmissible evidence from being suggested to the jury by any means, such as making statements or offers of proof or asking questions in the hearing of the jury."*

TRIAL STRATEGY

When the Jury Hears What It Should Not Hear, You Run the Risk of

1. Having a good verdict reversed on appeal.
2. Having a good trial halted with a mistrial.
3. Turning the trial judge into one whose broad discretion may not be wielded in your favor.
4. Causing the jury to think you are being unfair, especially if the judge reprimands you in front of the jury.

A Simple "May We Approach the Bench, Your Honor?" Is the Professional Way of Handling the Problem.

It was held error for the judge to adopt a "no side bar" rule (*U.S. v. Ledesma,* 632 F.2d 670 [7th Cir. 1980]). The judge will decide whether to use a side bar conference or to excuse the jury from the courtroom. The latter is usually necessary where there are complex problems. There is nothing wrong with either counsel suggesting, "This may take a while, your Honor," since side bar conferences should be brief and as few as possible.

Sec. 1.06 Use PLAIN ERROR When All Else Fails Rule 103(d) provides:

"Nothing in this rule precludes taking notice of plain errors affecting SUB-STANTIAL RIGHTS although they were not brought to the attention of the court."

TRIAL STRATEGY

Since Plain Error Is Seldom Granted

1. Don't rely on it.
2. Use it only as last resort when appeal was not properly protected.
   A. argue justice
   B. pray!

The levels of error are: (1) harmless error, (2) reversible error, and (3) plain error. Plain error is reversible, but it has that characteristic of being so reversible that it cannot be let stand, even where counsel has not acted properly for his or her client.

In reviewing effect of prejudice, one court established these factors: (1) degree of initial prejudice, (2) effectiveness of corrective measures, and (3) importance of defendant's credibility in view of strategy of government's other evidence (*U.S. v. Semensohn,* 421 F.2d 1206 [2nd Cir. 1970]).

Even though prosecutor had told jury of conviction of defendant THAT DID NOT EXIST, court held there was no plain error, holding the strong case against defendant as the reason for their decision (*U.S. v. Georgalis,* 631 F.2d 1199 [5th Cir. 1980]). The "Plain Error" rule applies in civil cases but only where "exceptional circumstances" present (*Allied International, Inc. v. International Longshoreman's Assoc.,* 814 F.2d 32 [1st Cir. 1987]). It is more likely that the rule will be used in a criminal case, where the confrontation clause is so important (*U.S. v. Mouszin,* 785 F.2d 682 [9th Cir. 1986]). *Mouszin* applied plain error where there were "foundational deficiencies."

Plain error as a concept would be unnecessary if attorneys did their job adequately; inadequate representation in a criminal case is often the basis for plain error. Court found plain error where series of court-appointed attorneys had failed to object to hearsay evidence (*Government of the Canal Zone v. Pinto,* 590 F.2d 1344 [5th Cir. 1979]).

Inaccurate reference to defendant as "illegal alien" would obviously prejudice and was deemed plain error (*Rojas v. Richardson,* 703 F.2d 186 [5th Cir. 1983]). In criminal cases if there is "grave doubt" as to whether error had substantial influence, conviction must be set aside (*Kotteakos v. U.S.,* 328 U.S. 750 [1946]).

The more basic the right, the greater the chance plain error will be applied.

Example ──

Right to be present at trial (*Rushen v. Spain,* 464 U.S. 114 [1983]); improper comment on defendant's silence (*U.S. v. Hasting,* 461 U.S. 114 [1983]); violation of right to counsel (*Moore v. Illinois,* 434 U.S. 220 [1977]); fourth amendment violation (*Chambers v. Maroney,* 39 U.S. 42 [1970]).

HISTORICAL NOTE

> Plain error has been a part of American jurisprudence since the Bill of Rights was adopted. Its growth under the Warren Court in basic constitutional situations (such as right to counsel, and right to remain quiet), and the broadening into civil cases, has been reaffirmed by Rule 103(d).

The question is, "Did it really make a difference?" There was reversal where the evidence was "critical" (*Contractor's Utility Sales Co., Inc. v. Certadi-Tel Products,* 638 F.2d 1085 [7th Cir. 1981]). Deliberate comment re polygraph must be reversed, even though court told jury to disregard comment (*U.S. v. Murray,* 784 F.2d 188 [6th Cir. 1986]).

Reversal where "uncorroborated" identification (*Harris v. Wainright,* 760 F.2d 1148 [11th Cir. 1985]). Reversal where "must have been in forefront of jurors' minds" (*U.S. v. Ruffin,* 575 F.2d 346 [2nd Cir. 1978]). No reversal where exclusion of evidence would not necessarily result in an acquittal (*U.S. v. Brantley,* 786 F.2d 1322 [7th Cir. 1986]). The court can conduct an in-camera inspection (*U.S. v. Odom,* 736 F.2d 404 [4th Cir. 1984]). The court can defer ruling if based on substantial grounds (*U.S. v. Barletta,* 644 F.2d 50 [1st Cir. 1981]).

Court should require independent proof of conspiracy before admitting statement (*U.S. v. Reda,* 765 F.2d 715 [8th Cir. 1985]). Opening statement by accused's lawyer in prior trial admitted as admission where inconsistent statement was assertion of fact (*U.S. v. McKeon,* 738 F.2d 26 [2nd Cir. 1984]).

Court required to hold hearing before admitting an admission by silence (*U.S. v. Sears,* 663 F.2d 896 [9th Cir. 1981]). Films should be reviewed outside presence of the jury (*Brandt v. French,* 638 F.2d 209 [10th Cir. 1981]).

Sec. 1.07 Ask the Judge to Consider Everything (Even Inadmissible Evidence) When Making Preliminary Determination   Rule 104(a) provides that "PRELIMINARY QUESTIONS" concerning "**qualification of a person to be a witness,**" "**the existence of a privilege,**" OR "**the admissibility of evidence**" shall be determined by the court, and in so doing, "is not bound by the rules of evidence except those relating to privilege."

Rule 104(a) is subject to Rule 104(b), which provides:

> "When the relevancy of evidence depends upon the fulfillment of a condition of fact, the court shall admit it upon, or subject to, the introduction of evidence sufficient to support a finding of the fulfillment of the condition."

Rule 104(a) is one of the most important of all rules of evidence. It gives rise to the "104(a) HEARING," at which counsel can obtain a ruling.

In determining preliminary questions, the judge becomes the trier of fact. He or she may consider hearsay, and other inadmissible evidence, as long as the evidence is not privileged. Whether a child is competent to testify may depend upon what the child is saying, and whether or not a hearsay statement is against interest may be determined only after examining the hearsay statement.

A preponderance of evidence is usually required re co-conspirator statement (otherwise jury would find "guilt" in order to decide "admissibility,") but in all other preliminary questions, a prima facie showing will suffice. Courts constantly say the evidence goes to the weight, not the admissibility, if there is any good reason to admit the evidence.

Where perception is present under Rule 602, competency under Rule 601 is accepted if witness has *anything* that is probative. Expert evidence will be "competent" if Rule 702 is satisfied.

Rule 104(a) ends with the words, ". . . is not bound by the rules of evidence except with respect to privilege." This means attorney cannot be forced to give privileged testimony to determine if the statement is hearsay. It does not mean hearsay cannot be used to determine if a third party was present when statement took place between attorney and client—a determination necessary to the question of whether or not the communication was privileged.

TRIAL STRATEGY

In Arguing Preliminary Question of Competency, Privilege or Admissibility

1. Present
   A. need to admit and
   B. reliability of evidence or
   C. reason to exclude
      (1) unreliability and
      (2) prejudice

Use All Evidence Available, Including Inadmissible Evidence, in Arguing Your Point.

Ruling on qualification of witness is reversible only if "clearly erroneous" (*Garbincus v. Boston Edison Co.,* 621 F.2d 1171 [1st Cir. 1980]). If, however, irrelevant evidence is admitted that is prejudicial, such may warrant a reversal (*U.S. v. Cote,* 744 F.2d 913 [2nd Cir. 1984]).

Business records could not be admitted where court did not make finding of precondition of admissibility and no foundation laid (*In Re Fine Paper Antitrust Litigation,* 751 F.2d 562 [3rd Cir. 1984]). If court is unable to obtain stipulation re transcript, each party can present its version of tape recording and let jury decide (*U.S. v. Rengifo,* 789 F.2d 975 [1st Cir. 1986]).

Court erred in not letting all circumstances surrounding confession be given to the jury, including "psychological environment" (*Crane v. Kentucky,* 106 S. CT 2142 [1986]). A strictness applies in criminal cases that is not found in civil cases. In all cases, however, the court can exercise discretion.

Sec. 1.08 If You Want a Limiting Instruction, Present One to the Court

Rule 105 provides:

> *When evidence which is admissible as to one party or for one purpose, but not admissible as to another party or for another purpose is admitted, the court, UPON REQUEST, shall restrict the evidence to its proper scope and instruct the jury accordingly.*

TRIAL STRATEGY

Instructing Jury on Evidence During Trial May Result from

1. Court acting *sua sponte*:
   A. to avoid plain error Rule 103(d) or
   B. so **"the truth may be ascertained"** Rule 102 or
2. By counsel.
   Rule 105 clearly states **"Upon Request."**
   Don't wait for the judge to do your job!

Trial lawyers know too well that telling the jury to ignore what they have heard is what the Supreme Court of the United States has called "unmitigated fiction" (*Kruelwitch v. U.S.,* 336 U.S. 440 [1949]). That fiction is a challenge, however, and not an excuse for failing to accept responsibility.

You should object, make a proffer, move to strike, request instructions, and move for mistrial, when such action is appropriate. How convincingly you do this may turn a "fiction" into a "reality."

Example ——————————————————————————————————————

Fact that your client changed his testimony since deposition on minor point may be admissible re credibility, but of no substantive use. By requesting judge to give limiting instruction you accomplish two things:

1. You try to limit effect of the evidence at the very moment the jury hears the damaging evidence.
2. You set yourself up for summation:

   "You remember the judge instructed you that . . . and you will, of course, keep your oath and promise to follow the court's instruction."

TRIAL STRATEGY

Think in Terms of the Kind of Instruction You Want

1. Curative instruction.
   The court admonishes the jury to disregard improper evidence.
2. Limiting instruction.
   The court instructs the jury as to limited purpose or limited parties as to properly admitted evidence.
   IMPORTANT: When you request a limiting instruction have a proposed instruction ready to present to the judge.

Court held co-defendant's confession implicating defendant so prejudicial, it was as though there had been "no instruction at all" (*Bruton v. U.S.*, 391 U.S. 123 [1968]). Where DEA agent testified that a drug informant told him defendant was owner of certain marijuana, court held following limiting instruction (or any instruction) "INSUFFICIENT" to preclude jury from concluding defendant owned the marijuana:

> "Now ladies and gentlemen of the jury, I am going to allow him to tell us what the informant told him, not for the truth of what the informant said, but just to show why he did what he did after he received that information, and for that purpose only" (*U.S. v. Rodriguez*, 524 F.2d 485 [5th Cir. 1975]). HOWEVER, plain error did not rescue defendant, who failed to request limiting instruction (*U.S. v. Garcia*, 530 F.2d 650 [5th Cir. 1976]).

TRIAL STRATEGY

In Every Case Involving a Limiting Instruction, Argue Rule 403, Because Its Lack of Effectiveness May Cause

1. Unfair prejudice
2. Confusion of issues or
3. Misleading the jury

In Fact, Giving a Limiting Instruction May Be Like "Waving a Red Flag in Front of the Jury" (*Lakeside v. Oregon*, 435 U.S. 333 [1978]).

IMPORTANT: Limiting instruction may limit as to (1) purpose or (2) parties, but must be: (1) specific and (2) timely (*U.S. v. Thiron*, 813 F.2d 146 [8th Cir. 1987]).

Sec. 1.09 Ask for Immediate Presentation of That "Which Ought, in Fairness to Be Considered Contemporaneously"   Rule 106 provides:

"When a writing or recorded statement or part thereof is introduced by a party, an adverse party may require the introduction at that time of any other part or any other writing or recorded statement which ought in fairness to be considered contemporaneously with it."

TRIAL STRATEGY

Use Rule 106 to Require That the Whole Story Be Told Contemporaneously if Possible to Avoid

1. MISLEADING nature of the evidence.
2. INADEQUATE remedy by offering the rest of the story too late.

See Advisory Committee Notes on Rule 106.

Where one of four channels was offered into evidence re an air crash, all four channels were ordered to be considered at the same time, as "integral parts" of the story (*In Re Air Crash Disaster At JFK On June 24, 1975*, 635 F.2d 67 [2nd Cir. 1980]). The rule does not require introduction of portions that are either relevant or explanatory (*U.S. v. Soures*, 736 F.2d 87 [3rd Cir. 1984]).

TRIAL STRATEGY

In Arguing to Require "Rest of Evidence" Be Introduced Now, Show

1. "Fairness" requires it.
2. "Misleading" nature of evidence.
3. "Inadequacy" of later presentation of the evidence.
4. "Full significance" of evidence can be understood by jury if presented now.
5. "Rule of completeness" means jury entitled to hear complete part of story contemporaneously.

REMEMBER: Rule 106

1. DOES NOT limit right to wait for cross-examination.

2. DOES permit including in the "rest of" or "related papers" some evidence that may not otherwise reach the jury.

The Advisory Committee made it clear that Rule 106 only applies to written documents. Despite *Advisory Committee's Notes On Rule 106,* court may require introduction of additional testimony contemporaneously under Rule 611(a) (control by court over mode and order of interrogation and presentation). If the "related" or "rest of" the writing includes hearsay, admissibility is at discretion of trial judge (*U.S. v. Apuzzo,* 245 F.2d 416 [2nd Cir. 1957]).

NOW THE RULES AND CITE THEM WITH AUTHORITY

Sec. 1.10 The Need to Master the Rules "You simply do not understand the hearsay rule," is what a federal judge told a high-priced lawyer, in open court, in front of his client and others. Another federal judge told lawyers attending a seminar, "Don't walk into a courtroom unless you can cite certain rules of evidence verbatim and by rule number."

State and federal judges are becoming impatient with lawyers who claim to be trial lawyers, but who haven't reached the basic threshold of trial practice. Mastering the rules of evidence is absolutely essential to the trial of lawsuits.

A lawyer who has not mastered the rules is like a carpenter who cannot hammer a nail. There are certain tools of any trade that are indispensable.

Lawsuits are won with evidence that is admitted at trial. It is only through the proper introduction of evidence that it passes from the lawyer's briefcase to the trier of the fact.

For centuries, courts have protected litigants from the introduction of improper evidence. It is nothing short of malpractice for that protection to be waived, merely because counsel has not bothered to learn the rules of evidence.

Lawyers spend months preparing for trial, mastering material they may never use again. Mastering the rules of evidence is a form of preparation that will serve the attorney in every lawsuit he or she will ever try.

Most procedural and substantive law can be researched leisurely in a law library. Law relating to evidence must be mastered, in advance, subject to being called upon on a moment's notice in the heat of battle.

A trial lawyer is proud of his profession, and devotes his or her life to a career in the courtroom. It is inconceivable that he or she would not devote the time required to master the rules of evidence. Without a thorough understanding of these rules, a lawyer is not prepared for trial.

Sec. 1.11 Start With the Federal Rules A good trial lawyer must be able to walk into any federal or state court and feel comfortable with the rules of evidence. He or she should, therefore, start by mastering the Federal Rules of Evidence.

Speed in obtaining the answer is imperative to the trial lawyer who must respond during trial in a split second. He or she can find the answer faster if he trains himself or herself from the start by looking for the answer in one of the areas of evidence law covered by the federal rules.

KNOW THE LAW

You can find the "Area of Law" that includes your problem, if you MEMORIZE THE ELEVEN ARTICLES:

Article One: General Provisions
Article Two: Judicial Notice
Article Three: Presumptions in Civil Actions and Proceedings
Article Four: Relevancy and Its Limits
Article Five: Privileges
Article Six: Witnesses
Article Seven: Opinions and Expert Testimony
Article Eight: Hearsay
Article Nine: Authentication and Identification
Article Ten: Contents of Writing, Recordings, and Photographs
Article Eleven: Miscellaneous Rules

Practice finding the article needed for special problems of evidence.

Examples ──

1. Prosecutor attempts to introduce certain photos just to shock the jury. RELEVANCY. ARTICLE FOUR. (Rule 4.03 provides, "Although relevant, evidence may be excluded if its probative value is substantially outweighed by the danger of unfair prejudice. . . .")
2. Witness wants to refer to a summary. CONTENTS OF WRITINGS, RECORDINGS, AND PHOTOGRAPHS. ARTICLE TEN. (Rule 1006 provides, "the contents of voluminous writings, recordings and photographs which cannot conveniently be examined in court may be presented in the form of a chart, summary or calculation.")
3. "The lady pointed at the Defendant." HEARSAY. ARTICLE EIGHT. (Rule 801(a) provides a statement may be a "nonverbal conduct of a person, if it is intended by him as an assertion.")
4. Judge relies upon hearsay to determine if certain evidence is admissible. GENERAL PROVISIONS. ARTICLE ONE. (Rule 104(a) provides that in deciding preliminary questions concerning admissibility, the court "is not bound by rules of evidence except those with respect to privilege.")
5. Counsel attempts to impeach his or her own witness. WITNESSES. ARTICLE SIX. (Rule 607 provides, "The credibility of a witness may be attacked by any party, including the party calling the witness.")
6. At extradition proceeding, counsel bases objection on provision of FRE. MISCELLANEOUS RULES. ARTICLE ELEVEN. (Rule 1101(d)(3) provides the FRE does not apply to extradition proceedings.)
7. Counsel attempts to have newspaper introduced as evidence. AUTHENTICATION AND IDENTIFICATION. ARTICLE NINE. (Rule 902(6)

provides "extrinsic" evidence of authentication as condition precedent to admissibility is not required, "with respect to newspapers.")

8. Judge is asked to apply state law as to privilege in civil case. PRIVI-LEGES. ARTICLE FIVE. (Rule 501 provides in civil action where state law provides the rule of decision, the privilege of a witness . . . "shall be determined in accordance with state law.")

9. In a civil case the judge took judicial notice of a fact, and counsel requests instruction as to conclusiveness of that fact. JUDICIAL NOTICE. ARTI-CLE TWO. (Rule 201(g) provides in a civil case the judge shall instruct the jury to accept as conclusive, any fact judicially noticed.)

10. What effect does presumption have on burden of proof? PRESUMPTIONS IN CIVIL ACTIONS AND PROCEEDINGS. ARTICLE THREE. (Rule 301 provides, "A presumption imposes on the party against whom it is directed the burden of going forward with evidence to rebut or meet the presumption, but does not shift to such party the burden of proof in the sense of the risk of nonpersuasion.")

11. When can a lay witness give an opinion? OPINIONS AND EXPERT TESTIMONY. ARTICLE SEVEN. (Rule 701 provides a lay witness can only give opinions or inferences which are, "(a) rationally based on the perception of the witness and (b) helpful to a clear understanding of his testimony or the determination of a fact in issue.")

Once a trial lawyer can find his or her way into the FRE, and work his or her way through each provision of those rules, he or she can walk into every federal court and most state courts and promptly furnish the rule of evidence for each question. Even in the states which have not adopted the FRE, the courts are moving toward this approach to evidence, and the federal rule is at least a model for comparison.

Case decisions are adding light to the rules, and state law differences (even where most of FRE has been adopted) are adding depth to the trial lawyer's understanding of the law of evidence. He or she must begin, however, by mastering the FRE.

Sec. 1.12 Where to Find the Answer Look within the appropriate article and you will find the appropriate rule. KNOW the rule, and you will have the answer. UNDERSTAND the rule and you can apply it.

How to Apply a Rule

Learn the law, then apply it to an

Example ────────────────────────────────────

Rule 801(d)(1) provides that before a prior statement by a witness can qualify as not being hearsay, by definition, the statement must have been given at a "trial, hearing, OR OTHER PROCEEDING, or at a deposition." Knowing this rule is important, but it is also necessary to know what is meant by "other proceeding." It has been held that testimony before a grand jury IS another proceeding, but a statement before a notary public at the police station IS NOT.

The challenge, the feeling of accomplishment, and the fascination that make evidence the most exciting area of trial law can be summed up in two sentences:

1. Every trial lawyer can enjoy the art of advocacy that is demanded of him or her in mastering the rules of evidence.

2. That same trial lawyer can spend the rest of his or her career finding new fact situations to which he or she can apply these rules.

Sec. 1.13 Studying the Text of the Rules   This book gives the reader the full text of the FRE and following each rule the reader will find examples, common law references, historical notes, and other important information.

The secret to mastering the rules of evidence is to approach each rule with the basic questions:

(1) How Important Is the Rule?

EXAMPLE: Rule 801 gives "Definitions" of hearsay and is so important, every word of this lengthy rule must be memorized.

(2) How Does This Rule Relate to Other Rules?

EXAMPLE: Rule 401 defines "Relevancy," but Rule 403 begins with, "Although relevant . . ." and sets forth important conditions under which relevant evidence must be excluded.

(3) How Can You Make Your Task Easier by Mastering Duplicate Provisions?

EXAMPLE: When you master Rule 803(24), the catchall exception to hearsay whether or not declarant is available, turn to Rule 804(b)(5), which is exactly the same rule as applied where declarant is not available.

(4) How Can Titles of Articles and Rules Help Master the Rules?

EXAMPLES: Article Seven is entitled "OPINIONS AND EXPERT TESTIMONY." By knowing the title, the reader not only knows it deals with opinion evidence, but knows this is where to find provisions relating to court-appointed experts. Rule 408 is entitled "Compromise And Offers To Compromise," and once those few words are memorized, the reader is well on the way to owning that rule.

(5) How Can Words and Phrases Help Learn the Rules?

EXAMPLE: Rule 804(b)(5) and 803(24) are long paragraphs, but the overall hearsay exception can be understood by memorizing four words, "equivalent, circumstantial, guaranties, of trustworthiness."

(6) How Can Degrees of Mastery Be Established?

> EXAMPLE: Rule 403 is short enough and important enough to memorize verbatim. Rule 801 is the longest rule that must be memorized, so set priorities by memorizing Rule 801(a) and 801(c) immediately. *THIS IS A MUST!* Next study 801(d) and then the magic phrases under 801(d)(1) ("inconsistent with his testimony," "consistent . . . and is offered to rebut an express or implied charge . . ." and "one of identification"). Then memorize the magic phrases of 801(d)(2) ("his own statement," "manifested his adoption or belief in its truth," "by a person authorized by him to make a statement concerning the subject," "agent or servant concerning a matter within the scope of his agency or employment, made during the existence of the relationship," and "by a co-conspirator of a party during the course and in furtherance of the conspiracy." *PUT ALL THIS TOGETHER AND YOU HAVE MASTERED RULE 801, AND YOU HAVE A FIRM BASIS FOR UNDERSTANDING THE HEARSAY RULE.*

Sec. 1.14 Understanding Is Remembering   The easiest way to remember a rule is to understand it as you memorize it. Memorizing alone will accomplish little, and a rule will only stay memorized if the words mean something.

Example ───

Rule 607 provides: "The credibility of a witness may be attacked by any party, including the party calling him." These are sixteen simple words that can be memorized by a person who has never attended law school. The trial lawyer, however, must know pages of history that led to this departure from the traditional, "Your Honor, he is impeaching his own witness." Knowing how radical this departure was causes red lights to flash for the trial lawyer, and he or she will remember that some states that have adopted the federal rules, have not adopted this provision.

The more a trial lawyer knows about a particular rule, the better his or her chances are of quoting it verbatim.

Example ───

The title of Rule 412 is "Rape Cases; Relevance of Victim's Past Behavior." The trial lawyer's appreciation for the value of cross-examination reminds him that only a strong public policy reason could limit cross-examination in rape cases. He or she will know in advance that this is limited to "the past sexual behavior of a rape victim," and these key words will stick with him or her. If certain requirements are met, (1) past sexual behavior with persons other than accused can be introduced by accused to show "whether the accused was or was not, with respect to the alleged victim, the source of semen or injury," and (2) past sexual behavior with the accused can be introduced by accused to show whether the alleged victim consented to the sexual behavior with respect to which rape or assault is alleged." AGAIN, these key words can be remembered best if the trial lawyer first analyzes the effort made by the rule-makers to be fair and balance the accused's problem of defending himself or herself, and the victim's problem of being persecuted for prosecuting.

This book brings to life each rule by attaching to it examples, historical notes, and other comments. This is how a rule becomes meaningful to the trial lawyer and how it becomes a permanent part of his or her vocabulary.

Sec. 1.15 Examples, Historical Notes, and Case Decisions As Tools   This book brings to life the rules and law with examples, historical notes, case decisions, and other references, for two reasons:

1. This additional background is a valuable part of the trial lawyer's understanding of the rule; and

2. It is a valuable tool in the lawyer's mastering of the rule.

The common law is based on case decisions, a law degree is based on a certain number of hours in which the students discuss examples, and a trial lawyer's art of advocacy is based on his or her constant inquiry into why a law or a fact is what it is.

It is the search for a rule that gives it validity and justifies its becoming a part of what we remember the law of evidence to be.

Example ──

The term "excited utterance" was unknown to lawyers not many years ago and today is not a term with which laymen are familiar. Even a reading of Rule 803(2) and its explanation that this is a statement relating to a startling event or condition made while the declarant was under the stress of excitement caused by the event or condition does not make the term perfectly clear. Clarity arrives only after we review in our minds the historical concept of res gestae, and its shortcomings, and as we apply examples and read case decisions. We find courts talking about "spontaneous responses" and the "lapse of time" between event and statement. If a witness is still nervous and reacting to the excitement, we understand the witness is acting without calculating, and we understand why we give more value to the statement.

Trial lawyers study law journals, such as the *ATLA Reporter,* and state counterparts, such as the *AFTL Journal.* These journals include an evidence section, and each month a quick look at the synopsis reminds the reader of a rule and solidifies his or her mastery of it.

The annotations of a rule, and treatises discussing a rule add depth to our understanding. The more a trial lawyer knows about a rule, the more he or she can discuss it intelligently, and the more he or she has mastered it.

Sec. 1.16 Apply Rules to Actual Situations   Every case in a trial lawyer's filing cabinet involves at least one problem of evidence. In reviewing a file, or preparing a trial notebook or trial brief, the trial lawyer should go through the process of applying the proper rule of evidence.

There is no better practice in applying a rule than to apply it to an actual situation. Too often a trial lawyer is content to know he or she is right. The judge may want to know WHY he or she is right.

Example ──

The statement was not admissible under 801(d)(2)(d) because it was an admission made by an agent concerning "a matter within the scope of his agency," but was not made while the relationship existed. GIVE UP? OF COURSE, NOT! Was the statement made "by a person authorized by him to make a statement concerning the subject?" If so, is it admissible under 801(d)(2)(c)?

Applying rules to actual situations gives the rules added meaning. It also expands the trial lawyer's ability to unravel situations as they fit into the rules and speeds up the process, as required in the heat of battle.

Sec. 1.17 Learn Key Words and Phrases The Rules of Evidence have a certain vocabulary that the trial lawyer must make his vocabulary. By properly using a few words from a rule, the judge will know that the lawyer knows the rule.

Examples _____

"Refusing to testify" makes a witness "unavailable" (Rule 804(a)(2)). "Not subject to reasonable debate" suggests a judicial notice type statement (Rule 201(b)). "Habit of a person" or "Routine practice of an organization" may be admissible (Rule 406). "Each part of the combined statements conforms with an exception" tells you what you need to know about hearsay within hearsay (Rule 805). "Offered for another purpose" is an exception to such relevancy questions as remedial measures (Rule 407) and liability insurance (Rule 411). "Probative value is substantially outweighed" suggests relative evidence that may be excluded (Rule 403). "Plain error, affecting substantial rights" suggests special appellant treatment (Rule 103(d)). "Protect witness from harassment or embarrassment" offers a possible objection (Rule 601(a)). "Qualified as an expert by knowledge, skill, experience, training or education" gives the criteria for qualifying as an expert (Rule 702). "Question of fact preliminary to admissibility of evidence" are matters for court and may be determined by use of inadmissible evidence (Rule 1101(d)(1)). Experts are "required to disclose the underlying facts or data on cross-examination" (Rule 705). "Startling event or condition" gives rise to an excited utterance (Rule 803(2)). "Stating the specific grounds of objection" is a WARNING to every trial lawyer (Rule 103(a)(1)). "Secure fairness" is the purpose of the rules (Rule 101). "Statement made in the course of plea discussions" is inadmissible (Rule 410(4)). "State of mind, emotion, sensation, or physical condition" is a hearsay exception (Rule 803(3)). "Timely objection or motion to strike" is timely suggestion for trial lawyers (Rule 103(a)(1)). "Tendency to make . . . more probable or less probable" is the basis of relevancy (Rule 401). "Type reasonably relied upon by experts in the particular field in forming opinions or inferences" describes proper basis for an expert opinion (Rule 703). "Unable to procure his attendance . . . by process or other reasonable means" reminds the trial lawyer he or she had better get those subpoenas out, if he or she intends to use a witness by deposition [Rule 804(a)(5)]. "Unfair to admit the duplicate" suggests the liberal federal rule isn't THAT liberal (Rule 1003). "Which ought in fairness be considered contemporaneously" provides means of interrupting a presentation of evidence to avoid unfairness (Rule 106). "Once had knowledge, but now has insufficient recollection to enable him to testify fully and accurately" is the crux of the recorded recollection exception (Rule 803(5)). "Kept in the course of a regularly conducted business activity" are the key words of the Records of Regularly Conducted Activity exception [Rule 803(6)]. "EQUIVALENT, CIRCUMSTANTIAL, GUARANTEES OF TRUSTWORTHINESS" broadened the hearsay rule as an overall exception that formed a compromise between expanding and discording the hearsay rule [Rule 803(24) and Rule 804(b)(5)].

"Had an opportunity and similar motive" is now the test for use of former testimony under certain conditions [Rule 804(b)(1)]. "Contrary to the declarant's pecuniary or proprietary interest," "tended to subject him to criminal or civil liability," or "render invalid a claim" are what statements against interest are all about (Rule 804(b)(3)). "Contents of voluminous writings, recordings or photographs which cannot conveniently be examined in court" form the basis for using a "chart, summary or calculation" (Rule 1006).

ALL OF THE ABOVE EXAMPLES MUST BE MASTERED! There is simply no excuse for a trial lawyer not knowing them. Master them as rapidly as possible. Then go on to conquering the entire rule.

Example ——————————————————————————————

The entire paragraph of recorded recollection should be memorized as soon as possible. Start with "once had knowledge, but now has insufficient knowledge." Then add the words, "to enable the witness to testify fully and accurately." Then memorize the entire rule:

Rule 803(5) *Recorded Recollection.* A memorandum or record concerning a matter about which a witness once had knowledge but now has insufficient recollection to enable the witness to testify fully and accurately, shown to have been made or adopted by the witness when the matter was fresh in the witness's memory and to reflect that knowledge correctly. If admitted, the memorandum or record may be read into evidence but may not itself be received as an exhibit, unless offered by an adverse party.

SOLVING EVIDENCE PROBLEMS BEFORE TRIAL

Sec. 1.18 Analyze Evidence and Problems of Evidence Early   An early study of evidence is absolutely necessary. What evidence is needed, and how to get that evidence admitted, should be given top priority.

TRIAL STRATEGY

Open Your File and Ask

1. What evidence is needed to "make your case"?
2. What additional evidence will make your lawsuit attractive to the jury?
3. What legal problems are involved in getting these two areas of evidence admitted?
4. What evidence can hurt your case?
5. What "law of evidence" can keep that evidence from being admitted?

During the heat of trial, many questions of the law of evidence are presented, and the trial lawyer must "shoot from the hip." A study of this challenge that faces every trial lawyer discloses that much of this can be avoided. Nearly all evidence problems can be foreseen, and it is the trial lawyer's duty to try to foresee them, so he or she can prepare for them.

Examples _____

1. During trial counsel attempts to show that a repair was made after the accident. Counsel knew from the date of a deposition that he or she would try to have this evidence admitted. Had he found another purpose, he or she might have gotten it admitted under Rule 4.07.
2. During trial, counsel attempts to exclude evidence that is relevant but prejudicial to his/her client. He knew this would be a problem, since his/her first interview with the client. He or she should have studied Rule 403 to see if his/her circumstances came within the "prejudicial" provision of this important rule.

Sec. 1.19 Use Discovery to Eliminate Need for Evidence   Once a trial lawyer knows what evidence he or she wants admitted and what evidence he or she wants excluded, he or she can prepare to accomplish both tasks. This demands early analysis.

TRIAL STRATEGY

Plan Early How Discovery Can

1. Obtain admissions as to what otherwise would have to be proven.
2. Discover what may lead to an evidence-saving substitute.
3. Perpetuate for trial testimony and exhibits that establish facts you must prove.
4. Learn about unfavorable evidence so you can:
    A. find law that will exclude it
    B. confine its impact through pretrial or motion in limine
    C. find evidence to rebut it

Discovery tools should include interrogatories, oral and written depositions, and requests for admissions. Each should be studied with the "evidence substitute" possibilities in mind.

Too often counsel fails to utilize the written deposition. The few questions he wants to ask a doctor, or a witness in another city, need not require retaining local counsel, or require further time and expense that might cause this bit of evidence to be slighted.

Examples ──

1. Counsel must prove that a witness who now lives in another city gave the defendant notice. Proving notice through other means may be costly and consume time prior to trial and during trial. Counsel can serve notice of written deposition, in which he or she asks a few preliminary questions, and then, "Did you serve notice to the defendant?" With a minimum of time and expense, counsel has proven an essential element of his or her case.
2. Counsel knew at time of filing original pleading he must show net worth of defendant as a part of his punitive damage proof. Through the use of interrogatories he has proof of net worth long before trial.
3. Defendant has denied certain facts in his pleading that he could not deny when asked under oath with particularity. Through a request for admissions counsel may obtain the evidence he needs for trial.
4. During oral deposition, defendant admits he or she drove through a red light. This may make the testimony of several witnesses unnecessary.

Sec. 1.20 File Motion In Limine   The motion in limine enables counsel to obtain the trial court's position on an evidentiary ruling in advance of trial. This valuable tool enables counsel to (1) prepare with knowledge of the court's position and (2) avoids unfavorable evidence from reaching the jury (with a motion to disregard that is too little, too late).

TRIAL STRATEGY

Use Motion in Limine Effectively

1. File the motion in limine.
2. Obtain a court ruling.
3. Pursue an adverse ruling at trial.
    A. to protect appeal
    B. in case something has happened at trial that has changed the judge's position

---

A motion in limine should be filed far in advance of trial, so presentation of evidence can be planned with the court's ruling in mind. Also, knowing the court's position on the question answered by the motion may tell something about the court's position on other matters.

Examples ──

1. Counsel files a motion in limine to exclude a matter that would hurt his case. The judge denies the motion, stating he does not feel the jury would be prejudiced by such evidence. During voir dire, counsel can expect that the judge will not excuse prospective jurors for cause because of such evidence.

2. Counsel files motion in limine asking that evidence be admitted under Rule 803(1), as a present sense impression. The court rules the evidence will be admitted. Without the ruling, counsel would have to bring in other witnesses to testify as to the now admitted fact.

Sec. 1.21 Stipulate Where Possible   A lawsuit is the result of counsel, or their clients, being unable to agree on basic issues, but that does not mean they cannot stipulate and agree on certain matters of proof.

TRIAL STRATEGY

A Trial Lawyer Should Stipulate If:

1. Time can be saved at trial.
2. Time and trouble of bringing certain witnesses or exhibits to trial can be avoided, or
3. Putting the jury to sleep can be avoided.

Unless:

1. By stipulating, the matter stipulated will be presented with less impact, or
2. By stipulating you will open the door to other evidence being presented with less impact.

It is important to find a balance between shortening the trial, and losing the effect of the evidence. REMEMBER, studies have shown that witnesses who testify in detail are more readily believed, and remembered longer than those who give a brief account of what happened.

Weigh evidence with the dramatic impact factor in mind. Study each potential stipulation with a "winning your lawsuit" objective.

Examples _____

1. An accountant is testifying and is about to put the jury to sleep. Even if it is opposing counsel who may get blamed for this boring presentation, it is YOUR LAWSUIT that is not being heard by the jury. If you know what the bottom line is going to be, STIPULATE.
2. Your expert is about to tell the jury why he is the world's greatest expert in his field; you have done this with talent and tact, and the jury is about to become very impressed by your expert. Opposing counsel is willing to admit the witness's expertise. Graciously thank him or her for his or her confidence in your expert, but DON'T STIPULATE.
3. Opposing counsel is willing to stipulate as to what your doctor would say on a simple issue. You will pick up a little more impact by having the doctor

there, but it would be expensive and would disrupt the presentation of other evidence. WEIGH THESE FACTORS CAREFULLY BEFORE YOU DECIDE WHETHER OR NOT TO STIPULATE.

Sec. 1.22 Judicial Notice   The law of judicial notice will be found in Sections 2.01 and 2.02. You should review evidentiary problems prior to trial, to avoid the need for evidence once you are satisfied the court will accept judicial notice as a substitute for a particular proof.

Sec. 1.23 List Documents and Method of Proof   The only way counsel can make sure he or she proves his or her case is to list all elements and how to prove each one. This should be found immediately behind one of the dividers of the trial notebook, such as "EVIDENCE."

TRIAL STRATEGY

Establish Method of Proof in Writing

Element of Proof	*Source of Proof*
1. Ownership of auto	Def. Depo. P.4 l. 6
2. Estimate of speed of auto	Pl. testimony
	John Green testimony
3. Negligence of Def. "He was swerving"	Testimony of Mary Brown. Rule 803(2)?
4.	
5.	
6.	

Notice, under paragraph 3, counsel has question as to Rule 803(2). This alerts him to an evidence problem. (Does the statement qualify as an "excited utterance"?)

By listing what must be proven, and how each element will be proven, evidence problems are resolved long before trial. This also alerts counsel to the need for other evidence, if it is determined the first proof will not be admitted.

Sec. 1.24 Prepare for and Benefit from the Pretrial Conference   The trial lawyer should not try to dodge pretrial responsibility by saying, "Pretrial isn't all that great in my county, or in my state." Pretrial may be what counsel makes it, and even where pretrial is not the custom, the judge may call one if told such a conference may prompt a settlement or cut a few hours off the trial time.

TRIAL STRATEGY

Use the Pretrial Conference Effectively

1. Prepare for it in advance.
2. Prepare a complete pretrial statement, even if one is not required.
3. Check which exhibits, including photos and charts, were used at deposition; list them and all other exhibits you will use (if permitted in your jurisdiction, list "all exhibits used at deposition," and all others not used at deposition), and have them marked or ready for marking.
4. Make a list of possible stipulations.
5. Acquire a complete understanding of the use of depositions and other discovery.
6. Acquire an understanding of any special arrangements pertaining to medical witnesses.
7. Agree upon such matters as proof of life expectancy.
8. Make sure pleadings are in order prior to the pretrial.
9. Make sure all witnesses will be available for the jury week.
10. Detail your damages, and organize any exhibits relating to them.
11. If a motion in limine has been filed, get this resolved at pretrial.
12. Make sure the list of witnesses is complete and the information accurate (some attorneys who "play games" with the court find they cannot use a witness they relied on).
13. Make sure discovery has been completed.
14. Make a sincere effort to settle before the pretrial conference, and have client available by phone, or in person, in case a settlement opportunity arises.

SUBSTITUTES FOR EVIDENCE AND HOW TO USE THEM

Sec. 1.25 Dismiss Certain Allegations by Motion   By filing a motion to dismiss, or a motion to make more definite and certain, counsel can rid the pleadings of certain "legal garbage." As long as an allegation remains a part of the pleadings, counsel must gather evidence to rebut the allegation.

Often a complaint will include several counts, though counsel filing the complaint expects to prevail on only one or a few of the counts. Try to get rid of those extra counts by motion.

If the complaint asks for punitive damages, make sure there are sufficient allegations to sustain such a claim. If there is not, move to strike that part of the pleadings.

TRIAL STRATEGY

Avoid Need to Defend Frivolous Allegations

1. Move to dismiss.
2. Move to make more definite and certain.
3. Move to strike from pleadings.
4. Move for sanctions (Federal Rule 11 and state counterparts).

Sec. 1.26 Move for Summary Judgment   What cannot be stricken by motion, often can be stricken by summary judgment. Even though allegations survive the pleading stage, they may not survive the further attack of affidavits, depositions, and other supporting documents.

TRIAL STRATEGY

Continue Attack on Frivolous Allegations

1. File necessary motions.
2. Conduct sufficient discovery.
3. File motion for summary judgment.
4. Attach supporting affidavits and exhibits.
5. Argue for partial or total summary judgment.

Every allegation that is eliminated by summary judgment, is one more allegation or defense that need not be proved. Winning a lawsuit is winning on many issues, and many battles can be won before the real war begins.

Sec. 1.27 Lessen Evidence Through Stipulation   A trial lawyer does not know what opposing counsel will stipulate to until he or she asks. Trial strategy demands proper use of opportunities to stipulate. See Sec. 1.21.

Though it is important to consider stipulations with trial strategy in mind, stipulations should also be considered as a means of saving preparation time, trial time, and the expense of litigation. Let the court know you are willing to stipulate to all that does not compromise your client's lawsuit, and solicit the court's help in trying to obtain a stipulation from opposing counsel.

TRIAL STRATEGY

Consider the Potential of Stipulation in Such Matters As:

1. Use of depositions.
2. Order of proof.
3. Use of exhibits.
4. Acceptance of exhibits into evidence.
5. Qualification of expert.
6. Conclusion of expert.
7. Question of liability.
8. Amount of certain damages.
9. Life expectancy data.
10. Cause of death.
11. Causal relation of medical bills.
12. *Nearly every other element of proof.*

Sec. 1.28 Presumptions and Judicial Notice The law of presumptions is found in Sec. 3.01. The law of judicial notice is found in Secs. 2.01 and 2.02. Presumptions and judicial notice can avoid the need to prove with evidence.

Sec. 1.29 Don't Plead More Than You Need to Prove The Brandeis brief was not known for its brevity, and another Justice, Abe Fortas, insisted on pleading fifty points, if fifty points could be pled. The trial lawyer, however, must decide how much to plead when he or she decides how much to prove.

TRIAL STRATEGY

1. If you can obtain as much money from one count and you are sure of that count, adding counts may detract from your cause and cause the jury to feel you have lost on an issue not really important to you.
2. Plead punitive damages if you can prove them. Consider the fact such pleadings may detract from your proof and persuasion of actual damages.
3. Collectibility must always be an important consideration.
   EXAMPLE: If a jury will give you $75 thousand on actual damages, but if you claim punitive damages, and they give you $50 thousand actual and $50 thousand punitive, you have increased your judgment by $25 thousand. However, if you can only collect "actual" from the insurance company, your "collectible" judgment is $25 thousand less than if you had not plead punitive damages.

The principal purpose of litigation is (a) proving liability, (b) establishing damages, and (c) collecting the judgment. All three of these objectives must be kept in mind during the pleading stage.

This is why your list of proof should be completed at the pleading stage. *PLAN WHAT YOU CAN PROVE! Then, plead what enables you to PROVE YOUR CASE!*

Sec. 1.30 Admit What Will Not Hurt
"Conflict is the essence of drama," whether that drama is in the theatre or in the courtroom. (*How To Use Courtroom Drama To Win Cases,* Edward T. Wright, Prentice-Hall, 1987.) The trial lawyer must decide early which conflicts he or she can win, and which ones he or she should avoid.

Good trial lawyers who represent insurance companies have earned a lot of money admitting liability. It is simply easier to argue the question of damages, if that is the only real issue, if you are not diverting the jury's attention to a losing issue of liability.

Conceding can apply to a single issue, a single fact, or to a major part of the lawsuit. In certain cases, such as insanity or entrapment, counsel may have to toss all other defenses to the wind.

TRIAL STRATEGY

Consider Conceding That Which Really Concedes Nothing

1. Where refusing to admit the obvious will damage your credibility—consider conceding.
2. Where refusing to admit the obvious will damage *your lawsuit's* credibility—consider conceding.
3. Where refusing to stipulate will only slow down the trial and make your presentation less dramatic—consider conceding.
4. Where admitting will not hurt, but will help your relationship with the court—consider conceding.
5. When admitting a weak point will direct the jury's attention to a strong point—consider conceding.
6. Review your "Proof List" with an effort; delete "losers" by admitting them.

Sec. 1.31 Avoid "Needless Presentation of Cumulative Evidence"
"Waste of time" was not a legal term until the adoption of the Federal Rules of Evidence. Rule 403 provides that, although relevant, evidence may be excluded because of considerations of "undue delay," "waste of time," or "needless presentation of cumulative evidence."

The drafters of the rules thought that needless cumulative evidence was such a waste of time, they made special reference to it. What they were telling the trial lawyer was, "Once you prove a point, go on to something else."

This does not lessen trial counsel's duty to "prove a point." The rules generally do not tell him/her to use one, two, or three witnesses. Trial strategy remains at the discretion of the trial lawyer until he or she abuses it, and then the trial judge is given wide discretion in carrying out the purpose of the rule.

There is nothing in Rule 403 that is in conflict with good trial strategy. This rule, in fact, is a reminder to every trial lawyer that he or she is under no duty to put the jury to sleep.

Using the term "waste of time" puts the message in words everyone can understand. Check the proof list and apply that list to good trial strategy, and you will present the kind of evidence that will not delay the trial.

TRIAL STRATEGY

Limit Cumulative Evidence to

1.   What will prove a point.
2.   What will add dramatic impact to the point.
3.   What will avoid needless possible contradiction among witnesses.

The following table shows whether or not states adopting the Federal Rules of Evidence adopted substantially same provisions relative to the rules discussed in this chapter:

	Rule 103	Rule 104	Rule 105	Rule 106
ALASKA	Yes	No	No	Yes
ARIZONA	Yes	Yes	Yes	Yes
ARKANSAS	No	Yes	Yes	Yes
COLORADO	Yes	Yes	Yes	Yes
DELAWARE	Yes	Not (b)	Yes	Yes
FLORIDA	Not (b)	Not (d,c)	Yes	Yes
HAWAII	Yes	Yes	Yes	Yes
IDAHO	Yes	Not (d)	Yes	Yes
IOWA	Not (b,d)	Not (d)	Yes	Yes
MAINE	Yes	Yes	Yes	Yes
MICHIGAN	No	Yes	Yes	Yes
MINNESOTA	Yes	Not (b)	Yes	No
MISSISSIPPI	Yes	Yes	Yes	Yes
MONTANA	Yes	Not (b)	Yes	No

	Rule 103	Rule 104	Rule 105	Rule 106
NEBRASKA	Yes	No	Yes	Yes
NEVADA	Yes	Yes	Yes	Yes
NEW HAMPSHIRE	Yes	Yes	Yes	Yes
NEW MEXICO	Yes	Yes	Yes	Yes
NORTH CAROLINA	Yes	Yes	Yes	Yes
NORTH DAKOTA	Not (g)	No	Yes	Yes
OHIO	Not (a)	Yes	Yes	Yes
OKLAHOMA	Yes	Yes	Yes	Yes
OREGON	Yes	Yes	Yes	No
RHODE ISLAND	Yes	Yes	Yes	Yes
SOUTH DAKOTA	Yes	Yes	Yes	Yes
TEXAS	Yes	Yes	No	Yes
UTAH	Yes	Yes	Yes	Yes
VERMONT	Yes	No	Yes	Yes
WASHINGTON	Yes	Yes	Yes	Yes
WEST VIRGINIA	Yes	Yes	Yes	Yes
WISCONSIN	Yes	Yes	Yes	Yes
WYOMING	Yes	Yes	Yes	Yes

Rule	Subject
103	Rulings on Evidence
104	Preliminary Questions
105	Limited Admissibility
106	Remainder of or Related Writings or Recorded Statements

See Section 12.02 for Discussion of the Law in Non-FRE States Relative to Rules Discussed in This Chapter.

2

JUDICIAL NOTICE

See Federal Rules of Civil Procedure
Article Two: Judicial Notice

Sec. 2.01 Determine Availability of Judicial Notice Rule 201 provides for judicial notice of "adjudicative facts." (Adjudicative facts are facts of the lawsuit being tried.) When the court takes judicial notice of a fact, it is not necessary to introduce evidence to prove that fact.

TRIAL STRATEGY

Request Judicial Notice Be Taken and Show Court: Fact Not Subject to Reasonable Dispute Because

1. Generally known within territorial jurisdiction of trial court, *or*
2. Capable of accurate and ready determination by resort to sources whose accuracy cannot reasonably be questioned.

Judicial notice can be taken at any stage of the proceeding, even on appeal. It can be taken upon request of counsel, or by court, without request. The Court MUST take judicial notice if requesting counsel SUPPLIES THE NECESSARY INFORMATION. (Rule 2.01[d])

If counsel finds the court will take judicial notice of a certain fact, that fact need not be proven with another method. That is why it is necessary to find out whether or not judicial notice will be taken (Sec. 2.02).

In a civil case the jury is instructed that it must accept as evidence that which has been judicially noticed. In a criminal case, the jury is instructed that it "MAY, but is not required, to accept as conclusive, any fact that is judicially noticed" (Rule 2.01[g]).

Sec. 2.02 Request Judicial Notice—IN ADVANCE The use of judicial notice may depend upon a timely request for its substitute for evidence.

TRIAL STRATEGY

Pursue the Use of Judicial Notice by

1. Requesting stipulation from opposing counsel.
2. Ruling by judge prior to trial.
3. Making request at trial.
4. Giving opposing counsel "opportunity to be heard as to propriety of taking judicial notice," Rule 201(e).
5. Have evidence ready until judicial notice committed.

The "proof list" must show how each element will be proven. If an element, or fact within an element, is to be proven by judicial notice, that element must remain a "tentative proof" until a commitment from the court or opposing counsel can be obtained.

Many trial lawyers feel judicial notice is discretionary, and feel that substitute evidence is usually easier and wiser than taking your judge to task with an appeal. When taking judicial notice is important to your cause, however, the court should be reminded of judicial notice and appropriate law.

TRIAL STRATEGY

Show Court Mandatory Nature of Judicial Notice

1. Court *"shall* take judicial notice if requested by a party and supplied with the necessary information," Rule 201(d).
2. Court *"shall* instruct the jury to accept as conclusive any fact judicially noticed," (civil case), Rule 201(g).

The rules set the guidelines as to what is an adjudicative fact, but courts must interpret the rules on a case-by-case basis. If in doubt, REQUEST!

TRIAL STRATEGY

Argue That Facts Judicially Noticed Include

1. Location of streets, commercial nature of neighborhood, location of cities, and approximate distance between locations;
2. Policies, history, records of certain groups, and governmental entities;
3. Facts from books, newspapers, and similar sources;
4. Court records, personnel, and activities.

The following table shows whether or not states adopting the Federal Rules of Evidence adopted substantially the same provisions relative to the rules discussed in this chapter:

	Rule 201
ALASKA	No
ARIZONA	Not (g)
ARKANSAS	Not (g)
COLORADO	Yes
DELAWARE	Yes
FLORIDA	Yes
HAWAII	Yes
IDAHO	Yes
IOWA	Yes
MAINE	Not (g)
MICHIGAN	Yes
MINNESOTA	Yes
MISSISSIPPI	Yes
MONTANA	Yes
NEBRASKA	Yes
NEVADA	plus
NEW HAMPSHIRE	+law
NEW MEXICO	Yes
NORTH CAROLINA	Yes
NORTH DAKOTA	Yes
OHIO	Yes
OKLAHOMA	Yes
OREGON	+law
RHODE ISLAND	Yes
SOUTH DAKOTA	Not (g)
TEXAS	Not (g)
UTAH	Yes
VERMONT	Yes
WASHINGTON	Yes
WEST VIRGINIA	Yes
WISCONSIN	Yes
WYOMING	Yes

Rule   Subject

201   Judicial Notice of Adjudicated Facts

See Sec. 12.02 for Discussion of the Law in
Non-FRE States Relative to the Rules
Discussed in This Chapter.

3

PRESUMPTIONS

See Federal Rules of Evidence
Article Three: Presumptions In Civil Actions And Proceedings

Sec. 3.01   Rely Upon Presumptions

Sec. 3.01 Rely Upon Presumptions   The Federal Rules of Evidence provide for presumptions in civil cases only. FRE Rule 301 provides, *a presumption imposes on the party against whom it is directed the burden of going forward with evidence to rebut or meet the presumption, but does not shift to such party the burden of proof in the sense of risk of nonpersuasion, which remains throughout the trial upon the party on whom it was originally cast.*

HISTORICAL NOTE

> At Common Law There Was a Dispute
>
> 1. Under one theory, when a presumption was rebutted, the presumption remained in the case, and was considered by the jury with other evidence.
> 2. Under the "bursting bubble" theory, once the presumption was rebutted, it was no longer to be considered.
>
> Rule 301 Adopted the "Bursting Bubble" Rule the Classic Example
>
> 1. Plaintiff must prove notice to Defendant, and does so by showing a letter was mailed.
> 2. It is presumed that letter-mailed is letter-received, so at this point plaintiff has proven receipt of notice.
> 3. Defendant shows he did not receive letter and judge (not jury) must decide if the presumption has been rebutted.
> 4. Judge decides presumption has been rebutted and the presumption of delivery is out of the case and is not to be considered by the jury.

The presumption merely requires the other party to come up with evidence. If a party introduces certain evidence that entitles proponent to a presumption, that evidence (a proven fact) gives life to the presumption (a presumed fact).

Examples ───

Discrimination Cases:

> 1. *Proven Fact:* Plaintiff is qualified, but was fired.
> 2. *Presumed Fact:* Defendant discriminated.
> 3. *Rebuttal Evidence:* Firing was necessary for reasons of economy and not related to discrimination.
> 4. *Plaintiff Then:* Has burden of showing real reason for firing was discrimination.
>
> (burden never shifted)

Will Contest:

> 1. *Proven Fact:* Testator declared incompetent to manage his affairs.
> 2. *Presumed Fact:* Testator lacked capacity to make will.
> 3. *Rebuttal Evidence:* Psychiatrist convinces judge that testator had "mental capacity to make will."
> 4. *Plaintiff Then:* Proves mental incapacity with other evidence, and cannot rely upon the presumption to show lack of capacity.

Rule 302 provides, "a presumption respecting a fact which is an element of a claim or defense as to which state law provides the rule of decision is determined in accordance with state law." The *Erie v. Thompson* doctrine, 304 U.S. 64 (1938) of applying state law where it provides a rule of decision applies to presumptions. However, only where the issue or claim "has its source in state law" (*Maternity Yours, Inc. v. Your Maternity Shop, Inc.*, 234 F.2d 538 [1956]).

Examples ──

1. Auto accident tried in federal court under diversity. State law applies.
2. Patent case tried in federal court re federal law but under diversity, state law on presumptions does not apply.

It is generally held that Rule 302 applies only to "substantive presumptions" affecting a claim or defense, and not to "tactical presumptions" involving a "lesser aspect of the case." The presumption that "mailing" means "delivery" does not really affect substantive rights and here, as in close cases, federal rule is applied.

Examples ──

Substantive Presumptions Include:

1. Presumption directors of corporation acted in good faith.
2. Presumption driver was authorized by owner to operate vehicle.
3. Presumption of death after seven-year unexplained absence.
4. Presumption bailee's negligence caused the damage to goods delivered to him in good condition.

The Supreme Court of the United States has held that a presumption in a criminal case can be constitutional only if there is a "rational connection" between the proven fact and the presumed fact (*Barnes v. U.S.*, 412 U.S. 837 [1973]). Where New York law presumed occupants of car to be in possession of deadly weapon in the car, the presumption was "permissive" and with proper instruction was found constitutional (*County Court of Ulster County v. Allen*, 442 U.S. 140 [1979]).

TRIAL STRATEGY

In Opposing Presumption in Criminal Case, Argue

1. All elements of crime must be proven beyond a reasonable doubt.
2. That burden never shifts.
3. Instructing jury that "jury may regard the basic facts as sufficient evidence of the presumed fact," but "*does not require it to do so*" is crucial. Standard 303, Unadopted Rule 303, generally followed in federal courts (*Francis v. Franklin*, 41 U.S. 307 [1985]).
4. There must be a "rational connection" between the proven fact and presumed fact.

The following table shows whether or not states adopting the Federal Rules of Evidence adopted substantially same provisions relative to the rules discussed in this chapter:

	Rule 301
ALASKA	No
ARIZONA	No
ARKANSAS	No
COLORADO	Yes
DELAWARE	Yes
FLORIDA	Yes
HAWAII	No
IDAHO	Yes
IOWA	No
MAINE	No
MICHIGAN	No
MINNESOTA	No
MISSISSIPPI	Yes
MONTANA	No
NEBRASKA	Yes
NEVADA	Yes
NEW HAMPSHIRE	Yes
NEW MEXICO	No
NORTH CAROLINA	Yes
NORTH DAKOTA	Yes
OHIO	Yes
OKLAHOMA	No
OREGON	No
RHODE ISLAND	No
SOUTH DAKOTA	Yes
TEXAS	No
UTAH	Not (b)
VERMONT	No
WASHINGTON	No
WEST VIRGINIA	Yes
WISCONSIN	Yes
WYOMING	No

Rule	*Subject*
301	Presumptions In General In Civil Actions And Proceedings

See Sec. 12.02 for Discussion of the Law in Non-FRE States Relative to the Rules Discussed in This Chapter.

4

MAKE RELEVANCY DEPEND UPON WHETHER IT HELPS OR HURTS YOU

See Federal Rules of Evidence
Article Four: Relevancy And Its Limits

Sec. 4.01 Know the Relevancy Test Rule 401 states clearly that relevant evidence is evidence having any tendency to make the existence of any fact that is of consequence to the determination of the action more probable or less probable than it would be without the evidence. Rule 402 states simply, "evidence which is not relevant is not admissible."

Rule 402 also states that relevant evidence may or may not be admitted. Therein lies the need to know the law, and the challenge to effective use of trial strategy.

TRIAL STRATEGY

If Evidence Will Hurt You Try to Exclude It by Showing

1. "Rule 401 situation"—evidence is irrelevant, or
2. "Rule 403 situation"—although relevant:
   A. prejudice
   B. confusion
   C. waste of time or
3. Relevant, but exception applies:
   A. improper use of character evidence (Rule 404) or improper method of proving character (Rule 405)
   B. evidence *not* in conformity with habit or routine practice (Rule 406)
   C. was subsequent remedial measure (Rule 407)
   D. was compromise or offer to compromise (Rule 408)
   E. was payment of medical or similar expense (Rule 409)
   F. related to plea discussions (Rule 410)
   G. improper reference to liability insurance (Rule 411)
   H. improper reference to rape victim's past behavior (Rule 412)

Mastering Rule 401 is one of the most important challenges in the law of evidence. In determining what makes a fact to which the witness is testifying less probable, the court can consider many factors, including the bias of the witness (*U.S. v. Abel*, 105 S.St. 465 [1984]).

TRIAL STRATEGY

The Simple Relevancy Test

1. Is evidence probative of proposition offered?
2. Is proposition of consequence in determining action?

(*U.S. v. Hall*, 653 F.2d 1002 [5th Cir. 1981])

The courts have offered several means of mastering relevancy. One approach is to identify terms of relevancy relationship:

1. Describe item of evidence offered.

2. Define consequential fact to which it is directed.

3. Hypothesis required to infer consequential fact from evidence.

(U.S. v. Mann, 590 F.2d 361 [1st Cir. 1978]).

Example ⎯⎯⎯⎯⎯⎯⎯⎯⎯⎯⎯⎯⎯⎯⎯⎯⎯⎯⎯⎯⎯⎯⎯⎯⎯⎯⎯⎯⎯⎯⎯⎯⎯⎯⎯⎯⎯⎯

1. PROFFERED EVIDENCE: A, an Israeli, was recent acquaintance of B, an adult Israeli traveling alone, who was arrested carrying cocaine.
2. CONSEQUENTIAL FACT: A paid C, a teenage Australian travelling with him, to carry cocaine in her girdle from Peru to San Juan in 1977.
3. HYPOTHESIS REQUIRED: Must show a rational connection between the two and prosecution failed to do so.

Rule 401 requires that direct examination have some relevant purpose (*U.S. v. Pintac,* 630 F.2d 1270 [8th Cir. 1980]). "Bolstering" is not irrelevant but must satisfy the Rule 403 "undue delay" requirement (*Snow v. Reid,* 619 F.Supp. 579 [S.D. NY 1985]).

HISTORICAL NOTE

"*Materiality*" is no longer an issue. "Any fact that is of consequence to determination of the action" is admissible (*U.S. v. Carriger,* 592 F.2d 312 [Cir. 1978]).

The court has broad discretion and shall use its "experience, judgment and knowledge of human motivation and conduct" (*U.S. v. Williams,* 545 F.2d 47 [8th Cir. 1976]). *Williams* made it clear this discretion will not be disturbed unless "clear showing of abuse of discretion."

PROPER RULE OF THUMB: "Whether reasonable man might believe probability of truth of consequential fact to be different if he knew of proffered evidence" (*U.S. v. Brashier,* 548 F.2d 1315 [9th Cir. 1976]).

Weight or significance of evidence is NOT important if it tends to prove or disprove a matter under consideration, U.S. v. American Cyanamid Co., 427 F.Supp. 859 (S.D. NY 1977). IMPORTANT: The slightest degree of relevancy usually means the evidence is admissible.
MASTER RULE 401 BY APPLYING IT TO:

Examples ⎯⎯⎯⎯⎯⎯⎯⎯⎯⎯⎯⎯⎯⎯⎯⎯⎯⎯⎯⎯⎯⎯⎯⎯⎯⎯⎯⎯⎯⎯⎯⎯⎯⎯⎯⎯

1. *Immigration Hearing:* Conditions in defendant's homeland and inconsistent enforcement of immigration laws NOT RELEVANT (*U.S. v. Hernandes,* 693 F.2d 996 [10th Cir. 1982]).

2. *Police Brutality:* Fact officer accused of brutality had been suspended for bribery NOT RELEVANT (*Lenard v. Argento,* 699 F.2d 874 [7th Cir. 1983]).
3. *Drug Sale:* Even though defendant had not joined co-conspirator in a sale, the sale was RELEVANT (*U.S. v. Torres,* 685 F.2d 921 [5th Cir. 1982]).
4. *Embezzlement Prosecution:* Past bankruptcy NOT RELEVANT, present bankruptcy RELEVANT, because it shows defendant was under financial pressure (*U.S. v. Reed,* 700 F.2d 638 [11th Cir. 1983]).
5. *Forseeability:* Evidence of other route in railroad yard makes forseeability of plaintiff's presence more probable, hence RELEVANT (*Hopkins v. Baker,* 553 F.2d 1339 [D.C. 1977]).
6. *Criminal Action:* Evidence of tip as to defendant's criminal activities NOT RELEVANT, since not necessary to show why police investigated him (*U.S. v. Mancillas,* 580 F.2d 1301 [7th Cir. 1978]).
7. *Sex with Co-Ed:* Evidence of sex with co-ed NOT RELEVANT since defendant did not know co-ed made herself available to induce his participation (*U.S. v. Carriger,* 588 F.2d 278 [5th Cir. 1979]).
8. *Belief Act Was Authorized:* Evidence that defendant was told labor union constitution "flexible" RELEVANT, to show he thought he was authorized to do what he did (*U.S. v. Rubin,* 591 F.2d 278 [5th Cir. 1979]).
9. *Value of Collateral:* Evidence concerning amount realized on collateral RELEVANT to show collateral was overvalued (*U.S. v. Kreimer,* 609 F.2d 126 [5th Cir. 1980]).
10. *Lacks Propensity:* Expert testimony that defendant "lacks propensity to commit violent act" RELEVANT. ("Peaceable man would more likely be planting turnips than shooting at passing aircraft.") (*U.S. v. Webb,* 625 F.2d 709 [5th Cir. 1980]).
11. *Self-Defense:* In assault case, victim's prior stabbing is RELEVANT on issue of self-defense (*U.S. v. Greschner,* 647 F.2d 740 [7th Cir. 1981]).
12. *Attempted Rape:* Two red dots shown on photo of victim's back, taken two days after alleged attempted rape, RELEVANT (*U.S. v. Weeks,* 10 Fed. Ev. Rep. 670 [4th Cir. 1982]).
13. *Relationship of Parties:* Evidence of relationship of parties RELEVANT where it tends to make party's respective position less credible (*Brockelsby v. U.S.,* 767 F.2d 1288 [9th Cir. 1985]).
14. *Resisting Arrest:* Evidenced man shot and killed by officer was wanted for robbery RELEVANT, to show he had reason to resist (*Bowden v. McKenna,* 600 F.2d 282 [1st Cir. 1979]).
15. *Discrimination:* Previous discrimination RELEVANT, to show intent to discriminate (*Allen v. County of Montgomery,* 788 F.2d 1485 [11th Cir. 1986]).
16. *Financial Situation:* Evidence of prospective tenant's financial situation RELEVANT, to show discrimination and not financial inability as a reason for denying lease to tenant (*Thronson v. Meisers,* 800 F.2d 136 [7th Cir. 1986]).
17. *Post-Complaint Conduct:* Post-complaint conduct RELEVANT, to show pre-complaint discrimination (*E.E.O.C. v. Sheet Metal Workers,* 463 F.Supp. 388 [D.C. MD 1978]).
18. *False Complaint:* Letter from fellow prisoner showing how to file false

complaint RELEVANT when found in possession of person making complaint (*Carter v. Hewitt,* 617 F.2d 961 [3rd Cir. 1980]).

19. *Pathological Gambler:* Experts do not agree on connection between "pathological gambling" and failure to pay taxes, so NOT RELEVANT. (*U.S. v. Shorter,* 618 F.Supp. 255 [D.C. DC 1985]).

20. *Weapons:* Weapons tend to prove intent to promote and protect narcotics conspiracy, so presence of guns RELEVANT (*U.S. v. MARINO,* 658 F.2d 1120 [6th Cir. 1981]).

21. *Drug Money:* Evidence of real-estate transactions RELEVANT, to show effort to conceal drug money (*U.S. v. Towers,* 775 F.2d 184 [7th Cir. 1985]).

22. *False Passport:* Testimony he obtained false passport using non-Jewish name to outwit Arab investors NOT RELEVANT, since it showed *motive* and not *intent* (*U.S. v. Wasman,* 5 Fed. Ev. Rep. 590 [S.D. FL 1979]).

23. *No Prior Claim:* Lack of prior claim RELEVANT to the defense, since defendant had no knowledge of dangerous propensity of product (*Kolopa v. General Motors,* 716 F.2d 373 [6th Cir. 1983]).

24. *Accident Expert:* If expert's opinion as to accident based on facts "significantly different," NOT RELEVANT (*Barnes v. General Motors,* 547 F.2d 275 [5th Cir. 1977]).

25. *Other Passenger:* Proof other passenger sustained "only slight injuries," NOT RELEVANT (*Perkins v. Volkswagen of America, Inc.,* 596 F.2d 681 [5th Cir. 1979]).

26. *Armed at Arrest:* Fact defendant charged with UNARMED robbery was armed at time of arrest, NOT RELEVANT (*U.S. v. Ferreira,* 821 [1st Cir. 1987]).

27. *Escape:* Evidence defendant tried to escape pending trial RELEVANT, to show "conscience of guilt" (*U.S. v. Guerrero,* 18 Fed. Rule Serv. 87 [9th Cir. 1985]).

28. *Blood Type:* Court considered (1) defendant had Type O, (2) 45 percent of population has Type O, (3) other prisoners not tested, (4) defendant only person with cut, (5) blood on weapon was Type O, RELEVANT *(U.S. v. Bari,* 750 F.2d 1169 [2nd Cir. 1984]).

29. *Videotape Experiment:* Whether videotape or similar experiment is RELEVANT, at sound discretion of trial judge (*Randall v. Warnaco,* 677 F.2d 1226 [8th Cir. 1982]).

30. *Destroying or Concealing Evidence:* Destroying or concealing evidence RELEVANT as to credibility (*Berkley Photo v. Eastman Kodak Co.,* 603 F.2d 263 [2nd Cir. 1979]). GOOD DISCUSSION.

31. *Child Abuse:* Though fact victim of child abuse had child born out of wedlock may affect its relevancy if of DUBIOUS VALIDITY (*Dyer v. MacDougall,* 201 F.2d 265 [2nd Cir. 1952]).

32. *Reinforcing Credibility:* Reporting alleged bribe to business partner RELEVANT as reinforcing witness credibility (*U.S. v. Iconetti,* 406 F.Supp. 554 [E.D. NY 1976]).

33. *Civil Rights:* Police officer being sued for shooting motorist showed plaintiff was drunk—RELEVANT, to show he acted as defendant alleged and that defendant was afraid (*Saladino v. Winkler,* 609 F.2d 1211 [7th Cir. 1979]).

34. *Personal Life:* Plaintiff's sexual activity, gambling and drinking RELE-VANT as to "diminishing social life" of brain-damage victim in personal injury case (*U.S. v. Schipani,* 289 F.Supp. 43 [E.D. NY 1968]).
35. *Briefcase Contents:* Ski mask and gun found in briefcase RELEVANT as not being what is usually found in briefcase (*U.S. v. Eatherton,* 519 F.2d 603 [1st Cir. 1975]).
36. *Nude Photos and Prophylactics:* In sex offense prosecution, possession by defendant of nude photo (*State v. Johnsons,* 67 N.W. 2d 639 [MN 1954]) or possession of prophylactics (*State v. Stone,* 83 S.E. 2d 543 [NC 1954])—NOT RELEVANT.
37. *Tax Returns:* Previous income tax return RELEVANT, to show state of mind when defendant filed non-conforming return (*U.S. v. Kalsky,* 610 F.2d 548 [8th Cir. 1979]).

Sec. 4.02 Know the Major Relevancy Exception   Rule 403 provides:

"Although relevant, evidence may be excluded if its probative value is substantially outweighed by the danger of:

> unfair prejudice,
> confusion of issues, or
> misleading the jury, or

by considerations of:

> undue delay,
> waste of time, or
> needless presentation of cumulative evidence."

This is not only the major relevancy exception, but probably the single most important rule of evidence. THE TRIAL LAWYER MUST COMMIT IT TO MEMORY.

TRIAL STRATEGY

Use Rule 403 Effectively by Showing

1. Evidence is inflammatory.
2. Less prejudicial evidence can accomplish same purpose.
3. Evidence is UNFAIRLY prejudicial.
4. Evidence is misleading.
5. Evidence is confusing.
6. Evidence is waste of time.
7. Evidence causes undue delay.
8. Evidence is needless presentation of cumulative evidence.

If you are attempting to have 403-type evidence admitted, argue the converse. REMEMBER: (1) courts favor admission, and (2) the level of relevancy has a low threshold.

One court reminded trial lawyers of their duty to show "client's tragic misfortune," even if injuries are gruesome (*Auerbach v. Philadelphia Transportation Co.*, 221 A.2d 172 [PA 1966]). Argue that the 403 drama was one created by defendant and he must live with the fact the jury may be outraged over his conduct and the result of it. Committing a gruesome crime does not immunize defendant from *gruesome* proof (*Rivers v. U.S.*, 270 F.2d 435 [9th Cir. 1959]).

MASTER RULE 403 BY APPLYING IT

Examples ───

1. *Extreme Pain:* Video showing extreme pain EXCLUDED under 403 (*Thomas v. C. G. Tate Construction*, 465 F.Supp. 566 [D.C. S.C. 1979]).

2. *Character Witnesses:* Where party put on character witness, not entitled to produce twenty five more character witnesses (*Cumulative v. Edwards*, 702 F.2d 529 [5th Cir. 1983]); judge limited character witnesses to three (*U.S. v. Johnson*, 730 F.2d 683 [11th Cir. 1984]).

3. *"Opening The Door":* Court excluded evidence of defendant's improper conduct in matter not before court; on cross-examination defendant implied he did not participate in the other scheme. *This opened the door!* Prosecution could then show defendant's participation in the other scheme (*U.S. v. Johnson*, 730 F.2d 683 [11th Cir. 1984]).

4. *Limiting Trial Hours:* At outset, court announced plaintiff would have eighteen hours to present his products liability case, and defendant would have fifteen hours in which to respond. HELD: Courts "must exercize strict control over the length of trials, and are therefore entirely within their rights in setting reasonable deadlines in advance and holding parties to them." "Though practice of placing rigid hours on a trial is discouraged, eighteen hours is not unreasonable and judgment affirmed." Trusting, "in future the able district judge will not try to cut the slice so thinly" (*Flaminio v. Honda*, 733 F.2d 463 [7th Cir. 1984]). In complex anti-trust suit, twenty-eight days set by court *(M.C.I. Communications Corp. v. Am.Tel&Tel Co.*, 708 F.2d 1081 [7th Cir. 1983]).

5. *Negative Factors Presented:* An EEOC "reasonable cause" determination is RELEVANT, but trial judge may exclude it if *"sufficient negative factors"* present (*Johnson v. Yellow Freight Systems*, 734 F.2d 1304 [8th Cir. 1984]).

6. *Convictions, Lawsuits and Other Acts:* It has been argued that Rule 609 admitting convictions only if its probative value "outweighs its prejudicial effect" applies only to criminal cases, but civil case would still have to stand the BALANCING TEST of 403. Fact defendant previously with person arrested for narcotics violation EXCLUDED (*U.S. v. Mann*, 590 F.2d 361 [1st Cir. 1978]). Court's failure to balance in brief reference to rape conviction was harmless error, and did not abuse discretion "in allowing very limited questioning" re prior civil action (*Czatka v. Hickman*, 703 F.2d 317 [8th Cir. 1983]). Previous wrongful acts (drug involvement) did not confuse or prejudice the jury (*U.S. v. Evans*, 697 F.2d 240 [8th Cir.

1983]). Prior conviction cannot be used to demonstrate "a propensity to commit crime" (*Carter v. Hewitt,* 617 F.2d 961a [3rd Cir. 1980]).

7. *Motel Rape Victim:* In suit against motel for not preventing rape, (1) summary of crimes committed in area, (2) security measures taken by other hotels in area, (3) customs and practices of other motels in area; "If sufficiently similar," ADMITTED (*Anderson v. Malloy,* 700 F.2d 1208 [8th Cir. 1983]).

8. *Photos:* Photos of victim's "superficial abrasions and lacerations" sustained after the alleged rape, admitted to show act was nonconsensual—NOT PREJUDICIAL (*U.S. v. One Feather,* 702 DF.2d 736 [8th Cir. 1983]). Admitting motion pictures is at "sound and broad discretion" of trial judge. Here, the films depicted an experiment illustrating a theory of the case, and dissimilarities between experiment and actual conditions go to weight and not admissibility (*Szeliga v. General Motors,* 728 F.2d 566 [1st Cir. 1984]). Movie that accurately depicted device ADMITTED (*Saturn Mfg. v. Williams,* 713 F.2d 1347 [8th Cir. 1983]). "Day in life" film ADMITTED, except for part aimed solely at sympathy (*Grimes v. Employer's Mutual,* 73 FRD 607 [D.Alaska 1977]). Color and black and white photo ADMITTED, since they both added credibility to pathologist (*People v. Linderen,* 402 N.E. 2d 238 [IL 1980]). Video showing force of water hose used by prison guards ADMITTED (*Slaken v. Porter,* 737 F.2d 368 [4th Cir. 1984]).

9. *Stipulations and Rule 403:* Stipulation need not be accepted as a substitute for proof, but does offer means of avoiding a 403 problem. Here, however, the judge said, "it sounds as if on both sides the background . . . is going to be brought out by somebody at some time and it may be an exercize in futility to start out withholding part of it from the jury" (*U.S. v. Gottesman,* 724 F.2d 1517 [11th Cir. 1984]). Had defense admitted intent, the need for the evidence would have been less, and the 403 factor would have outweighed the need—ADMITTED (*U.S. v. Webb,* 625 F.2d 709 [5th Cir. 1980]). Stipulation cannot rob party of use of evidence that gives its "fair and legitimate weight" (*Parr v. U.S.,* 255 F.2d 86 [5th Cir. 1958]). Stipulation will not avoid inflammatory photo (*U.S. v. Kaiser,* 545 F.2d 467 [5th Cir. 1977]), unless photo goes too far (*Ryan v. United Parcel Service,* 205 F.2d 362 [2nd Cir. 1953]). Requiring government to accept stipulation as to cause of death in assassination explosion would "dilute value of proof" (*U.S. v. Sampol,* 636 F.2d 621, [DC Cir. 1980]).

10. *Destroying Documents:* Evidence defendant had destroyed documents was more than "inflammatory rhetoric," it was "legitimate challenge" to credibility, and as each new fact came to light the court reassessed its relevancy to credibility and enlarged the scope of permissible inquiry into the witness's action (*Berkey v. Eastman Kodak,* 603 2d 263 [2nd Cir. 1979]).

11. *Informant Money:* In cross-examining informant, defense counsel can make it clear informant was paid by the FBI but cannot make "the same point, over and over" (*U.S. v. Toner,* 728 F.2d 115 [2nd Cir. 1984]).

12. *Toxic Tort Case:* In toxic tort case, plaintiff study ADMITTED, since defendant had an opportunity to challenge methodology and findings (*Kehm v. Procter & Gamble,* 724 F.2d 613 [8th Cir. 1983]).

13. *Trial Within Trial:* Evidence of later "flight incident" EXCLUDED

because of lack of similarity of proof of causation, hence a mini-trial within a trial resulting in "undue delay, waste of time, and needless presentation of cumulative evidence" (*Moe v. Avions Marcel Dassault-Brequet Aviation,* 727 F.2d 917 [10th Cir. 1984]).

14. *UNFAIR prejudice:* Admitting letter by defendant that admitted danger of roll-bar tractor would prejudice defendant's case, but such is not UNFAIR prejudice, so ADMITTED (*Dollar v. Long Mfg.,* 561 F.2d 613 [5th Cir. 1977]).

15. *Additional Witnesses:* Where evidence would require several rebuttal witnesses, tendency is to EXCLUDE (*Box Maxfield v. American Motors,* 637 F.2d 1033 [5th Cir. 1981]).

16. *Dissimilar Exhibits:* Exhibits of 25-gallon and 40-gallon fuel cells would only confuse the jury in a case involving a 31-gallon cell (*Rigby v. Beech Aircraft,* 548 F.2d 288 [10th Cir. 1977]).

17. *Charts:* Conversation times on chart must match conversation times stipulated, or it would merely confuse jury (*In Re Air Crash Disaster At John F. Kennedy International Airport,* 635 F.2d 67 [2nd Cir. 1980]).

18. *Drug Found On Person:* Court must make sure evidence of drug found on person won't just incite and confuse jury (*U.S. v. Green,* 548 F.2d 1261 [6th Cir. 1977]).

19. *Superfluous Statement:* Witness identified defendant as person he knew in prison. Fact defendant had been in prison was IRRELEVANT and highly prejudicial (*U.S. v. Anderson,* 584 F.2d 849 [6th Cir. 1978]).

20. *Homosexuality:* Fact person is homosexual can be so prejudicial that counsel must spell out clearly its relevancy (*U.S. v. Millen,* 594 F.2d 1085 [6th Cir. 1979]).

21. *Excising:* "Explosive portions" can be excised and 403 problem avoided (*U.S. v. McManaman,* 606 F.2d 919 [10th Cir. 1979]).

22. *The Klan:* Membership in Ku Klux Klan RELEVANT to conspiracy charge and entrapment defense and unavoidable, but on other issues, probative value low and potential for prejudice high (*U.S. v. Sickles,* 524 F.Supp. 506 [E.D. PA 1981]).

23. *Instruction:* Hair from ski mask admitted because of its probative value, but jury was made well aware of the limitations of the evidence (*U.S. v. Hickey,* 596 F.2d 1082 [1st Cir. 1979]).

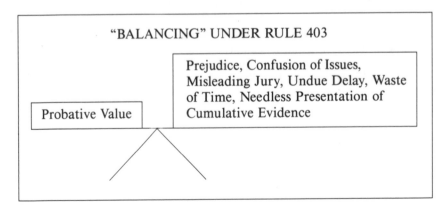

"BALANCING" UNDER RULE 403

Prejudice, Confusion of Issues, Misleading Jury, Undue Delay, Waste of Time, Needless Presentation of Cumulative Evidence

Probative Value

Under Rule 403 judge decides to proffer fact *if believed* versus prejudice (*Bowden v. McKenna,* 600 F.2d 282 [1st Cir. 1979]). The jury must decide whether to "credit the evidence" (*Ballou v. Henri Studios,* 656 F.2d 1147 [5th Cir. 1981]). "Evidence is prejudicial when it tends to have some adverse effect upon a defendant beyond tending to prove the fact or issue that justified its admission into evidence" (*U.S. v. Figueroa,* 618 F.2d 934 [2nd Cir. 1980]).

"UNFAIR PREJUDICE" is deciding of case "on an improper basis, commonly, though not necessarily an emotional one" (*Committee Notes,* Rule 403).

TRIAL STRATEGY

Show Prejudice Under Rule 403

1. Prejudice is *unfair.*
2. Probative value outweighed.

"Unfair prejudice" is accompanied by "misleading" and "confusing" as reasons to exclude under 403. While prejudice brings emotional factors to the attention of the court, misleading and confusing can be based on the mode of presentation, proper procedure, and the goal of finding the truth.

SHOW CONFUSION AND MISLEADING UNDER RULE 403

1. Introduces new issues.
2. Detracts from main issue by:
   A. confusing jury as to importance of main issue
   B. confusing jury with facts that detract from proper proof
   C. taking time from main issue

The "danger of" part of Rule 403 deals with *unfair prejudice, confusion of issues,* and *misleading the jury;* while the *considerations of* part deals with *undue delay, waste of time,* and *needless presentation of cumulative evidence.* More than one of these factors will usually be found in a 403 problem.

TRIAL STRATEGY

Use Rule 403 to Show Trial Will Be Improperly Prolonged

1. Needless cumulative evidence.
2. Evidence will lead to unnecessary evidence.
3. Probative value not worth time.
4. Detracts from real issues.
5. May require waiting for rebuttal witnesses.

The use of photos, video, movies, charts, demonstrations, in-court experiments and out-of-court experiments are loaded with 403 problems. See subparagraph 8 of this section. Be ready to proceed with your presentation without having any evidence excluded.

TRIAL STRATEGY

Argue Need to Admit Your Photos

1. Each photo adds something to your proof.
2. Inflammatory nature outweighed by probative value.
3. Inflammatory nature created by conduct of defendant.
4. Photos necessary for an effective presentation of your case.
5. Photos eliminate need for witnesses, demonstrations, and other evidence.

There is no rule of evidence in which the trial court uses broader discretion than under Rule 403. ("Only where court acted arbitrarily or irrationally will the ruling be disturbed") (*U.S. v. Robinson*, 560 F.2d 507 [2nd Cir. 1977]). That is why it is important for the trial lawyer to:

1. Have a "feel" for what should be excluded, and

2. Have a willingness to argue reasons for admitting or excluding under this rule.

HISTORICAL NOTE

Rule 403 does not include "SURPRISE" as a reason for excluding relevant evidence, as was done at common law. *Continuance is now proper remedy for "Surprise".*

See Sec. 6.08 for discussion of Rule 403 as applied to criminal convictions and impeachment.

Sec. 4.03 When Is Character Evidence Admissible? Rule 404 provides that "evidence of a person's character or trait of character is not admissible for the purpose of proving action in conformity therewith on a particular occasion." EXCEPT:

1. "Evidence of a pertinent trait of character offered by an accused, or by the prosecution to rebut the same."

2. "Evidence of a pertinent trait of character of the victim of the crime offered by an accused (or by the prosecution) to rebut the same, or evidence of a character trait of peacefulness of the victim, offered by the

prosecution in a homicide case to rebut evidence that the victim was the first aggressor."

3. "Evidence of the character of a witness as provided in rules 607, 608 and 609."

Rule 404(b) provides that:

"Evidence of other crimes, wrongs, or acts is not admissible to prove the character of a person in order to show action in conformity therewith. It may, however, be admissible for other purposes, such as proof of **motive, opportunity, intent, preparation, plan, knowledge, identity, or absence of mistake or accident.**"

TRIAL STRATEGY

In Objection to Character Evidence, Argue

1. Court must balance a conviction's probative value against its prejudicial character (*Luck v. U.S.,* 348 F.2d 763 [D.C. Cir. 1965]).
2. Where crime identical, extreme potential for prejudice (*People v. Rist,* 16 Cal. 2d 211 [CA App. 1961]).

Where character is an issue in the case, it may be proven. Where it is NOT an issue, it must comply with the exceptions of Rule 404.

TRIAL STRATEGY

When You Can Use Character Evidence

1. When character is in issue (*U.S. v. Schell,* 692 F.2d 672 [10th Cir. 1982]).
2. Pertinent trait of accused.
   A. offered by accused
   B. offered by prosecution in rebuttal
   [Rule 404(a)(2)]
3. Pertinent trait of victim.
   A. offered by accused
   B. offered by prosecution in rebuttal
   [Rule 404(a)(2)]
4. Trait of peacefulness of homicide victim.
   A. offered by prosecution to rebut that victim was aggressor
   [Rule 404(a)(2)]

5. Credibility of witness may be attacked by showing character for truthfulness or untruthfulness.
    A. but, character for truthfulness can only be used after truthfulness attacked

    [Rule 608(a)]

6. Inquire on cross-examination of witness's character for truthfulness or untruthfulness:
    A. in discretion of court
    B. if probative of truthfulness or untruthfulness
    C. in attacking or supporting credibility
    D. not including conviction of crime.

    [Rule 608(b)(1)]

7. Inquire of another witness on cross-examination of character for truthfulness or untruthfulness (as to which character the witness being examined has testified):
    A. in discretion of court
    B. if probative of truthfulness or untruthfulness
    C. in attacking or supporting credibility
    D. not including conviction of crime.

    [Rule 608(b)(2)]

8. Attack during cross-examination credibility of witness with evidence that he or she has been convicted of a crime:
    A. by eliciting from him or establishing by public record
    B. if crime punishable by death or imprisonment in excess of one year
    C. if court determines probative value outweighs prejudicial effect
    D. involved dishonesty or false statement (regardless of punishment)
    E. if more than ten years since conviction or release from confinement, whichever is later
        (1) unless court determines conviction over ten years has probative value outweighing prejudicial effect "in the interest of justice"
        (2) provided, ten-year-old conviction cannot be used without notice and "fair opportunity to contest use of such evidence"
    F. not admissible of pardon, annulment or similar procedure
    G. juvenile conviction not admissible unless
        (1) used against other than accused
        (2) offense one that could be used against adult
        (3) court satisfied admission "necessary for a fair determination of innocence or guilt"

    [Rule 609]

9. Other crimes, wrongs or acts, if not to show activity in conformity therewith, but for other purposes, such as:
   A. motive
   B. opportunity
   C. intent
   D. preparation
   E. plan
   F. knowledge
   G. identity
   H. absence of mistake or accident
   [Rule 404(b)]

Rule 404 must be considered with Rule 403, so evidence of prior or subsequent acts must:

1. Direct toward "establishing a matter in issue other than Defendant's propensity to commit the crime."

2. Show other act is "similar enough and close enough in time to be relevant to the matter in issue."

3. Be clear and convincing.

4. Have probative value not "substantially outweighed by the danger of unfair prejudice" (*U.S. v. Schackelford,* 738 F.2d 776 [7th Cir. 1984]).

Courts have held "a jury is entitled to know the circumstances and background of a criminal charge." Under this "res gestae" approach, evidence can be introduced "for the purpose of providing the context in which the crime occurred." (Held, evidence of drug activity admitted in charge of illegal possession of firearms, where jury learned the firearms were found during a drug raid (*U.S. v. Moore,* 735 F.2d 289 [8th Cir. 1984]).

Where character evidence would have little probative value, defendant's guilt overwhelming, and evidence would take a great deal of time, not error to exclude (*McCluney v. Jos. Schlitz Brewing Co.,* 728 F.2d 924 [7th Cir. 1984]). Defendant not permitted to call informant to testify that on two occasions defendant had not accepted opportunity to engage in arms deal, since such would not show predisposition (*U.S. v. Toner,* 728 F.2d 115 [2nd Cir. 1984]).

Sec. 4.04 How Is Character Evidence Proven? Rule 405 provides that character evidence may be proven as follows:

"(a) *Reputation or Opinion:* In all cases in which evidence of character or a trait of a person is admissible, proof may be made by *testimony as to reputation or by testimony in the form of an opinion.* On cross-examination, inquiry is allowable into *relevant specific instances of conduct.*

(b) *Specific Instances of Conduct:* In cases in which character or a trait of character of a person is an essential element of a charge, claim, or defense, proof may also be made of *specific instances of that person's conduct.*"

HISTORICAL NOTE

"[Or] by testimony in the form of opinion" was not known at common law (though reputation testimony has been described as opinion evidence in disguise).

The Advisory Committee refused to expand method of "specific instances" except where character is in issue (or cross-examination), because though most logical, it also causes most prejudice, confusion, surprise, and consumption of time [*Advisory Committee Notes,* Rule 405(a)].

Court can avoid battle of experts by not letting psychiatrist testify as to "personality type" (*U.S. v. MacDonald,* 688 F.2d 224 [4th Cir. 1982]). But, in assault case, psychiatrist should be permitted to testify defendant more likely to hurt self than others (*U.S. v. Staggs,* 553 F.2d 1073 [7th Cir. 1977]). In defamation action, documents pertaining to character must be produced (*Pagano v. Hadley,* 100 FRD 758 [D.C. DC 1984]).

Evidence of earlier fraud is evidence of intent to commit fraud, in this case (*U.S. v. Fitterer,* 710 F.2d 1328 [8th Cir. 1983]). Evidence woman was raped by defendant while being robbed, ADMITTED to show her credibility to "observe and form lasting impression" (*Thomas v. State,* 615 S.W. 2d 361 [AS 1981]).

TRIAL STRATEGY

When Can You Show Character Through "Special Instances"?

1. "On *cross-examination* inquiry is allowable into *relevant specific instances of conduct*" [Rule 405(a)].

2. "In cases in which *character or trait of character is an essential element* of a charge, claim or defense, proof may be made of *specific instances of that person's conduct*" [Rule 405(b)].

Acts "inextricably intertwined" with charged acts can be admitted (*U.S. v. McCrary,* 699 F.2d 308 [11th Cir. 1983]). Evidence one victim beat another not admissible in involuntary manslaughter case (*U.S. v. Kill Ree,* 691 F.2d 412 [8th Cir. 1982]). Reputation and opinion can show character, but victim's previous act of violence NOT ADMITTED, to support self-defense, since defendant not aware of prior acts at time of killing (*Halfacre v. State,* 639 S.W. 2d 734 [AS 1982]).

Where defendant established alibi with testimony of a good family relation-ship, prosecution could proceed as follows:

Q. In fact, on one occasion some time ago, you injured your father rather severely, did you not?

A. No, I didn't. It wasn't severely, it was pretty minor.

> COUNSEL: Your Honor, I am going to object to going into this once again. If it is character evidence, it is not relevant, and is not permissible under Rule 404.

> COURT: Objection overruled on the grounds previously stated under 404(a)(1).

> WITNESS: Do you want me to tell you about it?

Q. Yes, I would.

A. I can remember like it happened yesterday. . . . Well, I reached over and grabbed the knife and stabbed him in the ass.
(*U.S. v. Dahlin,* 734 F.2d 393 [8th Cir. 1984]).

TRIAL STRATEGY

In Cross-Examining Character Witnesses

1. Have "good faith" basis for questions relative to specific acts.
2. Question witness's familiarity with people where witness lives, works, and spends his or her time.
3. Question witness's familiarity with the reputation of those people.
4. Ask specifically where, when, and from whom witness learned of the reputation.
5. Show any bias on part of witness.
6. Show any bias on part of those upon whom the reputation is based ("only black living in white neighborhood").
7. Question witness's familiarity with reputation personally (investigator not allowed to testify as to what people told him) (*U.S. v. Pezzal,* 643 F.2d 632 (2 Cir. 1981]).
8. If you know of improper basis for reputation, PURSUE IT. "Johnny was unpopular because he refused to perjure himself when the others were caught stealing, isn't that right?"
9. If you know witness is concealing good character traits, PURSUE IT. "Didn't you tell John everyone liked him and couldn't believe this about him?"

10. Inquire about specific instances.
    "Were you aware that he admitted . . ."
11. Avoid arguing with witness.
    "Would you change your mind if you assumed the defendant is guilty of this?" (*U.S. v. Williams*, 738 F.2d 172 [7th Cir. 1984]).
12. Argue importance of special instance if 403 argument advanced.
13. Attack factual basis of an opinion.
14. Limit cross-examination to character trait covered on direct examination.
15. Where character is in issue, pursue the specific instances (opposing counsel is given thorough opportunity because of importance of character issue, so you should cross-examine with same thoroughness).
16. Witness giving opinion should be required to comply with Rule 701 if lay witness (perception) and if expert, then with Rule 702 (special qualification that will assist trier of fact), and Rule 702 (based on what experts in the particular field reasonably rely upon).
17. Ask witness about statements made by party.
    "Didn't defendant tell you he was involved in counterfeiting?" (Held Proper—"other crime" admissible to show intent, etc. (*U.S. v. Thompson*, 730 F.2d 82 (8th Cir. 1984]).
18. Avoid testimony that can cause mistrial.
    "Where were you when defendant told you that?"
    "We were in prison" (*U.S. v. Sostarich*, 684 F.2d 606 [8th Cir. 1982]).

Sec. 4.05 How to Prove Habit or Routine Practice   Closely akin to character evidence is Rule 406, which provides:

> *Habit; Routine Practice* Evidence of the habit of a person or of the routine practice of an organization whether, corroborated or not and regardless of the presence of eyewitnesses, is relevant to prove that the conduct of the person or organization on a particular occasion was in conformity with the habit or routine practice.

REMINDER: *Habit* relates to a person, and *routine practice* relates to an organization. Organization includes corporations and all formal and informal entities.

Dentist testimony that he routinely and regularly informed patients of potential risks ADMITTED (*Meyer v. U.S.*, 464 F.Supp. 317 [Dist. Colo. 1979]). Failure to file income tax returns for prior years ADMITTED in prosecution for failure to file current return (*U.S. v. Luttrell*, 612 F.2d 396 [8th Cir. 1980]). Fact deceased took certain bus regularly, ADMITTED to show he was passenger on the bus prior to being run over (*Howard v. Capitol Transit Co.*, 97 F.Supp. 578 [D.C. DC 1951]).

TRIAL STRATEGY

Prove Habit or Routine Practice

1. Show behavior frequent.
   Four convictions of public intoxication in three and one-half years insufficient to show "regularity" (*Reyes v. Mo. Pacific R.R.*, 589 F.2d 791 [5th Cir. 1979]);
   However, a six-pack, four times a week did suffice (*Keltner v. Ford*, 748 F.2d 1265 [8th Cir. 1984]).
2. Show behavior consistent.
   "Ratio of reactions to situations is important" (*Wilson v. Volkswagen*, 561 F.2d 494 [4th Cir. 1977]).
3. Show time of behavior.
   Discrimination dating back two years, ADMITTED (*Commonwealth v. Porter*, 659 F.2d 306 [3rd Cir. 1981]).
4. Use witness who knows of the "habit" or "routine practice."
   Agent permitted to testify as to "normal procedures" in executing warrant, though he had never observed execution of warrant (*U.S. v. Queseda*, 754 F.2d 1190 [5th Cir. 1985]).
5. Ignore fact there was eyewitness or you have no corroborating witness (*Cereste v. N.Y., New Haven & Hartford*, 231 F.2d 50 [2nd Cir. 1956]).
6. Have the person, if available, testify as to his or her habit.
7. Tie in behavior with negligent acts (or other evidence) that goes to the issue being tried.
8. Rebut 403 objection by showing probative value and lack of prejudice (*balancing* is important).
9. Offer opinion and specific instances.
   Rule 406 is silent on method of proof, and Congress decided to let courts decide on a case-by-case basis; but original 406 included opinions and specific instances as a method, and no real objection to it has come from Congress or the courts. In showing opinion evidence show
   A. personal knowledge
   B. helpful to trier of fact.

Sec. 4.06 How to Get "Subsequent Remedial Measures" Admitted   Rule 407 provides,

> "When, after an event, measures are taken which, if taken previously, would have made the event less likely to occur, evidence of the subsequent measures

is not admissible to prove negligence or culpable conduct in connection with the event."

The rule further provides such exclusion not required . . . . "when offered for another purpose, such as proving ownership, control, or feasibility of precautionary measures, if controverted, or impeachment."

HISTORICAL NOTE

> Nearly a hundred years ago, the Supreme Court of the United States reaffirmed the public policy of not admitting subsequent remedial measures, holding such evidence (correcting conveyor belt) "is calculated to distract the minds of the jury from the real issue and to create a prejudice against the defendant" (*Columbia Railroad v. Hawthorne,* 144 U.S. 202 [U.S. 1892]).
>
> For plaintiff's counsel to seek relief from this public policy, arguing its illogic will not suffice; exceptions must be found, some of which are included in Rule 407.

Since negligence of defendant is not in issue in strict liability case, this rule not applicable (*Unterberger v. Snow Co.,* 630 F.2d 599 [8th Cir. 1980]). But see (*DeLurea v. Winthrop Laboratories,* 697 F.2d 222 [8th Cir. 1983]). Exclusion applies only "to prove negligence or culpable conduct," ADMITTED to show specifications required in action against architect for negligent supervision (*Hennington v. Hennington,* 714 F.2d 773 [8th Cir. 1983]).

Where plaintiff had been raped in motel (defendant), defendant's counsel asked one of the owners of the motel whether police chief had talked to him about putting in peepholes:

A. He felt like we had six-foot picture windows right next to the door. If we put peepholes in, it would be false security.

Q. Did you follow the officer's recommendation in that regard?

A. Yes. We did not put peepholes in at that time.

> ON REDIRECT, plaintiff's counsel asked if he understood correctly, that peepholes were not feasible. Witness again explained this was not feasible and was a false sense of security.

> THEN, plaintiff's counsel introduced evidence that peepholes were later installed.

ADMITTED ON APPEAL: "The plaintiffs were entitled to show affirmatively that these devices were feasible, and furthermore to impeach the credibility of defendants by showing that, although the defendants testified they had done everything necessary for a secure motel, and that chain locks and peepholes would not be successful, they, in fact, took further security measures after (plaintiff) was raped, and in fact, installed the same devices that they testified could not be used successfully" (*Anderson v. Malloy,* 700 F.2d 1208 [8th Cir. 1983]).

"Remedial measure" includes repairing a condition (*Knight v. Otis Elevator Co.,* 596 F.2d 84 [3rd Cir. 1979]), discharge of negligent employee (*Elliot v. Webb,* 98 FRD 293 [D. Idaho 1983]), adopting a new regulation (*Ford v. Schmidt,* 577 F.2d 408 [7th Cir. 1978]), or adopting a new policy (*Hall v. America Steamship Co.,* 688 F.2d 1062 [6th Cir. 1982]).

Most courts have held recall letters from auto manufacturers *are* admissible (*Rozier v. Ford Motor Co.,* 573 F.2d 1332 [5th Cir. 1978]), but see *Vockie v. G. M.,* 66 FRD 57 (E.D. PA 1975). Complying with the National Vehicle Safety Act should be reason for making the changes (*Farner v. Paccan,* 562 F.2d 518 [8th Cir. 1977]).

TRIAL STRATEGY

Get Subsequent Remedial Measure Admitted

1. Show third party made the remedy (*Steele v. Wiedemann Machine Co.,* 280 F.2d 380 [3rd Cir. 1960]).
2. Show defendant was forced to make the remedy by regulation (*Louisville & Nashville Railroad v. Williams,* 370 F.2d 380 [5th Cir. 1966]).
3. Show evidence is offered to prove ownership, if controverted (Rule 407).
4. Show evidence offered to prove control, if controverted (Rule 407).
5. Show evidence offered in rebuttal re "feasibility of precautionary measure" (*Doyle v. U.S.,* 441 F. Supp. 701 (D.C. SC 1977]), usually where defendant claimed
   A. proper care exercised
   B. corrective measures not feasible
6. Show evidence is of an "additional measure" (*Brown v. Link Belt Corp.,* 565 F.2d 1107 [9th Cir. 1977]).
7. Show evidence offered as "alternative means" of public safety (*Chute v. U.S.,* 449 F. Supp. 172 [D. MA 1978]).
8. Show evidence will help jury understand scene of accident. Photo taken after accident and after remedial measure ADMITTED with instruction to ignore the change (*Lebrecht v. Bethlehem Steel,* 402 F.2d 585 [2nd Cir. 1968]).
9. Argue for admission on theory public policy is *not* served by excluding proper evidence. *Remember,* the court has considerable discretion.
10. Show change made *before* accident (not subsequently) though delivered after the accident (*Ramos v. Liberty Mutual Insurance Co.,* 615 F.2d 715 [5th Cir. 1980]).

11. If defendant showed conditions at time of accident, plaintiff can show the change.
12. Argue purpose of evidence is not to show negligence.
13. Argue in products liability case that 407 simply does not apply.

Sec. 4.07 How to Use "Plea Discussions" and "Negotiations"   Rule 408 provides,

"Evidence of (1) furnishing or offering or promising to furnish, or (2) accepting or offering, or promising to accept, a valuable consideration in compromising or attempting to compromise a claim which was disputed as to either validity or amount, is not admissible to prove liability for or invalidity of the claim or its amount."

The rule also provides;

"Evidence of conduct or statements made in compromise negotiations is likewise not admissible." The rule *does not exclude* "evidence otherwise discoverable," or if offered for another purpose, such as "bias or prejudice of a witness, negativing a contention of undue delay, or proving an effort to obstruct a criminal investigation or prosecution."

Rule 410 *pertains to criminal matters* and provides:

"Except as otherwise provided in this rule, evidence of the following is not, in any civil or criminal proceeding, admissible against the defendant who made the plea or was a participant in the plea discussions:

(1) *a plea of guilty which was later withdrawn;*
(2) *a plea of nolo contendere;*
(3) *any statement made in the course of any proceedings under Rule 11 of the Federal Rules of Criminal Procedure or comparable state procedure regarding either of the foregoing pleas; or*
(4) *any statement made in the course of plea discussions with an attorney for the prosecuting authority which do not result in a plea of guilty or which result in a plea of guilty later withdrawn. However, such a statement is admissible (i) in any proceeding wherein another statement made in the course of the same plea or plea discussions has been introduced and the statement ought in fairness be considered contemporaneously with it, or (ii) in a criminal proceeding for perjury or false statement if the statement was made by the defendant under oath, on the record and in the presence of counsel.*

TRIAL STRATEGY

You Are Attempting to Exclude

1. Offers to compromise.
2. Compromises.
3. Conduct during negotiations.
4. Statements during negotiations.

Though Mexican law considers an offer to settle to be a "binding and conclusive" admission of liability, evidentiary law is procedural, hence law of the forum applied and offer excluded (*Morris v. LTV Corp.,* 725 F.2d 1024 [5th Cir.]). Where settlement with one defendant was introduced to show no valid claim against second defendant, EXCLUDED (*Quad/Graphics v. Fass,* 742 F.2d 1230 [7th Cir. 1983]).

HOWEVER, the fact there were negotiations was admitted to show a party had knowledge of pertinent issues (*Breuer Elec. Mfg. v. Tornado Systems of America,* 687 F.2d 182 [7th Cir. 1982]). Testimony as to prior suit between the parties was admitted to show hostility between the parties (*American Family Life Assurance v. Teasdale,* 733 F.2d 559 [8th Cir. 1984]).

A *payment of* a claim is not excluded (*U.S. v. Hooper,* 596 F.2d 219 [7th Cir. 1979]). There must have been a DISPUTE PENDING at the time of the conduct, or statements or the evidence to be EXCLUDED (*Deere & Co. v. International Harvester,* 710 F.2d 1551 [Fed. Cir. 1983]).

"Negotiations" can be questioned during discovery if the testimony may lead to admissible evidence (*Manufacturing Systems, Inc. of Milwaukee v. Computer Tech.,* 99 FRD 335 [D.C. Wisc. 1983]). The judge must BALANCE encouraging settlements with evaluating credibility of witnesses (*Reichenach v. Smith,* 528 F.2d 1072 [5th Cir. 1976]).

TRIAL STRATEGY

In Arguing for Admission of "Negotiations" Show

1. Evidence is "otherwise discoverable."
   EXAMPLE: During negotiations defendant documents were used that were not prepared for negotiations. They were admitted at trial—but contra if prepared specifically for the negotiations (*Ramada Development v. Rauch,* 644 F.2d 1097 [5th Cir. 1981]).
2. Evidence shows "bias or prejudice."
   EXAMPLE: Witness who is testifying had settled his case, and jury

had right to know this may have influenced his testifying (*John McShain, Inc. v. Cessna Aircraft,* 563 F.2d 632 [3rd Cir. 1977]).

3. Evidence negates a claim of undue delay.
    EXAMPLE: Jury is led to believe plaintiff did not take certain action as soon as reasonable, and plaintiff can then rebut the evidence that negotiations were the reason (Rule 408).

4. Evidence shows an effort to obstruct criminal investigation or prosecution.
    EXAMPLE: An agreement is made to settle a case if no criminal charges are brought (such is admissible, Rule 408).

5. No claim or dispute was pending.
    EXAMPLE: Offer made to settle a case before claim or suit filed, ADMITTED (*U.S. v. Peed,* 714 F.2d 7 [4th Cir. 1983]).

6. Evidence offered to show surrounding circumstances.
    EXAMPLE: To show why certain refunds were made in a labor dispute, it was necessary that jury know there was an agreement on that issue (*U.S. v. Wilford,* 710 F.2d 439 [8th Cir. 1983]).

7. Need for the evidence outweighs prejudice.
    EXAMPLE: Where certain promises made during negotiations were not kept, there was a need to admit (*County of Hennepin v. AFG Industries,* 726 F.2d 149 [8th Cir. 1984]).

In a criminal case there must be negotiations in progress, or Rule 410 does not apply (*U.S. v. Robertson,* 582 F.2d 1356 [5th Cir. 1978]). Where U.S. Attorney has authorized F.B.I. agent to negotiate, defendant's statements cannot be used, though defendant did not originally attend the meeting for that purpose (*U.S. v. Grant,* 622 F.2d 308 [8th Cir. 1980]).

TRIAL STRATEGY

To Keep Plea Bargaining Statement Out

1. Show accused exhibited an actual subjective expectation to negotiate a plea at the time.
2. Accused's expectation was reasonable under the circumstances (*U.S. v. Robertson,* 582 F.2d 1356 [5th Cir. 1978]).

Where defendant "breaches" the agreement and pleads not guilty, still NOT ADMISSIBLE (*U.S. v. Grant,* 622 F.2d 308 [8th Cir. 1980]). It must be shown, however, that defendant was contemplating a plea (*U.S. v. Jimenez-Diaz,* 659 F.2d 562 [5th Cir. 1981]).

TRIAL STRATEGY

In Civil and Criminal Cases It Is Important to Make It Clear That Any Statements About to be Made by Client or Counsel, Are Made "Assuming the
Facts Are As You Say . . ."

Sec. 4.08 When Can Payment of Medical Expenses and Similar Expenses Be Used? Rule 409, the Good Samaritan Rule, provides that,

> "*Evidence of furnishing or offering or promising to pay medical, hospital, or
> similar expenses occasioned by an injury is not admissible to prove liability for
> the injury.*"

"LIABILITY FOR INJURY" is the only purpose for which this evidence is
excluded. Where this is the purpose of the testimony, however, there is a strong
public policy that such evidence should be excluded (*Winningham v. Travellers,*
93 F.2d 520 [5th Cir. 1937]).

The "other purposes" include payment to driver as evidence of permission
of driver to operate the vehicle (*Employer's Mutual v. Mosqueda,* 317 F.2d 609
[5th Cir. 1963]) and using maintenance payments to show status as seaman
(*Savoie v. Otto Candies, Inc.,* 692 F.2d 363 [5th Cir. 1982]). Statements made after
apologizing and paying bills was admitted (*Sims v. Sowle,* 395 P.2d 133 [OR
1964]). There need not be a "disputed claim."

Trial courts have wrestled with the statements that include payment of
medicals and admissions of liability. It is the "payment" that is inadmissible, not
the statements that accompany them. Courts have been reluctant to let evidence
in if the jury will learn of medical payment, but sometimes the sacrifice of good
evidence is too great.

TRIAL STRATEGY

Argue Jury Entitled to Hear Important Evidence, Though Jury Will Also
Learn of Medical Payment

1. Try to separate admissible from inadmissible.
   EXAMPLE: "I was drunk, here is one thousand dollars for medical
   bills." Certainly "I was drunk" is an admission that must reach the
   jury—perhaps by having the witness testify to that admission—
   but not the rest of the sentence.
2. Show damages are reasonable by showing defendant would not
   have paid them if they were not.
   EXAMPLE: Defendant paid $100 thousand for a series of operations,
   but denies liability. By arguing the need for proof on damages, at

least a stipulation as to reasonableness can be obtained, and if not, argue the evidence is not being used to prove liability. BALANCING is important here as in all relevancy problems, and the court should encourage a stipulation.

3. Request that any problem be cured by instruction.
   EXAMPLE: "I know you are injured badly, and I will pay for the medical bills." When defendant later denies the plaintiff was really injured, try to separate the two statements; if you can't, tell the judge to instruct the jury it is not to use the statement as proof of liability. IMPORTANT: Do not try to play games with the court by indirectly telling the jury they *should* consider the evidence as proof of liability. Appellate courts often quote from final arguments, and such tactics do not impress juries, trial courts, or appellate courts.

Sec. 4.09 How Can the Jury Learn About "Liability Insurance?" Rule 411 provides

"Evidence that a person was or was not insured against liability is not admissible upon the issue whether the person acted negligently or otherwise wrongfully. This rule does not require the exclusion of evidence of insurance against liability *"when offered for another purpose, such as proof of agency, ownership or control, or bias or prejudice of a witness."*

Statement by plaintiff's counsel during cross-examination and closing argument that the Commonwealth and not the individual defendant would pay the verdict should not have been permitted (*Catrambone v. Bloom,* 13 Fed. R.Ev.Serv. 1707 [M.D. PA 1983]). Where insurance company was a proper defendant and liability insurance was admissible, it was still error to tell jury the amounts of the policies (*Reed v. General Motors,* 773 F.2d 660 [5th Cir. 1985]).

TRIAL STRATEGY

How Jury Learns of Liability Insurance

1. During voir dire (*Kiernan v. Van Schaik,* 347 F.2d 775 [3rd Cir. 1965]).
   EXAMPLE: "Are you, or any member of your family, employed by or have a financial interest in State Farm Insurance Company?"
2. To show bias or prejudice.
   EXAMPLE: Insurance company employee's statement is introduced. Jury has a right to know the statement was taken from a person who may be biased (*Mideastern Contracting Corp. v. O'Toole,* 55 F.2d 909 [2nd Cir. 1932]).

3. To show agency, ownership or control.
   EXAMPLE: Ownership of the vessel was an issue. Plaintiff showed defendant carried liability insurance. This was ADMITTED to show ownership (*Dobbins v. Crain Bros., Inc.,* 432 F.Supp. 1060 [W.D. PA 1976]).

4. Not offered to prove liability and not prejudicial.
   EXAMPLE: Attorney who handled cases for insurance carrier who insured defendant testified that plaintiff's doctor could not be believed. Plaintiff's counsel should have been permitted to cross-examine the witness on his association with the insurance company. Court pointed out that Rule 403 was NOT "designed as a blanket exclusion of evidence of insurance" without a showing of prejudice (*Charter v. Chleborad,* 551 F.2d 246 [8th Cir. 1977]).

5. Where insurance issue is a part of highly probative evidence.
   EXAMPLE: Statement was necessary to establish liability, but it included a reference to insurance. The primary part of the statement is what was being used to make the case on negligence, so the evidence was ADMITTED (*Garee v. McDonnell,* 116 F.2d 79 [7th Cir. 1940]).
   HOWEVER:
   A. *must act in good faith*
   B. *must sever insurance part of statement, if possible*
   C. *court must give appropriate instruction*
   IMPORTANT: Don't ruin a good case with a mistrial, only to have jurors tell you they assumed there was insurance anyway!

Sec. 4.10 When Is "Past Sexual Behavior" of Rape Victim Relevant? Rule 412 provides:

"Notwithstanding any other provision of law, in a criminal case in which a person is accused of rape, or assault with intent to commit rape, reputation or opinion evidence of the past sexual behavior of an alleged victim of such rape or assault is not admissible" (Rule 412[a]).

Rule 412(b) provides such evidence not admissible EXCEPT:

1. Specific instances admitted if "constitutionally required to be admitted," and

   A. written motion filed

   B. written offer of proof filed

   C. judge decides proffer justifies hearing

       D. hearing in chambers in which judge finds relevant and probative value outweighs unfair prejudice or

  2. Specific instances admitted if offered by accused and show (1) source of semen or injury is sex with other than accused, or (2) consent to the rape or assault (sex with accused) and

       A. written motion filed

       B. written offer of proof filed

       C. judge decides proffer justifies hearing

       D. hearing in chambers in which judge finds relevant and probative value outweighs unfair prejudice

Under Rule 412(c)(1) the motion must be filed 15 days before trial, unless judge finds due diligence or newly arisen evidence. Rule 412(c)(2) provides for hearing in chambers, including questioning of victim. Rule 412(d) defines "past sexual behavior" as being other than the alleged rape or assault for which accused is being tried.

Denying psychiatric exam of rape victim is within spirit of Rule 412 (*Government of Virgin Islands v. Scuito*, 623 F.2d 869 [3rd Cir. 1980]). Defendant could not cross-examine as to other rape allegations of the victim, since offered re consent, and this exception applies only to sex with accused (*U.S. v. Nez*, 661 F.2d 1203 [10th Cir. 1981]).

Where accused did not give notice under Rule 412, he could not introduce specific instances for purpose of attacking credibility, since victim's character not put in issue and, under Rule 608(a), specific instances could not then be used (*U.S. v. Lavallie*, 666 F.2d 1217 [8th Cir. 1981]). Rape shield laws do not restrict defendant's Sixth Amendment right to confront and cross-examine witnesses (*Bell v. Harrison*, 670 F.2d 656 [6th Cir. 1982]).

Court prohibited "fishing expedition" into victim's social and sexual life, stating if accused wanted to find out about pattern of conduct, he should have done so before trial (*Bell v. Harrison*, 670 F.2d 656 [6th Cir. 1982]). Court properly refused evidence of victim's past sexual behavior to show condition of vaginal area, since such did not relate to the "injury" exception (*U.S. v. Shaw*, 824 F.2d 601 [8th Cir. 1987]).

"DATE RAPE" CASES have been viewed differently by trial judges, and this area of the law is beginning to reach appellate courts. It has been held in sentencing, that where defendant assumed alleged victim was consenting, and it became apparent that she was not, the accused's state of mind becomes very important, including *what he thought of victim's lack of chastity* (*U.S. v. Fox*, 24 MJ 110 [C. MA 1987]).

The following tables show whether or not states adopting the Federal Rules of Evidence adopted substantially same provisions relative to the rules discussed in this chapter:

	Rule 401	Rule 402	Rule 403	Rule 404	Rule 405	Rule 406
ALASKA	Yes	Yes	Yes	Yes	Yes	Yes
ARIZONA	No	No	Yes	Yes	Yes	Yes
ARKANSAS	Yes	Yes	Yes	Yes	Yes	Yes
COLORADO	Yes	Yes	Yes	Yes	Yes	Yes
DELAWARE	Yes	No	Yes	Yes	Yes	Yes
FLORIDA	Yes	Yes	Yes	Yes	Yes	Yes
HAWAII	Yes	Yes	Yes	No	Yes	Yes
IDAHO	Yes	Yes	Yes	Yes	Yes	Yes
IOWA	Yes	Yes	Yes	No	Yes	Yes
MAINE	Yes	Yes	Yes	Not (b)	No	Yes
MICHIGAN	No	Yes	Yes	No	No	Yes
MINNESOTA	Yes	Yes	Yes	No	Yes	Yes
MISSISSIPPI	Yes	Yes	Yes	No	Yes	Yes
MONTANA	Yes	Yes	Yes	No	No	No
NEBRASKA	Yes	No	Yes	Yes	Yes	No
NEVADA	Yes	Yes	plus	Yes	Yes	Yes
NEW HAMPSHIRE	Yes	Yes	Yes	Yes	Yes	Yes
NEW MEXICO	Yes	Yes	Yes	Yes	Yes	No
NORTH CAROLINA	Yes	Yes	Yes	No	No	Yes
NORTH DAKOTA	Yes	Yes	Yes	Yes	Yes	Yes
OHIO	Yes	Yes	Yes	Yes	Yes	Yes
OKLAHOMA	Yes	Yes	Yes	Yes	Yes	Yes
OREGON	Yes	Yes	Yes	No	No	Yes
RHODE ISLAND	Yes	Yes	Yes	Yes	Yes	Yes
SOUTH DAKOTA	Yes	Yes	Yes	Yes	Yes	Yes
TEXAS	Yes	Yes	Yes	No	Yes	Yes
UTAH	Yes	Yes	Yes	Yes	Yes	Yes
VERMONT	Yes	Yes	Yes	Yes	No	Yes
WASHINGTON	Yes	Yes	Yes	Yes	No	Yes
WEST VIRGINIA	Yes	Yes	Yes	Yes	No	Yes
WISCONSIN	Yes	Yes	Yes	No	Yes	Yes
WYOMING	Yes	Yes	Yes	Yes	No	Yes

Rule	Subject
401	Definition of "Relevant Evidence"
402	Relevant Evidence Generally Admissible
403	Exclusion of Relevant Evidence On Grounds of Prejudice, Confusion, or Waste of Time
404	Character Evidence Not Admissible To Prove Conduct; Exceptions
405	Methods of Proving Character
406	Habit; Routine Practice

	Rule 407	Rule 408	Rule 409	Rule 410	Rule 411	Rule 412
ALASKA	Yes	No	Yes	Yes	Yes	Yes
ARIZONA	Yes	Yes	Yes	Yes	Yes	No
ARKANSAS	Yes	No	Yes	No	No	No
COLORADO	Yes	Yes	Yes	Yes	Yes	No
DELAWARE	Yes	Yes	Yes	No	Yes	Yes
FLORIDA	Mod	Yes	Yes	Yes	No	No
HAWAII	Yes	Yes	Yes	Yes	Yes	Yes
IDAHO	Yes	Yes	Yes	Yes	Yes	Yes
IOWA	plus	Yes	Yes	Yes	Yes	Yes
MAINE	No	No	Yes	Yes	No	Yes
MICHIGAN	Yes	Yes	Yes	Yes	Yes	No
MINNESOTA	Yes	Yes	No	Yes	Yes	No
MISSISSIPPI	Yes	Yes	Yes	Yes	Yes	Yes
MONTANA	Yes	Yes	No	Yes	Yes	No
NEBRASKA	Yes	Yes	Yes	Yes	Yes	No
NEVADA	Yes	Yes	Yes	Yes	Yes	Mod
NEW HAMPSHIRE	Yes	plus	plus	Yes	Yes	No
NEW MEXICO	Yes	Yes	Yes	Yes	Yes	No
NORTH CAROLINA	Yes	Yes	Yes	Yes	Yes	No
NORTH DAKOTA	Yes	Yes	Yes	Yes	Yes	No
OHIO	Yes	Yes	Yes	Yes	Yes	Yes
OKLAHOMA	Yes	Yes	Yes	Yes	Yes	No
OREGON	Yes	Yes	No	No	Yes	plus
RHODE ISLAND	No	Yes	Yes	Yes	Yes	No
SOUTH DAKOTA	Yes	Yes	Yes	Yes	Yes	No
TEXAS	plus	Yes	Yes	No	Yes	Yes
UTAH	Yes	Yes	Yes	Yes	Yes	Yes
VERMONT	Yes	Yes	Yes	Yes	Yes	No
WASHINGTON	Yes	Yes	Yes	No	Yes	No
WEST VIRGINIA	Yes	Yes	Yes	Yes	Yes	No
WISCONSIN	Yes	Yes	Yes	Yes	Yes	No
WYOMING	Yes	Yes	Yes	No	Yes	No

Rule	Subject
407	Subsequent Remedial Measures
408	Compromise and Offers to Compromise
409	Payment of Medical and Similar Expenses
410	Inadmissibility of Pleas, Plea Discussions, and Related Statements
411	Liability Insurance
412	Rape Cases; Relevance of Victim's Past Behavior

See Sec. 12.03 for Discussion of the Law in Non-FRE States Relative to the Rules Discussed in This Chapter.

5

PRIVILEGE IS A RIGHT—USE IT

See Federal Rules of Evidence
Article Five: Privileges

Sec. 5.01 When Does a Privilege Exist?   Rule 501, the only FRE rule relating to privilege, provides that, unless otherwise excepted, privilege shall be governed by *"the principles of common law as they may be interpreted by the courts of the United States in the light of reason and experience".* However, state laws shall apply in civil actions *"with respect to an element of a claim or defense as to which state law provides the rule of decision".*

EXAMPLE OF PRIVILEGE

Attorney-Client Privilege
IF:

1. Client (individual or corporate) seeks legal advice (directly or through another)

2. From an attorney admitted in any state (in his capacity as an attorney; directly or through representative [including secretary or paralegal])

3. In confidence (no third party present unless presence necessary in furtherance of the legal services, or for communication between attorney and client [privilege though accused's father present during interview]) and

4. Intended to be confidential (not to be made public),

THEN:

1. Any such communication is protected

2. Permanently

3. At any stage of the proceeding

4. From disclosure by client or attorney

5. Unless waived by:

   (a) Client, or

   (b) His estate etc.

By:

   (1) Consenting to publication, or

   (2) Making public

Where state and federal law apply to same claim, courts usually refuse to follow state policy. *(Wm. T. Thompson Co. v. General Nutrition Corp., Inc.,* 671 F.2d 100 [3rd Cir. 1982]). Where multi-state contact, law of forum usually applied. (See pre-FRE case, *Klaxon Co. v. Sentor Electric Mfg. Co.,* 313 U.S. 487 (1941) Law of state where deposition is being taken is usually applied. *(In Re Westinghouse,* 76 F.R.D. 47 [W.D. Va. 1977]), but see Restatement of Conflict of Laws, Second.

TRIAL STRATEGY

In Showing That Privilege Exists,
ARGUE:

1. Confidential communication.
2. Confidential relationship.
3. Community recognizes need for the privilege.
4. Need for confidence exceeds need for the evidence (including, other evidence available).

Though only one privilege rule was adopted by Congress, several rules were submitted by the Supreme Court, and are considered by courts. They include in-depth provisions relating to attorney-client, required reports privileged by statute (examples: FLORIDA: accident reports, MICHIGAN: property tax), parent-child or family, psychotherapist-patient, communications to clergy, trade secrets, secrets of state and other official information, and identity of informants.

REMEMBER:

1. "In light of reason and experience" suggests "case-by-case" approach

2. Privilege is "strictly construed" since it excludes otherwise admissible evidence. *Elkins v. U.S.,* 364 U.S. 206 (1960)

3. If close question, court will admit the evidence,

4. Proponent of the evidence must show "substantial need" and inability "without undue hardship to obtain substantial equivalents" (See F. Rules of Civil P. 26 (b)(3).

HUSBAND-WIFE PRIVILEGE: The United States Supreme Court has held it is the spouse-witness, and not the spouse-accused who decides whether the spouse-witness will testify. *Trammel v. U.S.,* 445 U.S. 40 (1980). There is no privilege where marriage no longer exists, or where marriage is a sham. There is split of authority as to admitting out of court statement where privilege would have been avoided in court statement.

MISCELLANEOUS PRIVILEGES: There was no PHYSICIAN-PATIENT privilege at common law, and none in FRE, but state law allowing such a privilege is accepted in federal courts. Where the communication is not for diagnosis or treatment, is for commitment or restoration, or re will contest, the privilege normally does not apply. Though some state courts recognize an accountant privilege, federal courts do not.

Sec. 5.02 Who Has the Privilege? In *Trammel,* the Supreme Court of the United States made it clear the spouse-witness decides whether or not to testify against the spouse-accused. However, the same Court held that a confidential communication between husband and wife belongs to either spouse giving the communication.

TRIAL STRATEGY

In arguing to the Court, WHO HAS THE PRIVILEGE, cite the unadopted, but persuasive, Recommended 503, re attorney-client privilege:

"Who may claim the privilege. The privilege may be claimed by the client, his or her client, his or her guardian or conservator, the personal representative of a deceased client, or the successor, trustee, or similar representative of a corporation, association, or other organization, whether or not in existence. The person who was the lawyer at the time of the communication may claim the privilege, but only on behalf of the client. His or her authority to do so is presumed in the absence of evidence to the contrary (see also, U.S. v. Juarez, 575 F.2d 267 [5th Cir. 1978]).

The Trustee may assert the privilege for Debtor [*Commodity Future Commission*, 105 S.Ct. 1986 (1985)]. Either present or past attorney may claim privilege, but if they differ as to client's desire, present attorney shall decide (*U.S. v. DeLillo*, 448 F.Supp. 840 [E.D. NY. 1978]). A spouse is presumed to be able to claim the privilege for an absent spouse (recommended 505). The privilege as to identity of an informant may be claimed by "an officer of the government, or of a state or subdivision thereof" (recommended 510).

Sec. 5.03 How Can a Privilege Be Waived?   A privilege is meaningless unless it is asserted. If a privilege is waived, evidence that is otherwise inadmissible will be admitted.

TRIAL STRATEGY

Avoid Waiving a Privilege By

1. Objecting at FIRST OPPORTUNITY.
2. Not giving such evidence VOLUNTARILY.
3. By NOT OPENING THE DOOR with other evidence, that, in fairness, makes the privileged evidence admissible.

Recommended 511 provides:

"A person upon whom these rules confer a privilege against disclosure of the confidential matter or communication waives the privilege if he or his predecessor while holder of the privilege voluntarily discloses or consents to disclosure of any significant part of the matter or communication. This rule does not apply if the disclosure is itself a privileged communication."

The client cannot testify that he was not advised, or not properly advised, then claim the privilege (*U.S. v. Miller,* 600 F.2d 498 [5th Cir. 1979]). Recommended 512, however, provides there is no waiver if the disclosure was compelled erroneously, or made without an opportunity to claim the privilege.

TRIAL STRATEGY

Avoid Waiving the Attorney-Client Privilege By:

1. Avoiding voluntary disclosure.
2. Avoiding "opening the door."
3. Avoiding interview of client with others present unless their presence is necessary to rendering of services or communication.
4. Obtaining information from corporate client through corporate employee who has the privilege.
5. Making sure confidence is intended.

Sec. 5.04 Criminal Privileges v. Civil Privileges   Rule 501 has special significance in the criminal trial. If not excepted by the Constitution, Federal Law, or Supreme Court rule, privilege "shall be governed by the principles of the common law as they may be interpreted by the courts of the United States in light of reason and experience."

The role of the informant is extremely important in a criminal trial. The privilege has long been recognized, and does not violate the confrontation protection (*McCray v. Illinois,* 386 U.S. 300 [1967]). The trial lawyer, however, must know when he can pierce that privilege.

TRIAL STRATEGY

Pierce the Privilege of Informant By:

1. Showing identity of informant has been disclosed.
2. Move for the court to determine (in camera) if "informant may be able to give testimony necessary to fair determination of guilt or innocence." (Force government to dismiss or disclose.)
   Court must BALANCE need to protect and need for fair trial (*Roviaro v. U.S.,* 353 U.S. 54 [1957]).

Investigative reports are privileged only to extent needed to encourage proper prosecution (*Black v. Sheraton,* 564 F.2d 531 [D.C. Cir. 1977]); *Denver P.P.A. v. Lichtenstein,* 660 F.2d 432 [10th Cir. 1981]). REMEMBER: Most privilege questions in criminal trials have been resolved in favor of the prosecution. However, this only increases the demand upon the criminal defense lawyer to insist that serious constitutional questions are involved, and the PROSECUTION MUST SHOW A NEED.

Sec. 5.05 Relying Upon the Privilege It is often to the trial lawyer's benefit that the privilege exists and that it not be waived or otherwise lost. To rely upon the privilege, counsel must first know under what circumstances a privilege will exist (see Sec. 11.01). Once a privilege exists, make sure it has not been waived (see Sec. 11.03).

In relying upon a privilege counsel should argue the need to protect the communication. This should be argued, even where there was no such privilege at common law (*Totten v. U.S.,* 92 U.S. 1057 [1876]), and more recent cases.

TRIAL STRATEGY

In Arguing for the Privilege Recite the Key Words of Rule 501

". . . shall be governed by the principles of the common law as they may be interpreted by the courts of the United States IN THE LIGHT OF REASON AND EXPERIENCE."

The privilege is often so important that damage is done once the information is made public, even if it does not reach the ears of the jury. In such a case, counsel has a serious responsibility to his client.

TRIAL STRATEGY

In Camera Proceedings Should Be Used Relative To:

1. Trade secrets.
2. Informants.
3. Other matters where the privilege is sensitive to public exposure.

Relying upon a corporate privilege has caused the courts considerable concern. For many years the "control group" test was followed by the courts, under which only communications between counsel and those in control were privileged (*Philadelphia v. Westinghaus*, 210 F.Supp. 483 [E.D. PA 1980]). However, in 1981 in UPJOHN, the court expanded the representatives of a corporation with whom the attorney could "communicate," not adopting a definite rule, but leaving the courts to a case-by-case approach (*Upjohn Co. v. United States*, 449 U.S. 383 [1981]).

TRIAL STRATEGY

In Claiming Work Product Privilege

Argue the evidence "reveals the attorney's mental process"
CITE: *Upjohn Co. v. United States*, 44 US 383 and *Hickman v. Taylor*, 329 US 495.

Sec. 5.06 Getting Around the Privilege   Privilege is contrary to the concept of admitting relevant evidence that can help determine an issue. In opposing the privilege, counsel must show a NEED for the evidence and a LACK OF HARM to those who have the privilege.

Each privilege has its own vulnerability:

TRIAL STRATEGY

If Attacking Marital Privilege Show

1. Failure to prove valid marriage.
2. Failure to prove communication (most courts require utterance, and not mere nonverbal communication).
3. Failure to prove intent that the communication be confidential (conversation private, and intended to be so).
4. Testimony of marital communication by third party (some courts accept eavesdropper's testimony unless obtained by betrayal or connivance of spouse).
5. Testimony pertained to spouses involvement in future or ongoing crimes (courts are not unanimous).

In addition to above communication privilege, there is a marital testimonial (refusing to testify) privilege that applies only in criminal cases, which can only be asserted by the testifier. It includes non-confidential matters, cannot be asserted after the marriage, and in some courts does not cover statements about events that occurred before the marriage.

TRIAL STRATEGY

In Attacking the Attorney-Client Privilege, Remember

1. Client must be seeking legal advice.
2. Attorney must be admitted in some states (his personnel included).
3. Communication must be in confidence.
4. Communication must be intended to be confidential.
5. Privilege has not been waived.
6. If document is subject to process if in possession of client, it is subject to process if in possession of attorney.
7. No privilege if it furthers crime or fraud.
8. Some courts hold communication from attorney to client is privileged only if it reveals client's confidences.
9. Identifying facts are not privileged, but courts are not in agreement as to client's identity, whereabouts, or fee arrangement.
10. Upjohn rule expanded those within corporation with whom communications by attorney are privileged.
11. No privilege where dispute arises between attorney and client (such as attorney suing for fee).

The following table shows whether or not states adopting the Federal Rules of Evidence adopted substantially same provisions relative to the rules discussed in this chapter:

	Rule 501
ALASKA	No
ARIZONA	No
ARKANSAS	No
COLORADO	No
DELAWARE	No
FLORIDA	Mod
HAWAII	No
IDAHO	No
IOWA	Yes
MAINE	No
MICHIGAN	No
MINNESOTA	No
MISSISSIPPI	No
MONTANA	No
NEBRASKA	No

	Rule 501
NEVADA	plus
NEW HAMPSHIRE	No
NEW MEXICO	No
NORTH CAROLINA	Yes
NORTH DAKOTA	No
OHIO	Yes
OKLAHOMA	plus
OREGON	No
RHODE ISLAND	Yes
SOUTH DAKOTA	No
TEXAS	Yes
UTAH	No
VERMONT	Yes
WASHINGTON	No
WEST VIRGINIA	No
WISCONSIN	Yes
WYOMING	No

Rule   Subject

501   Privileges-General Rule

See Sec. 12.04 for Discussion of the Law in Non-FRE States Relative to the Rules Discussed in This Chapter.

6

CHALLENGING COMPETENCY OF WITNESSES AND EVIDENCE

See Federal Rules of Evidence
Article Six: Witnesses

Sec. 6.01 Challenge Legal Competency of Witness
Rule 601 provides, "Every person is competent to be a witness except as otherwise provided in these rules." The trial judge has full discretion as to competency except as to requirements of Rule 602 that "a witness may not testify to matter unless evidence is introduced sufficient to support a finding that the witness has personal knowledge of the matter." Rule 602 further provides, "evidence to prove personal knowledge may, but need not, consist of the witness' own testimony," and that this rule is subject to Rule 703, relating to expert opinions.

HISTORICAL NOTE

1. At early common law, even parties to a lawsuit were not competent to testify.
2. Before Federal Rules of Evidence, counsel would often request hearing on competency of witness to show such matters as witness too young or too senile to testify.
3. Under Rule 601 the judge exercises discretion except to hear evidence of lack of preception.

Although insanity as such is no longer a ground for disqualifying a witness, see FRE 601, a district judge has the power, and in an appropriate case the duty, to hold a hearing to determine whether a witness should be allowed to testify because insanity has made him incapable of testifying in a competent fashion" (*U.S. v. Gutman,* 725 F.2d 417 [7th Cir. 1984]). The Court added, however, that the trial judge would be reversed only if there was a "clear conviction that he erred."

Rule 601 also provides that competency is to be decided by state law, where "State law provides the rule of decision." The same limitations applied to presumptions in Rule 302, however, apply to competency (see Sec. 2.04).

Federal courts have held that where federal question is involved, state law does not apply, but may be considered, and in doing so, the following is important:

1. *The need for uniformity throughout the nation.*
2. *Whether application of state law would conflict with federal policy underlying federal law.*
3. *Whether a uniform federal rule displacing state law would disrupt an area of traditional local concern (Hanes v. Mid-America Petroleum, Inc.,* 577 F.Supp. 637 [W.D. MO 1983]).

HISTORICAL NOTE

Rule 607 provides, *"The credibility of a witness may be attacked by any party, including the party calling the witness."* This is the federal rule's most radical departure from the common law. Courts were so accustomed to warning counsel about impeaching his own witness, that some states have refused to adopt this provision.

Though counsel may impeach his own witness, "It would be an abuse of the rule, in a criminal case for prosecution to call a witness that it knew would not give it useful evidence, just so prosecution could introduce hearsay evidence against the defendant in the hope that the jury would miss the subtle distinction between "impeachment and substantive evidence" (*U.S. v. Webster,* 734 F.2d 1193 [7th Cir. 1984]).

Example ———

Prosecution knew witness would deny the FBI agent's testimony, but put her on stand so they could impeach her with testimony of agent whose hearsay testimony could be used to impeach witness but could not have been used as substantive evidence—NOT ADMISSIBLE! (*U.S. v. Crouch,* 731 F.2d 621 [9th Cir. 1984]).

Sec. 6.02 Challenge "Personal Knowledge" of All Witnesses   Rule 602 retains for counsel his or her right to attack perception of witness. Though the judge has discretion in this matter, the trial lawyer has a duty to pursue the question of actual knowledge.

TRIAL STRATEGY

Attack Competence of Witness By Asking

1. Did witness PERCEIVE occurrence or have admissible opinion?
2. Can witness REMEMBER the perception so he or she can NOW give the testimony?
3. Can witness COMMUNICATE this evidence?
4. Is the testimony SINCERE, as shown by giving of oath or substitute?

Sec. 6.03 Challenge Degree of Competency As to Special Testimony   One of the modern problems relating to competency as to special testimony relates to testimony induced by hypnosis. There is still a conflict with some courts admitting "reliable" post-hypnosis testimony and some finding hypnosis may cause previous acceptable evidence to be inadmissible.

TRIAL STRATEGY

In Attacking Testimony Based on Post-Hypnosis Testimony, Show

1. Hypnotist not qualified psychiatrist or psychologist experienced in hypnosis.
2. Hypnotist not independent.
3. Information given hypnotist before session not recorded.

4. Before hypnosis, witness did not describe facts as he remembered them.
5. All contact between hypnotist and witness not recorded (video is preferred method).
6. Others present during session.

The above standards adopted in New Jersey and Oregon (*State v. Hurd,* 432 A.2d 86 [1981]; Ore. Rev. Stat. Sec. 136.675 [1981]). Federal Bureau of Investigation GUIDELINES: (a) Require written permission of witness (b) accept qualified physicians and dentists (c) need not work independently (*U.S. v. Valdez,* 722 F.2d 1196 [5th Cir. 1984]).

Another modern problem facing courts and counsel is the use of drugs by witnesses before testifying. The court must be alert to such situations and must decide whether or not a witness is competent to testify, and counsel must be alert to call this to court's attention (Rule 601).

Example ⎯⎯⎯⎯⎯⎯⎯⎯⎯⎯⎯⎯⎯⎯⎯⎯⎯⎯⎯⎯⎯⎯⎯⎯⎯⎯⎯⎯⎯

Court noticed witness' unusual manner and asked if he had used medication before testifying. Witness denied this but later said, "I don't feel good." Judge excused jury and asked if he would submit to a drug exam and witness agreed. Examining doctor testified that witness was under an influence while testifying, but was now free from such influence. Judge told jury what happened, told them to disregard the earlier testimony, then had witness testify again. APPELLATE COURT COMMENDED TRIAL JUDGE'S HANDLING OF MATTER (*U.S. v. Hyson,* 721 F.2d 856 [1st Cir. 1983]).

One of the main reasons for applying state law under Rule 601 was to preserve the state Dead Man's Statutes. Under such laws a person claiming against an estate is incompetent to present certain testimony that cannot be rebutted because the party is dead.

Each state law is different and most statutes have been heavily adjudicated. Most statutes can be easily waived (in Florida by using the witness' deposition at trial, and in Missouri by the mere taking of the deposition).

State law on competency is used only in cases based on state law. In a federal-question-based civil rights Section 1983 case, the court found, "compelling federal interest for refusing to apply state policy or procedure (*Langoria By Langoria v. Wilson,* 730 F.2d 300 [5th Cir. 1984]).

Rule 610 provides:

"Evidence of the beliefs or opinions of a witness on matters of religion is not admissible for the purpose of showing that by reason of their nature the witness' credibility is impaired or enhanced." The fact that witness religion rejects violence cannot be used to enhance credibility (*Government of Virgin Islands v. Peterson,* 553 F.2d 324 [3rd Cir. 1977]).

Sec. 6.04 Require the Oath   Rule 603 provides, "every witness shall be required to declare that the witness will testify truthfully, by oath or affirmation administered in a form calculated to awaken the witness' conscience and impress the witness' mind with the duty to do so." Counsel cannot question witness as to why he or she insists upon an affirmation rather than an oath (*People v. Wood*, 66 NY 2d 374 [NY 1985]).

When the witness refuses to give oath or affirmation, the judge simply refuses to let him or her testify (*U.S. v. Fowler*, 605 F.2d 181 [5th Cir. 1979]). Qualifying by affirmation instead of oath should be done outside the hearing of the jury (*U.S. v. Raab*, 394 F.2d 230 [3rd Cir. 1968]). The trial judge must be satisfied that some kind of ceremony did "awaken his conscience" (*U.S. v. Haro*, 573 F.2d 661 [10th Cir. 1978]).

TRIAL STRATEGY

Insist Upon Oath or Affirmation, To

1.   Impress upon witness seriousness of his or her testimony.
2.   Remind witness of perjury possibilities.

Sec. 6.05 Interpreters As Witnesses   Rule 604 provides that

"An interpreter is subject to the provisions of these rules relating to qualification as an expert and the administration of an oath or affirmation to make a true translation."

Federal Rules of Civil Procedure, Rule 43(f) and Federal Rules of Criminal Procedure, Rule 28, authorize the court to appoint interpreters; but FRE Rule 604 requires: he qualify as an expert as per Rule 702, and that he give the oath.

TRIAL STRATEGY

Handle Interpreter Situations Carefully

1.   In criminal cases make sure interpreter keeps defendant informed as to what *everyone in the courtroom* is saying.
2.   Avoid long conversations between witness and interpreter.
3.   Keep eye on jury, and adjust as you see how jurors are reacting to this unusual kind of testimony.
     A.   if they are bored, try to hurry it up!
     B.   if they seem confused, have interpreter stop and make sure jury is following testimony.

C. if sympathy is running for or against the witness because of the situation, EXPAND OR RETRACT this testimony, depending on whether this is helping or hurting.

Sec. 6.06 Incompetency of Judge or Juror As Witnesses

Rule 605 provides, "The judge presiding at the trial may not testify in that trial as a witness," and "no objection need be made in order to preserve the point." Rule 606(a) provides that at trial

"A member of the jury may not testify as a witness before that jury in the trial of the case in which the juror is sitting. If the juror is called so to testify, the opposing party shall be afforded an opportunity to object out of the presence of the jury."

The judge should not admit affidavit of lawyer on personal knowledge of attorney's trustworthiness (*Furtado v. Bishop*, 604 F.2d 80 [1st Cir. 1979]). The judge is disqualified from hearing contempt where charge based on disrespect toward him [*Fed. Rules Crim. Proc.* 42(b)].

TRIAL STRATEGY

If Judge Called As a Witness, Insist That He Either

1. Recuse himself and declare new trial.
2. Refuse to testify.
   (In criminal case, be alert to constitutional problem.)

The best way to avoid the juror-witness problem is to conduct a proper voir dire. Rarely does the need to testify arise during trial, but when it does, be prepared for it.

TRIAL STRATEGY

If Juror Called As Witness

1. Take action outside hearing of jury.
2. Argue Rule 606(a), insisting:
   A. jurors may side with testifying juror
   B. vigorous cross-examination of juror may offend other jurors
   C. juror-witness has not been sequestered like other witnesses

---

Rule 606(b) provides for inquiry into the validity of a verdict or an indictment:

> "a juror may not testify as to any matter or statement occurring during the course of the jury's deliberations or to the effect of anything upon that or any other juror's mind or emotions as influencing the juror to assent to or dissent from the verdict or indictment or concerning the juror's mental processes in connection therewith, EXCEPT THAT "a juror may testify on the question whether extraneous prejudicial information was improperly brought to the jury's attention or whether any outside influence was improperly brought to bear upon any juror." (nor may affidavit of juror be used for those purposes).

This rule protects jurors from inquiry into their "*subjective motivations and mental processes*" (*U.S. v. Green,* 523 F.2d 229 [2nd Cir. 1975]), but DOES stunt inquiry where "*substantial evidence of bias*" (*Smith v. Brewer,* 444 F.Supp 482 [S.D. IA 1978]). Juror telling non-juror during recess, "I think the black bastard is guilty," held not sufficient showing of prejudice to disturb finality of verdict (*Wright v. U.S.,* 559 NY Supp. 1139 [E.D. NY 1983]). Each state has its own rule as to what contact, if any, counsel can have with jurors after trial, so the trial lawyer must be careful not to violate any such rule.

Sec. 6.07 The Role of Attorney As Witness

No specific rule applies to attorneys as witnesses, as in the case of judges and jurors. It is only under Rule 601 that the judge can use his discretion and determine an attorney to be incompetent to testify.

The lawyer-as-witness problem is really a problem of ethics. The American Bar Association Code of Professional Responsibility EC-5-9 provides

> "If a lawyer is both counsel and witness he becomes more impeachable for interest and becomes a less effective witness . . . an advocate who becomes a witness is in the unseemly and ineffective position of arguing his own credibility. The rules of an advocate and a witness are inconsistent; the function of an advocate is to advance or argue the cause of another, while that of a witness is to state the facts objectively."

DR 5-102 provides that if it becomes apparent an attorney or his firm "ought to be called as a witness on behalf of his client, he shall withdraw from the conduct of the trial.

Rule 611(a) gives the court "reasonable control over the mode and order of interrogating witnesses and presenting evidence so as to make the interrogation and presentation effective for ascertainment of truth." This authority, plus the general competency determining powers of Rule 601 are used by courts to control testimony of attorneys.

TRIAL STRATEGY

Keep Attorney Testimony Out by Showing:

1. Attorney's testimony would exceed preliminary matter or undisputed matter.
2. This is a jury trial.
3. Court should not encourage or condone unethical conduct.
4. Attorney must withdraw or not testify, and withdrawing now would disrupt and prejudice the trial.
5. Attorney knew or should have known before trial he or she would be a witness.
6. The need for attorney's testimony is exceeded by ethical considerations and fairness.
7. Attorney could have had nonlawyer personnel obtain this evidence—they are not subject to the testify-or-withdraw problem (*U.S. v. Nyman,* 649 F.2d 208 [4th Cir. 1980]).
8. The attorney was not sequestered with other witnesses.
9. The attorney-witness should have resolved this problem at the pretrial conference.

The more of these points you can argue effectively, the better your chances are for excluding the testimony.

One court held the attorney could neither testify nor withdraw, since it was improper to testify, and court has complete control over withdrawing during trial (*U.S. v. Brown,* 417 F.2d 1068 [5th Cir. 1969]). Another court held, however, the attorney could testify, then suffer the consequences of his unethical conduct (*Universal Athletics Sales Co. v. American Gym, Inc.,* 546 F. Del. 530).

The courts usually have no problem letting attorneys testify on "preliminary" or "undisputed" matters. An assistant U.S. attorney was permitted to testify as to chain of custody of a letter, when he was the only one who could do it (*U.S. v. Trapnell,* 638 F.2d 1016 [7th Cir. 1982]).

Sec. 6.08 Attack Credibility By Attacking Competency   Rule 601 qualifies witnesses that were not competent to testify at common law. This increases the duty of the trial lawyer to attack the credibility of those once not permitted to testify.

Example _____

At common law, a child of a very young age could not testify because he was not competent. Under Rule 601 the child IS competent, BUT COUNSEL CAN CROSS-EXAMINE.

Competency is for the judge to decide. Once the judge decides the witness is competent, the jury becomes the judge of the credibility of the witness.

TRIAL STRATEGY

Attack Credibility

1. Show poor perception.
2. Show poor nature of evidence, such as hearsay or circumstantial.
3. Show age.
4. Show questionable mental capacity.
5. Show lack of physical capacity.
6. Show lack of memory.
7. Show effect of drugs or alcohol on witness's testimony.

and do it all with class!

REMEMBER: A *minimum* of qualification is needed to establish competency; a maximum of qualification is needed to establish credibility.

Rule 609 provides that credibility of a witness may be attacked with conviction of a crime, where crime was punished by death, or imprisonment for more than a year—where judge feels probative value outweighs prejudicial effect—or crime involves "dishonesty or false statement." EXCEPT: A crime which occurred more than ten years ago or "the conviction has been subject of a pardon, annulment, or other equivalent procedure based on a finding of innocence."

IMPORTANT: The U.S. Supreme Court has resolved a split of authority by holding that: "Federal Rules of Evidence 609(a)(1) requires a judge to permit impeachment of a civil witness with evidence of prior convictions regardless of ensuant unfair prejudice to the witness or the party offering the testimony" (*Green v. Bock Laundry Machine*, [Decided 5-22-89] 104 L.Ed. 2d 557). The Court's discussion suggests the broad discretion under FRE 403 to avoid prejudice is limited by the limitation of a specific rule and that in such cases balancing would not be permitted.

TRIAL STRATEGY

Obtain Proof of Conviction From:

1. Police records.
2. Court records.

Sec. 6.09 Competency and Sequestered Witnesses   Rule 615 provides:

"At the request of a party the court shall order witnesses excluded so that they cannot hear the testimony of other witnesses and it may make the order of its own motion." The rule does not authorize exclusion of:

"(1) a party who is a natural person, or
(2) an officer or employee of a party which is not a natural person designated as its representative by its attorney, or
(3) a person whose presence is shown by a party to be essential to the presentation of the party's cause."

TRIAL STRATEGY

Insist Upon the Right To:

1. Keep witness from adopting testimony of other witnesses.
2. Keep witness from avoiding conflicting testimony.

"Restraint on witnesses tailoring their testimony to that of earlier witnesses; and it aids in detecting testimony that is less than candid" (*Geder v. U.S.*, 425 U.S. 80 [1976]).

The court should instruct witnesses not to discuss testimony with others, EXCEPT THE ATTORNEY (*Potaschnick v. Port City Construction Co.*, 449 U.S. 820 [1980]). Witness cannot read daily transcript of what other witnesses are saying (*Miller v. Universal City Studios, Inc.*, 650 F.2d 1365 [5th Cir. 1981]).

The rule specifically provides for corporate representatives, and it has been held that a police officer can be the representative remaining in the courtroom (*U.S. v. Jones*, 687 F.2d 1265 [8th Cir. 1982]). If more than one person required as "representative," the request shall be made and court must have one representative in the courtroom during part of the trial, and another during other parts of the trial, or merely find the second representative to be a person necessary to the trial of the lawsuit.

Where it was shown presence of expert witness necessary to "management of case," court is bound to permit him to remain in the courtroom (*Morvant v. Construction Aggregates Corp.*, 570 F.2d 626 [6th Cir. 1978]). Non-experts, such as a mother who wants to be with a child victim, have been permitted to remain in the courtroom.

HISTORICAL NOTE

1. At Common Law, Judge Had Discretion. Rule 615 says court *shall* . . .
2. Request to "invoke the rule" or "invoke the rule on witnesses" has always constituted a request for sequestration, *and still does!*

IMPORTANT: Make sure opponent's sequestered witnesses are not in the courtroom, because the remedy for this violation is inadequate—(1) contempt, (2) telling the jury of the noncompliance, or (3) refusing witness' testimony. Although it is within court's discretion, courts simply do not exclude the noncomplying witness' testimony except under extremely rare circumstances (*U.S. v. Ell,* 718 F.2d 291 [9th Cir. 1983]).

Though Rule 615 does not mention it, the exclusion-of-witnesses rule is usually followed at depositions. If counsel cannot agree, the court may be called upon to use its discretion.

The following tables show whether or not states adopting the Federal Rules of Evidence adopted substantially same provisions relative to the rules discussed in this chapter:

	Rule 601	Rule 602	Rule 603	Rule 604	Rule 605	Rule 606	Rule 607
ALASKA	No	Yes	Yes	Yes	Yes	Yes	No
ARIZONA	No	Yes	Yes	Yes	Yes	No	No
ARKANSAS	No	Yes	Yes	Yes	Yes	Yes	Yes
COLORADO	No	Yes	Yes	Yes	Yes	Yes	Yes
DELAWARE	No	Yes	Yes	Yes	Yes	Yes	Yes
FLORIDA	Yes	Yes	plus	Yes	Yes	Yes	No
HAWAII	No	Yes	Yes	Yes	Yes	No	Yes
IDAHO	Yes	Yes	Yes	Yes	Yes	Yes	Yes
IOWA	Yes	Yes	Yes	Yes	Yes	Yes	Yes
MAINE	Yes	Yes	Yes	Yes	Yes	Yes	Yes
MICHIGAN	No	Yes	Yes	Yes	Yes	Yes	No
MINNESOTA	No	Yes	Yes	Yes	Yes	Yes	Yes
MISSISSIPPI	No	Yes	Yes	Yes	Yes	Yes	Yes
MONTANA	No	Yes	Yes	Yes	Yes	No	Yes
NEBRASKA	No	Yes	Yes	Yes	Yes	No	Yes
NEVADA	Yes	Yes	plus	Yes	Yes	Yes	Yes
NEW HAMPSHIRE	No	Yes	Yes	Yes	Yes	Yes	Yes
NEW MEXICO	No	Yes	Yes	Yes	Yes	Yes	Yes
NORTH CAROLINA	No	Yes	Yes	Yes	Yes	Yes	Yes
NORTH DAKOTA	No	Yes	Yes	Yes	Yes	No	Yes
OHIO	No	Yes	Yes	Yes	Yes	No	No
OKLAHOMA	Yes	Yes	Yes	Yes	Yes	Yes	Yes
OREGON	Yes	Yes	Yes	Yes	Yes	Yes	Yes
RHODE ISLAND	Yes	Yes	Yes	Yes	Yes	Yes	Yes
SOUTH DAKOTA	Yes	Yes	Yes	Yes	Yes	Yes	Yes
TEXAS	Mod	Yes	Yes	Yes	Yes	Yes	Yes
UTAH	No	Yes	Yes	Yes	Yes	Yes	Yes
VERMONT	No	Yes	Yes	Yes	Yes	Yes	Yes

	Rule 601	Rule 602	Rule 603	Rule 604	Rule 605	Rule 606	Rule 607
WASHINGTON	No	Yes	Yes	Yes	Yes	Mod	Yes
WEST VIRGINIA	No	Yes	Yes	Yes	Yes	Yes	Yes
WISCONSIN	Yes	Yes	Yes	Yes	Yes	Yes	Yes
WYOMING	No	Yes	Yes	Yes	Yes	No	Yes

Rule	Subject
601	General Rule of Competency
602	Lack of Personal Knowledge
603	Oath or Affirmation
604	Interpreters
605	Competency of Judge as Witness
606	Competency of Juror as Witness
607	Who May Impeach

	Rule 608	Rule 609	Rule 610	Rule 611	Rule 612	Rule 613	Rule 614	Rule 615
ALASKA	No	No	Yes	Yes	Yes	Yes	Yes	Yes
ARIZONA	No	No	Yes	No	Yes	Yes	Yes	Yes
ARKANSAS	Yes	Yes	Yes	Yes	No	Yes	Yes	No
COLORADO	Yes	No	Yes	Yes	Yes	No	Yes	Yes
DELAWARE	No	Yes	Yes	Yes	No	No	Yes	Yes
FLORIDA	No	Mod	Yes	Yes	Yes	No	Yes	No
HAWAII	Yes	No	Yes	Yes	Yes	No	Yes	Yes
IDAHO	Yes	Yes	Yes	Yes	Yes	Yes	Yes	Yes
IOWA	Yes	No	Yes	Yes	Yes	Yes	Yes	Yes
MAINE	No	No	Yes	No	Yes	Yes	Yes	Yes
MICHIGAN	No	No	Yes	No	No	No	Yes	Yes
MINNESOTA	Yes	No	Yes	Yes	Yes	Yes	No	Yes
MISSISSIPPI	Yes	Yes	Yes	Yes	Yes	Yes	Yes	Yes
MONTANA	Yes	No	Yes	No	Yes	Yes	Yes	Yes
NEBRASKA	Yes	No	Yes	Yes	No	Yes	Yes	Yes
NEVADA	Yes	Yes	Yes	Yes	Mod	Yes	Yes	Yes
NEW HAMPSHIRE	Yes	Yes	Yes	plus	Yes	Yes	No	Yes
NEW MEXICO	Yes	No	Yes	Yes	Yes	Yes	plus	Yes
NORTH CAROLINA	Yes	No	No	No	No	Yes	No	No
NORTH DAKOTA	No	No	Yes	Yes	No	Yes	No	Yes
OHIO	No	No	Yes	No	Yes	No	Yes	Yes
OKLAHOMA	Yes	Yes	Yes	Yes	Yes	Yes	Yes	Yes
OREGON	No	Yes	Yes	Yes	Yes	Yes	No	No
RHODE ISLAND	Yes	Yes	Yes	Yes	Yes	Yes	Yes	Yes
SOUTH DAKOTA	Yes	No	Yes	Yes	Yes	Yes	No	No
TEXAS	Yes	No	Yes	No	No	Yes	No	Yes

	Rule 608	Rule 609	Rule 610	Rule 611	Rule 612	Rule 613	Rule 614	Rule 615
UTAH	No	Yes	Yes	Yes	Yes	Yes	Yes	Yes
VERMONT	Yes	No	Yes	No	No	Yes	Yes	Yes
WASHINGTON	Mod	Yes	Yes	Yes	Yes	Yes	Yes	Mod
WEST VIRGINIA	Yes	No	Yes	Mod	Yes	Yes	Yes	Yes
WISCONSIN	Yes	No	Yes	Yes	Yes	Yes	Yes	Yes
WYOMING	Yes	Yes	Yes	Yes	No	Yes	Yes	Yes

Rule	*Subject*
608	Evidence of Character and Conduct of Witness
609	Impeachment By Evidence of Conviction of Crime
610	Religious Beliefs or Opinions
611	Mode and Order of Interrogation and Presentation
612	Writing Used To Refresh Memory
613	Prior Statement of Witness
614	Calling and Interrogation of Witness By Court
615	Exclusion of Witnesses

See Sec. 12.04 for Discussion of the Law in Non-FRE States Relative to the Rules Discussed in This Chapter.

7

HOW LAY AND EXPERT WITNESSES CAN HELP YOU

See Federal Rules of Evidence
Article Seven: Opinions And Expert Testimony

Sec. 7.01 How To Use Lay Opinions   Rule 701 provides:

"If the witness is not testifying as an expert, the witness' testimony in the form of opinions or inferences is limited to those opinions or inferences which are (a) rationally based on the perception of the witness AND (b) helpful to a clear understanding of the witness' testimony OR the determination of a fact in issue."

TRIAL STRATEGY

During Discovery Find Out What Lay Opinions as Well as Expert Opinions Will Be Put in Evidence

---

The same witness may testify as an expert witness and as a lay witness. He may be expert in regard to one part of his testimony, but a lay witness in regard to another part. Lay opinions are not based on qualifications of the witness, but upon PERCEPTION and HELPFULNESS.

TRIAL STRATEGY

In Offering Lay Opinion Show

    1. *Rationally based on perception.*
    2. *Helpful to*
        A. *clear understanding of his testimony or*
        B. *determination of a fact in issue*

MASTER RULE 701 BY APPLYING IT TO SPECIFIC EXAMPLES:

1. *Value of Property:* Owner of real property has special knowledge of it and can give opinion as to value (*U.S. v. 79.20 Acres of Land, More Or Less, Situated in Stoddard County, Missouri,* 710 F.2d 1352 [8th Cir. 1983]). Tiger cub owner could estimate value, based on offers he had received (*U.S. v. Laughlin,* 804 F.2d 1336 [5th Cir. 1986]). Could give "probable value" of crop, if water system had not failed (*Greenwood Ranches, Inc. v. Ski Construction Co., Inc.,* 629 F.2d 518 [8th Cir. 1980]). Owner can also give value of personalty, such as auto damaged in accident (*Meredith v. Hardy,* 554 F.2d 764 [5th Cir. 1977]).

2. *Discretion of court:* Admitting lay opinion is in sound discretion of trial court (*Bohannon v. Pegelow,* 652 F.2d 729 [7th Cir. 1981]). However, court abused discretion in excluding lay opinion of persons with

extensive personal knowledge of the operation of furnaces (*Joy Mfg. v. Sola Basic Industries, Inc.*, 697 F.2d 104 [3rd Cir. 1982]).

3. *Legal Opinions:* Lay witness cannot give a legal opinion (*Christiansen v. National Savings and Trust Co.*, 683 F.2d 520 [D.C. Cir. 1982]).

4. *Intent:* Testimony that he "understood the meaning" not proper way to show intent (*U.S. v. Phillips*, 600 F.2d 535 [5th Cir. 1979]). Daughter could testify she did not think one person believed another person was going to kill him (*John Hancock Mutual Life Ins. Co. v. Dutton*, 585 F.2d 1289 [11th Cir. 1978]).

5. *Drunkenness:* Drunkenness has always been accepted as a subject of lay opinion (*Singletary v. Secretary of Health, Education and Welfare*, 623 F.2d 217 [2nd Cir. 1980]).

6. *Nervous and Afraid:* Testimony that employees were "nervous and afraid" is saying what they perceived and is admissible (*Kerry Coal Co. v. United Mine Workers*, 637 F.2d 957 [3rd Cir. 1980]).

7. *Odors:* Border patrol officer could testify as to odor of marijuana (*U.S. v. Arrasmith*, 557 F.2d 1093 [5th Cir. 1977]). Testimony as to smell of dynamite after explosion admitted (*People v. Reed*, 164 N.E. 847 [IL 1929]).

8. *Injuries:* Police officer does not have to be doctor to describe "fresh scrapes on shoulder" (*In Re Deja Vu, Inc.*, 40 B.R. 316 [Bky. MA 1984]). Family permitted to tell effect scarring had on plaintiff's personality (*Drayton v. Jiffe Chemical Corp.*, 591 F.2d 352 [6th Cir. 1978]).

9. *Terms:* Employees were not permitted to testify as to what customer meant by word "coke" (*Coca-Cola v. Overland, Inc.*, 692 F.2d 1250 [9th Cir. 1982]). Witness was permitted, however, to interpret meaning of ambiguous language in conversation with accused (*U.S. v. Deperi*, 778 F.2d 963 [3rd Cir. 1985]).

10. *Seaworthiness:* Lay opinion on "seaworthiness" was admitted (*Sceib v. Williams-McWilliams Co., Inc.*, 628 F.2d 509 [5th Cir. 1980]).

11. *Speculation:* Witness cannot speculate, but where witness based his testimony on growing crop costs on his recollection of past experience, admitted (*Deitz v. Consolidated Oil & Gas, Inc.*, 643 F.2d 1088 [TX Cir. 1981]).

12. *Racial Discrimination:* Lay testimony that action was racially motivated admitted, though it goes to ultimate issue (*Bohannon v. Pegelow*, 652 F.2d 729 [7th Cir. 1981]).

13. *Cause of Accident:* Highway patrolman could testify that in his opinion car hit tandem wheels on truck (*Dogan v. Hardy*, 587 F.2d 967 [5th Cir. 1984]). However, officer could not testify as to why wheelchair tipped; source of such testimony unknown (*Meder v. Everest & Jennings, Inc.*, 637 F.2d 1182 [8th Cir. 1981]). There was no basis for lay opinion that

driver did all possible to avoid the accident, so inadmissible (*Gorby v. Schneier Tank Lines, Inc.,* 741 F.2d 1015 [7th Cir. 1984]).

14. *Bloodstains:* Lay witness could testify stains were bloodstains (*People v. Preston,* 173 N.W. 383 [IL 1930]).

15. *Gunshot:* Lay witness could testify as to opinion noise heard was gunshot (*People v. Singletary,* 391 N.E. 2d 440 [IL 1979]).

16. *Handwriting and Signature:* Lay witness can identify a person's handwriting or signature, based on personal knowledge (*U.S. v. Clifford,* 704 F.2d 86 [3rd Cir. 1983]); *U.S. v. Barron,* 707 F.2d 125 [5th Cir. 1983]).

17. *Sanity:* Lay witness opinion as to sanity can be given more weight by jury than expert testimony (*Greider v. Duckwoth,* 701 F.2d 1228 [7th Cir. 1987]). Osteopath could not testify as expert re sanity, but could give lay testimony (*Beck v. Gross,* 499 So. 2d 886 [FL App 1986]).

18. *Identity of Drug:* Lay witness can identify drug based on his drug use (*U.S. v. Sweeney,* 688 F.2d 1131 [7th Cir. 1982]).

19. *Conclusions:* Court refused to permit defendant to be asked if acts were "unlawful," "willful," or "conspired" (*U.S. v. Baskes,* 649 F.2d 471 [7th Cir. 1980]).

20. *Speed of Vehicle:* Trial courts have different degrees to which lay witness can give opinion as to speed. Basically, the witness cannot "guess" but he can give an "estimate." Some courts hold estimate can mean "approximately 60 miles per hour," but more often "very fast," and in at least one case, "he was going like a bat out of hell."

Sec. 7.02 Qualify the Expert   Rule 702 provides:

"If scientific, technical, or other specialized knowledge will assist the trier of fact to understand the evidence or to determine a fact in issue, a witness qualified as an expert by knowledge, skill, experience, training, or education, may testify thereto in the form of an opinion or otherwise."

TRIAL STRATEGY

In Qualifying the Expert, You *Must* Show

1. Witness has special knowledge.
2. In an area recognized by courts.
3. As being helpful to trier of fact.

You *should* also: Do this with drama, detailing and glamorizing the expert's qualifications (often by using a hypothetical, though not required by federal rules and by many state rules)

Qualifying a witness is not difficult, if the two-way test is satisfied: (1) witness must be qualified and (2) must have "knowledge, skill, experience, training or education" in the field (*Coleman v. Parkline Corp.*, 844 F.2d 863 [DC Cir. 1988]). Qualifying the expert *effectively* is an equally important task.

Beginning with voir dire, you must prepare the jury for the kind of expert testimony that will be presented. If a psychiatrist is going to testify, you must meet the challenge of those who aren't impressed by this profession—get them off the jury, or educate them as to the value of this kind of evidence. If you are going to rely upon a lay witness to give opinion on mental capacity, prepare all prospective jurors with comments bolstering the value of psychiatric evidence.

The expert is not qualified on the basis of education alone. An officer who investigated five hundred accidents gave an opinion on the cause of an accident (*Gladhill v. General Motors Corp.*, 73 F.2d 1049 [4th Cir. 1984]). Neighboring farmers could testify as to probable yield of crops (*Federal Crop Ins. v. Hester*, 765 F.2d 723 [8th Cir. 1985]). The agent from the Drug Enforcement Agency was permitted to testify as to typical characteristics of a drug addict (*U.S. v. Pugliese*, 712 F.2d 1574 [2nd Cir. 1983]).

HISTORICAL NOTE

The *Frye* test was adopted in 1923, holding that mere experiments should not be admitted, and scientific evidence must reach "general acceptance" in its "particular field" (*Frye v. U.S.*, 293 F. 1013 [DC Cir. 1923]). Rule 702 does not talk about "general acceptance," and courts are moving away from *Frye*. In *Williams*, it was held that courts cannot surrender to the scientific arena the responsibility of determining the reliability of evidence (*U.S. v. Williams*, 583 F.2d 1194 [2nd Cir. 1978]).

Courts have let experts testify as to hair samples (*U.S. v. Cyphers*, 553 F.2d 1064 [7th Cir. 1977]), reliability of eyewitness testimony (*U.S. v. Moore*, 786 F.2d 723 [5th Cir. 1986]), cephalometry (measuring of head re photo identification) (*U.S. v. Alexander*, 816 F.2d 164 [5th Cir. 1987]), post-traumatic stress (*U.S. v. Winters*, 729 F.2d 602 [9th Cir. 1984]), but not on polygraph tests (*U.S. v. Alexander*, 526 F.2d 161 [8th Cir. 1975]).

The fact that expert is not "specialist" goes to the weight, not the admissibility of his testimony (*Payton v. Abbott Labs*, 780 F.2d 147 [1st Cir. 1985]). It was within court's discretion to exclude expert's opinion of the effect of drugs, where not based on examination (*U.S. v. Rohrer*, 708 F.2d 429 [9th Cir. 1983]), but it was abuse of discretion not to accept expert's affidavit on motion for summary judgment, where expert had some knowledge that would help (*Bulthuis v. Rexall Corp.*, 777 F.2d 1353 [9th Cir. 1985]).

There are CONFLICTING VIEWS as to whether or not you should voir dire opponent's expert at the end of his being qualified. DISADVANTAGE: His qualifications should be determined before trial, and having him repeat qualifications gives him extra credit with the jury. ADVANTAGE: By conducting a voir dire immediately after he has testified as to his qualifications, you get a "crack at him" before he gives his opinion, and can lessen the effect of that opinion, if you can weaken his credentials in any way.

HELPFULNESS is the key word in qualifying an opinion, and the qualification process can be simple:

"Are you here today to give an opinion about . . . ?" (Subject helpful and in accepted area.)

"Yes, I am."

"What are your qualifications for giving such an opinion?"

Expert opinions must always satisfy Rule 401 by being relevant, and Rule 403 by being not only relevant, but having probative value that outweighs any unfair prejudice or waste of time. One court said the two important questions are probative value and experience of witness (*Hughes v. Hemingway Transport Inc.,* 539 F.Supp 130 [D.C. PA 1982]). Another court said "help" must be "appreciable help" (*Kline v. Ford Motor Co., Inc.,* 523 F.2d 1067 [9th Cir. 1975]). Expert, such as a Certified Public Accountant, could testify as a lay witness and as an expert witness (*Teen Ed, Inc. v. Kimball Intern, Inc.,* 620 F.2d 399 [3rd Cir. 1980]).

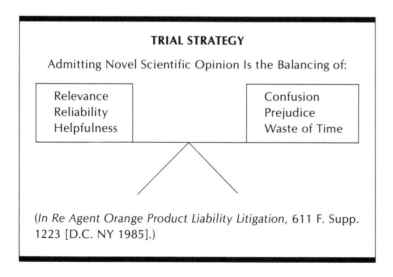

TRIAL STRATEGY

Admitting Novel Scientific Opinion Is the Balancing of:

| Relevance Reliability Helpfulness | Confusion Prejudice Waste of Time |

(*In Re Agent Orange Product Liability Litigation,* 611 F. Supp. 1223 [D.C. NY 1985].)

THE FUTURE OF FRYE: Courts don't want to abandon Frye, but are taking a harder look at what has "gained general acceptance." One court has held the polygraph test can be admitted, "if stipulated to, or if offered in evidence to impeach or corroborate testimony." (*U.S. v. Piccinonna,* 885 Fed. 2d 1529 [11th Cir. 1989]).

Sec. 7.03 Use The Basis of The Expert's Opinion   Rule 703 provides:

"The facts or data in the particular case upon which an expert bases an opinion or inference may be those perceived by OR made known to the expert at or before the hearing. If of a type REASONABLY RELIED UPON by experts in the particular field in forming opinions or inferences upon the subject, the facts or data need not be admissible in evidence."

HISTORICAL NOTE

To the common law rule has been added "OR BEFORE" and "NEED NOT BE ADMISSIBLE:"

Facts and Data Perceived By, Or Made Known To At OR BEFORE Hearing Of a type reasonably relied upon By Experts In The Particular Field. NEED NOT BE ADMISSIBLE

Some authorities have suggested that permitting experts to rely upon hearsay evidence for their opinion is the federal rule's most drastic departure from the common law. This is why some states have not fully adopted the rule.

The truth is, experts (especially doctors) do base their opinions on hearsay; if they are to be HELPFUL to the trier of fact, such experts must use a type of hearsay they rely upon reasonably often in the real world. The court must make a Rule 104(a) determination as to whether experts of the particular field "reasonably rely" upon such inadmissible evidence.

Courts are not in agreement as to "reasonable reliance." In *Zenith*, the court said it "is not what the court deems reliable, but what experts in the relevant discipline deem it to be" (*Matsushita Electric Industries, Inc. v. Zenith Radio Corp.*, 505 F.Supp 1313 [E.D.PA 1981]). It has been held, however, that merely producing an expert with no basis will not suffice (*Evers v. General Motors Corp.*, 770 F.2d 984 [11th Cir. 1985]).

Nothing in Rule 703 requires the hypothetical question and nothing prohibits it. When it is used, all basic facts must be included in the question, based on what is learned at or before trial.

TRIAL STRATEGY

When Using the Hypothetical Question, You Should Write It Out

1. To use in preparing the expert.
2. As a checklist when examining the expert, to make sure all elements are covered.
3. As an outline in argument.

A doctor could testify as to his opinion based largely upon statements in reports of employees of Medical Center For Federal Prisoners (*U.S. v. Bramlet*, 820 F.2d 851 [7th Cir. 1987]). However, state trooper could not give opinion based on statements from a driver (*Faires v. Atlas Truck Body Mfg. Co.*, 797 F.2d 619 [8th Cir. 1986]). The court refused to strike expert opinion based on a chemical test, where appellant argued test was the best evidence (*U.S. v. Gavic*, 520 F.2d 1346 [8th Cir. 1975]).

Where the expert states his opinion, and the court has accepted him as an expert, the basis of that opinion can well be a question of weight, and not admissibility (*Fischer v. State*, 312 N.E. 2d 04 [IN App. 1974]).

TRIAL STRATEGY

Use the Key Words in Conveying to the Jury the Basis of an Opinion

1. "Doctor, can you tell us with a reasonable degree of medical certainty, whether . . ."
2. "Doctor, assume that . . ."
   "Now doctor, assuming all of these facts are true, do you have an opinion based on a reasonable degree of medical certainty as to whether . . ."

The court held that a psychiatrist should have been permitted to testify his opinion was based on (and to disclose contents of) (1) evaluations of doctors and counselors, (2) reports submitted by expert, (3) facts of previous offense, and (4) statements defendant made to him (*People v. Anderson*, 495 N.E. 2d 485 [IL 1986]). This testimony, the reports, and similar papers must meet the Rule 403 test of unfair prejudice, however, before they can be admitted (*In Re Richardson-Merrill, Inc. "Benedictin" Liability Litigation*, 624 F.Supp. 1212 [S.D. OH 1985]).

The only substantive evidence is the opinion of the expert testifying, and if all of it is only the opinion of another expert, then the expert's opinion cannot be admitted (*O'Kelly v. State*, 607 P.2d 612 [NM 1980]). The Advisory Committee anticipated that the hearsay depended upon by the expert be "trustworthy."

Sec. 7.04 Disclosing the Basis of the Opinion　Rule 705 provides:

"The expert may testify in terms of opinion or inference and give his reasons therefor without prior disclosure of the underlying facts or data, unless the court requires otherwise. The expert may in any event be required to disclose the underlying facts or data on cross-examination."

HISTORICAL NOTE

At common law, the expert could not give an opinion without first disclosing, in court, the facts, data, or opinion upon which the opinion is based. It is possible under Rule 705 to put the expert on, qualify him as an expert, and then ask him his opinion.

Though a hypothetical question is no longer required, it is an impressive way to present an opinion. When a hypothetical question is used, the common law requirements must be met, including the question of every "material fact essential to the formation of a rational opinion" (*Harris v. Smith,* 372 F.2d 806 [8th Cir. 1967]).

TRIAL STRATEGY

Underlying Reasons for Opinion

1. *Must* be given:
   A. if court requires it.
   B. on cross-examination.
2. *Should* be given:
   A. where jury wants to know reason,
   B. where such evidence will dramatize the point being made by the expert,
   C. where you want to cover evidence on direct in a positive manner, that opposing counsel may cover on cross in a negative manner.

The old problem of assuming facts that are not in evidence no longer applies to experts under Rule 705. The Rule does not limit the expert to basing his opinion on facts that are in evidence (*Taylor v. Burlington Northern Railway Co.,* 787 F.2d 1309 [9th Cir. 1986]). The trier of fact now has more responsibility in weighing the value of the opinion, since one step in the process is no longer required.

In certain areas, support information is very important. In reconstructing an accident it must be shown that the opinion will be helpful to the jury and that there is "sufficient factual data" to show a "reasonably complete and accurate reconstruction" (*Le Mieux v. Bishop,* 209 N.W. 2d 379 [MN 1973]).

TRIAL STRATEGY

A Thorough Presentation of Expert Testimony Can Be Effective, and Simplification That Is Permitted Under Rule 705 May Not Be the Best Approach in Most Cases

1. Qualify the expert;

A. training and experience includes education, training, licensing, experience, special responsibilities, seminars, "how many times," "similar situations," and current periodicals.

B. special qualifications includes specialty, intensive training in a certain area, teaching assignments, writing, lecturing, studies, and communication with leaders in the field.

2. Familiarity with the problem, generally;

A. "expert" includes having qualifications that relate to the particular problem.

B. reliance on other data and opinions includes having knowledge beyond one's own expertise, as well as studying reports or consulting with experts in the field.

3. Familiarity with your client's problem.

A. investigation of client's problem, from which expert can give opinion based on what he perceives the problem to be.

B. reliance on factual data submitted. Expert suggests good opportunity to use a hypothetical question.

THEN YOU ARE READY FOR: "Doctor, can you give an opinion with a reasonable degree of medical probability ("reasonable degree of medical *certainty*" in some jurisdictions) that . . ."

Cross-examination has become more important under Rule 705, because much is left to the cross-examiner. One effective approach is to know as much as possible about the expert, what he has done, what he has said, and what he has written (especially if he has written for his profession). Also, the use of a treatise may be effective.

TRIAL STRATEGY

You Have Four Ways to Qualify a Treatise So You Can Use It in Cross-Examining an Expert

1. Where expert relied upon the treatise.
2. Where expert acknowledges relying upon such authorities, though not necessarily this one.
3. Where expert acknowledges the treatise to be authoritative.
4. Without acknowledgment by expert, you establish reliability of work by:
   A. proof, or
   B. judicial notice

(See *Bowers v. Garfield*, 382 F. Supp. 503 [D.C. PA 1974])

Sec. 7.05 Win With Ultimate Issue Opinions   Rule 704 provides:

> *"Testimony in the form of an opinion or inference otherwise admissible is not objectionable because it EMBRACES AN ULTIMATE ISSUE TO BE DECIDED BY THE TRIER OF FACT."*

Rule 704 was amended in 1984 by adding (b), which provides that in a criminal case, expert may not testify as to *"whether the defendant did or did not have the mental state or condition constituting an element of the crime charged or a defense thereto."* This amendment was intended to resolve the conflicts of expert insanity testimony (specifically after the Hinckley case), but was also aimed at the ultimate issue at end of trial, and not the other opportunities during trial where insanity evidence can still be introduced. "Every actual fact concerning the defendant's mental condition is still admissible" (*U.S. v. Edwards,* 819 F.2d 262 [11th Cir. 1987]).

HISTORICAL NOTE

> At early common law, lay and expert witnesses could not give an opinion "upon the ultimate issue" because such would "invade the province of the jury." Wigmore, other authorities, and the courts became critical of this rule which they regarded as meaningless and often preventing the jury from hearing helpful evidence. The Advisory Committee in its comments on Rule 704 pointed out that opinions were couched in such terms as "might" or "could," instead of using the more direct term "did," which proponent of the evidence should be entitled to use. Rule 704 put the problem to rest permanently by specifically providing that otherwise admissible evidence will not be excluded because it embraces the ultimate issue.

One key part of Rule 704 is found in the words "OTHERWISE ADMISSIBLE." There are hearsay problems and relevancy problems that often exclude the evidence. There is a built-in 403 problem, since letting a witness tell a jury what to decide could be misleading, confusing, or prejudicial.

Opinions relating to ultimate issue must also meet the Rule 702 test of being helpful to the trier of fact. Some courts are cautious to exclude opinions that don't really add to the evidence but do, in effect, tell the jury how to decide the case.

TRIAL STRATEGY

In Presenting Evidence of Opinion on the Ultimate Issue

1. You *cannot* "merely tell the jury what result to reach." (*Advisory Committee's Note To Rule 704*)
   a) EXAMPLES:
      "He is guilty"
      "He is liable"
      "He was negligent"

> 2. You *can* tell the jury, party to the action did or did not do the one thing that decides the outcome of the case.
> EXAMPLES: Opinion that Patty Hearst did act "under fear of death or grave bodily harm" (the only real issue to be decided in the case) (*U.S. v. Hearst,* 563 F.2d 1331 [9th Cir. 1977]). Her condition was deemed "unsafe," "dangerous," or "not according to standard of care."

Rule 704 was not the beginning of permitting an expert to testify as to the ultimate issue. In the *Alger Hiss* case, a 1950 court permitted an expert to testify as to whether or not Whitaker Chambers was telling the truth, when telling the truth was the only issue (*U.S. v. Alger Hiss,* 88 F.Supp. 559 [S.D. NY 1950]). It is this very issue, however, that surely has played a big role in causing court to deny the use of the polygraph test.

A hypothetical was excluded where conclusion was the same as that which must be reached by the jury for a verdict (*Matthews v. Ashland Chemical Inc.,* 770 F.2d 1303 [5th Cir. 1985]). Depicting accused as person in bank photo pretty much cinches the case for the prosecution, but that is no reason to exclude it (*U.S. v. Langford,* 802 F.2d 1176 [9th Cir. 1986]). Summary judgment affidavits are submitted for the very purpose of deciding the ultimate issue, but they must be based on facts (*Evers v. General Motors Corp.,* 770 F.2d 984 [11th Cir. 1985]).

Courts are careful not to let this rule shift the duty of determining law from the court to the jury. That is why legal conclusions do not come from the expert's testimony, but from the judge's instructions (see, *Adalman v. Baker, Watts, & Co.,* 807 F.2d 359 [4th Cir. 1986]).

In criminal cases under Rule 704(b), experts are to diagnose and explain their findings, but may not say whether defendant had a specific intent to kill (*U.S. v. Frisbee,* 623 F.Supp. 1217 [D.C. CA 1985]). Rule 704(b) did give the jury a greater responsibility, and courts permit extensive cross-examination on the issue of insanity, to make sure the jury is fully informed, and does not decide the ultimate issue on the basis of an opinion (*U.S. v. Alexander,* 805 F.2d 1458 [11th Cir. 1986]).

TRIAL STRATEGY

In Trying to Keep Out an Ultimate Issue Opinion, You Should Argue

1. Opinion not helpful.
2. Opinion is prejudicial.

Sec. 7.06 Beware The Court's Expert   Rule 706 provides the court *ON ITS OWN MOTION OR AT REQUEST OF PARTY* appoint an expert, with written duties as set forth by the court, copy to be filed with clerk, or at conference with participating attorneys. He shall "*advise parties of the witness' findings, if any; the witness' deposition may be taken by any party; and the witness may be called to testify by the court or any party. The witness shall be subject to cross-examination by each party, including a party calling the witness.*"

Expert shall receive reasonable compensation—in criminal case as provided by law, and in civil cases, in such proportion as court directs. Court may authorize disclosure to jury of such appointment. Each party can call its own experts.

The Advisory Committee stated candidly that the need for Rule 706 is based upon the "shopping for experts" whose testimony can be purchased. This same committee submitted Article Seven of Federal Rules of Evidence that increased the importance of the expert by

1. permitting expert to testify without first giving the basis of his opinion;

2. eliminating the hypothetical requirement;

3. permitting opinion to be based on inadmissible evidence, and

4. permitting an opinion on the ultimate issue.

The Advisory Committee realized court-appointed experts may overly impress the jury by their mere appointment. This is one reason experts are rarely appointed by the court, and when they are, often the jury is not told the expert was court-appointed.

Even in jury trials, the judge has great authority and trial lawyers are concerned that the judge may be influenced in rulings by his own expert. Despite all the shortcomings of swearing matches between experts and the skyrocketing cost of experts, they are very much a part of our adversary system.

TRIAL STRATEGY

Problems of Court-Appointed Expert

    1. Court may receive extraneous information.
    2. Expert may cover areas not anticipated.
    3. Your client may be charged with costs not anticipated.

These Problems Can be Avoided By

    1. Conference of judge, all counsel, and expert to establish guidelines.
    2. The guidelines should be made a part of a court order.

The following table shows whether or not states adopting the Federal Rules of Evidence adopted substantially same provisions relative to the rules discussed in this chapter:

	Rule 701	Rule 702	Rule 703	Rule 704	Rule 705	Rule 706
ALASKA	Yes	Yes	Yes	Yes	No	Yes
ARIZONA	Yes	Yes	No	No	Yes	No
ARKANSAS	No	No	Yes	Yes	Yes	Yes
COLORADO	Yes	Yes	Yes	Yes	Yes	Yes
DELAWARE	No	Yes	Yes	Yes	No	Yes
FLORIDA	Mod	Yes	Yes	Yes	Yes	No
HAWAII	Yes	Yes	Yes	Yes	No	No
IDAHO	Yes	Yes	Yes	Yes	Yes	Yes
IOWA	Yes	Yes	Yes	Yes	Yes	Yes
MAINE	Yes	Yes	Yes	Yes	Yes	Yes
MICHIGAN	Yes	Yes	No	Yes	Yes	Yes
MINNESOTA	Yes	Yes	Yes	Yes	Yes	Yes
MISSISSIPPI	Yes	Yes	Yes	Yes	Yes	Yes
MONTANA	Yes	Yes	Yes	Yes	Yes	No
NEBRASKA	Yes	Yes	Yes	Yes	Yes	No
NEVADA	Yes	Yes	Yes	Yes	Yes	No
NEW HAMPSHIRE	Yes	Yes	Yes	No	Yes	No
NEW MEXICO	Yes	Yes	Yes	Yes	Yes	No
NORTH CAROLINA	Yes	Yes	Yes	Yes	No	Yes
NORTH DAKOTA	Yes	Yes	Yes	Yes	Yes	Yes
OHIO	Yes	Yes	Yes	Yes	Yes	No
OKLAHOMA	Yes	Yes	Yes	Yes	Yes	No
OREGON	Yes	Yes	Yes	Yes	Yes	No
RHODE ISLAND	Yes	Yes	Yes	Yes	Yes	Yes
SOUTH DAKOTA	Yes	Yes	Yes	No	No	No
TEXAS	Yes	Yes	Yes	Yes	Yes	No
UTAH	Yes	Yes	Yes	Yes	Yes	Yes
VERMONT	Yes	Yes	Yes	Yes	Yes	Yes
WASHINGTON	Yes	Yes	Yes	Yes	Yes	Yes
WEST VIRGINIA	Yes	Yes	Yes	Mod	Yes	Yes
WISCONSIN	Yes	Yes	Yes	Yes	Yes	Yes
WYOMING	Yes	Yes	Yes	Yes	Yes	No

Rule	*Subject*
701	Opinion Testimony by Lay Witness
702	Testimony by Experts
703	Basis of Opinion Testimony by Experts
704	Opinion on Ultimate Issue
705	Disclosure of Facts or Data Underlying Expert Opinion
706	Court-Appointed Experts

See Sec. 12.05 for Discussion of the Law in Non-FRE States Relative to the Rules Discussed in This Chapter.

8

USE HEARSAY TO EXCLUDE UNFAVORABLE EVIDENCE— HOW TO GET AROUND THE HEARSAY RULE

See Federal Rules of Evidence
Article Eight: Hearsay

USE HEARSAY TO EXCLUDE UNFAVORABLE EVIDENCE

HOW TO GET AROUND THE HEARSAY RULE

USE HEARSAY TO EXCLUDE UNFAVORABLE EVIDENCE

Sec. 8.01 Know the Hearsay Rule   Every trial lawyer must MASTER the Hearsay Rule. This can be accomplished by knowing what questions must be answered and then finding the answers.

TRIAL STRATEGY

Be Able to Ask the Hearsay Questions

1. Is it an assertion? [Rule 801(a)]
2. Is it an out-of-court statement? [Rule 801(c)]
3. Is it offered to prove the matter asserted? [Rule 801(c)]
4. Is it a "not-hearsay" prior statement? [Rule 801(d)(1)]
5. Is it a "not-hearsay" admission by party-opponent? [Rule 801(d)(2)]
6. Is it an "availability of declarant immaterial" exception? [Rule 803]
7. Is it a "declarant unavailable" exception? [Rule 804]

During the heat of battle you must ask and answer all seven of these questions in a split second . . . you cannot possibly accomplish this analysis unless you thoroughly understand the hearsay rule and its many applications. You must know where to find each part of the Rule, then be able to take it apart and know how each part fits with another.

Example ———————————————————————————————

The first question is whether there is an ASSERTION. Start with the hearsay definition, found in Rule 801(c). It begins, "Hearsay is a statement . . . ." STOP! You simply cannot proceed until you know what a statement is. Back up to Rule 801 (a) which defines a statement:

"A 'statement' is (1) an oral or written assertion or (2) nonverbal conduct of a person, if it is intended by the person as an assertion."

So, in Rule 801 "Definitions" we find there can be no hearsay unless there is an assertion, because there can be no hearsay without a statement and no statement without an assertion.

ALWAYS START WITH THE DEFINITION OF HEARSAY
Rule 801(c) provides:

"Hearsay is a statement, other than one made by the declarant while testifying at the trial or hearing, offered in evidence to prove the truth of the matter asserted."

The trial lawyer not only must commit this to memory, but he must take it apart, look at it piece by piece, and completely understand each word of each phrase. We have looked at "Hearsay is a statement" and found those four introductory words are important. In Section 8.02 we will explore the challenges of "ASSERTION."

TRIAL STRATEGY

REMEMBER: The Two Most Common Hearsay Mistakes Made by Lawyers Is In Not Understanding

1. Is it an assertion? (See Sec. 8.02)
2. Is it offered to prove the matter asserted? (See Sec. 8.04)

Once you have established that it is an assertion, you proceed to the next part of Rule 801(c), which provides, "other than one made by the declarant while testifying at the trial or hearing . . ." That brings us to the next hearsay question, "Was it an out-of-court statement?"

We will discuss this in Sec. 8.02, but Rule 801 gives us one important clue. Rule 801(b) says, "A 'declarant' is a person who makes a statement." In the 801(c) definition of hearsay we find it is when the DECLARANT is testifying that it is an "in-court" statement.

Often the witness and the declarant is the same person. That the witness is testifying and the declarant is the person who made the statement becomes very important in determining whether the statement was made "in court."

The third, and most important part of Rule 801(c) is whether the statement is "OFFERED IN EVIDENCE TO PROVE THE TRUTH OF THE MATTER ASSERTED". Once it is shown the statement is shown to be "out-of-court", and that it IS a statement in that it "asserts something", then the crucial MATTER-ASSERTED test must be examined. See Sec. 8.04.

TRIAL STRATEGY

Keep Clear in Mind How "Definition Hearsay" Is Divided and Where It Is Found

1. Hearsay *exceptions* are found in Rules 803 and 804.
2. All "definition hearsay" is found in Rule 801.
    A. hearsay Rule 801(a), (b), and (c)
    B. not hearsay Rule 801(d)

Rule 801(d) provides:

"A statement is not hearsay if—(1) prior statement by witness or (2) admission by party-opponent." The two "not hearsay" by definition rules will be discussed in sections 8.05 and 8.06, but it is important to consider them as a part of Rule 801. They are NOT exceptions, they are a part of the definition rule.

HISTORICAL NOTE

For several centuries courts have recognized there is really no need for the right of a person to cross-examine himself, so admissions have been admitted under several theories. Though usually considered an exception to hearsay, the FRE drafters chose to make it "not hearsay" by definition. SAME RESULT!

Rule 802 states simply, "Hearsay is not admissible except as provided by these rules or by other rules prescribed by the Supreme Court pursuant to statutory authority or by Act of Congress."

Rule 805 provides, "Hearsay included within hearsay is not excluded under the hearsay rule if each part of the combined statements conforms with an exception to the hearsay rule provided in these rules."

TRIAL STRATEGY

Argue Hearsay Within Hearsay (Double Hearsay, Triple Hearsay, or Multiple Hearsay) Is Admissible Because

Each level of hearsay satisfies some part of rule (exception or by definition is not hearsay)

Example ————————————————————————

Witness testified his secretary told him defendant's secretary said a witness told her . . .

1. Secretary's statement admitted as vicarious admission
2. What secretary was told admitted as excited utterance (*U.S. v. Portsmouth Paving Corp.,* 694 F.2d 312 [4th Cir. 1982])

Rule 806 provides that when hearsay evidence is admitted, "the credibility of the declarant may be attacked, and if attacked may be supported, by any evidence which would be admissible for those purposes if declarant had testified as a witness". It further provides that there is no requirement that declarant be afforded an opportunity to deny or explain "statement or conduct by the declarant at any time, inconsistent with the declarant's hearsay statement."

TRIAL STRATEGY

In Offering Hearsay Evidence, Remember the Risk

1. Defendant offered his statement through another witness and found his criminal record admitted (*U.S. v. Lawson*, 608 F.2d 1129 [6th Cir. 1979]).
2. Testimony of witness that cocaine was not in home prior to defendant arrival was admitted under co-conspirator exception; defendant rebutted; prosecution then could introduce third statement of witness, supporting the hearsay (*U.S. v. Bernal*, 719 F.2d 1475 [9th Cir. 1983]).
3. Where prior convictions are used to support hearsay, request instruction limiting use to credibility (*U.S. v. Bovain*, 708 F.2d 606 [11th Cir. 1983]).

REMEMBER: Rule 806 permits supporting or attacking evidence but only that "which would be admissible for those purposes if declarant had testified as a witness." *Bovain* made it clear that evidence satisfying Rule 806 as to hearsay must also satisfy Rule 608 and Rule 609 as to witnesses, and everything that is done in the courtroom must satisfy Rule 403 as to unfair prejudice.

TRIAL STRATEGY

Don't Forget the "Forgotten Hearsay Exception"

Rule 801 defines hearsay, and Rules 803 and 804 give the exceptions.

HOWEVER, Rule 104 provides that in determining the admissibility of evidence, the trial judge "IS NOT BOUND BY THE RULES OF EVIDENCE EXCEPT THOSE WITH RESPECT TO PRIVILEGES."

Argue admissibility with hearsay evidence if hearsay is what you have!

Sec. 8.02 "In-Court" and "Out-of-Court" Statements

Rule 801(c) begins with, "Hearsay" is a statement, other than one made by the declarant while testifying at the trial or hearing. . . ." If it is an "in-court" statement, it is not hearsay, so you need not go further.

The common law talked about the "out-of-court" statements made by declarants, and whether or not the credibility of such declarants could be properly evaluated by the trier of fact. This was true, whether the statement was an oral one or contained in a written document.

It is the *statement* that is out of court, not the *declarant*. Whether or not the declarant testifies at trial does not matter.

Example ——————————————————————————————————————

Jones is on the witness stand testifying. Counsel introduces a letter Jones wrote six months earlier. "OBJECTION, Hearsay!" The statement being introduced IS an out-of-court statement, even though the witness is in Court. The letter may be admitted, but it must be viewed as hearsay and treated as such, and hearsay requirements must be satisfied.

Statement must be made WHILE TESTIFYING (*U.S. v. Sisto,* 534 F.2d 616 [5th Cir. 1976]).

One way to admit statement made out of court by in-court witness is to use Rule 801 (d), pertaining to certain prior consistent statements. This is the FRE answer to those who question the hearsay nature of statements made by a person who is in court and subject to cross-examination.

TRIAL STRATEGY

Whether the "Out-of-Court" Statement Is or Is Not Hearsay Matters Not
. . . *If Counsel Fails to Object!*

Sec. 8.03 Is It an Assertion? If it does not assert anything, it is not a statement, and it is not hearsay [Rule 801(a) and (c)]. The assertion may be "oral or written," or "nonverbal conduct," if intended as an assertion [Rule 801(a)].

HISTORICAL NOTE

> As early as 1830 English courts were wrestling with the matter of assertions, as in the famous will contest case in which it was argued whether or not letters written to deceased were such as would be written to a mentally competent person (*Wright v. Doe D. Tatham,* 2 Russ. & M. 1, 39 Eng. R. 295 [1830]).

When a person is asked who was present and he or she points at the defendant, that is a nonverbal assertion that the defendant was present. However, if the person merely scratched his or her head he or she would not be asserting anything.

When a witness is not really saying anything, his credibility is not at stake, trustworthiness is not in issue, and there is no need for cross-examination. Often counsel avoids a hearsay objection by showing the statement is not assertive, then loses the war because the court rules if the statement is not saying anything, why is it relevant?

Relevancy is often not a problem, however, where you want to show an act was done or a statement was made.

Example ——————————————————————————————————

People who called the establishment-under-investigation for bookmaking thought it was a place for making bets, so the calls were relevant to the issue of the case; but the people were calling to place bets, not to say it was a bookie place, so their calls were not assertive, hence admitted. It could certainly be argued that the calls "asserted" this is a gambling place (*U.S. v. Zenni,* 492 F.Supp. 464 [E.D. KY 1980]).

Where a photo of an unconscious person was introduced to show pain and suffering, it was held the person was not asserting anything, he was just lying there, but he told a great deal (*Grimes v. Employer's Mutual* 73 FRD 607 [D. AK 1977]). It should be remembered that how much a statement tells is not the question, but rather whether or not a non-verbal act was INTENDED to be an assertion.

From the time of *Tatham* in 1830 until the adoption of the Federal Rules of Evidence, implied assertions gave the courts considerable difficulty. The FRE simply took the position, rightly or wrongly, that if the declarant was not trying to say something, there is no real need to question him and hence no need for the statement to be considered hearsay.

TRIAL STRATEGY

When Asserting Assertions, Remember the Real Reasons for the Hearsay Rule

1. Protect against lack of perception.
2. Protect against lack of memory.
3. Protect against his or her "telling of the story."
4. Protect against his or her lack of integrity.

In Other Words, the Precious Right to Cross-Examine!

MASTER RULE 801(a) BY APPLYING IT TO EXAMPLES:

1. *Pointing:* By pointing at a vehicle, witness was asserting "this is the vehicle" (*U.S. v. Caro,* 569 F.2d 411 [5th Cir. 1978]).

2. *Nervousness:* Statement bank teller was shaking was not assertive (*Cole v. U.S.,* 327 F.2d 360 [9th Cir. 1964]).

3. *Failure to Complain:* Failure of passengers on a train to complain about temperature asserts nothing as to temperature (*Silver v. N.Y. Central Railway,* 105 N.E. 2d 923 [MA 1952]).

4. *Implied Assertions:* People who called to make bets did not intend to make an assertion, so police who heard the calls could testify and the implied assertions were not deemed hearsay (*U.S. v. Zenni,* 492 F.Supp. 464 [E.D. KY 1980]).

5. *Questions:* Where statement was merely an inquiry, there was no assertion, hence no hearsay (*Harrison v. State,* 680 S.W.2d 220 [TX Crim. App. 1984]).

6. *Postage Stamp:* A postage stamp does not say anything, unless you want it to assert that it went through a certain post office on a certain date (*U.S. v. Cowley,* 720 F.2d 1037 [9th Cir. 1983]).

7. REMEMBER: A photo of a person who did not know he was being photographed, and similar situations, cannot be assertions, because the person did not intend to assert anything.

Sec. 8.04 Is It Offered to Prove the Matter Asserted?

Rule 801(c) provides, "Hearsay" is a statement, other than one made by the declarant while testifying at the trial or hearing, OFFERED IN EVIDENCE TO PROVE THE TRUTH OF THE MATTER ASSERTED."

If the statement is offered for ANY PURPOSE other than to prove the truth of the matter asserted, it is NOT hearsay. A statement can be very relevant, yet not be offered to prove the matter asserted.

Example _____

Guagliato and Gutierrez were under investigation for drug conspiracy. Guagliato was arrested and agreed to call Gutierrez so the F.B.I. could tape the conversation:

Guagliato: Well, Don Jose was supposed to meet me in Guadalupe, right?

Gutierrez: You and Jose aren't worth a damn.

Guagliato: Why?

Gutierrez: Because you do not do things the way they are supposed to be done. Look, go to Motel 6 and wait for us in the motel.

Guagliato: In Ontario?

Gutierrez: And don't leave.

Guagliato: Okay, what name are you using in the motel?

Gutierrez: Fernando.

Guagliato: Well, the man and the cargo is real full and loaded, it's heavy.

Gutierrez: That, I don't know.

Guagliato: Heh?

Gutierrez: That, I don't know.

Guagliato: Look, I'm scared. I think someone has been following me. I'm not sure.

EVIDENTIARY PROBLEMS: Statements made by Guagliato were not those of co-conspirator under Rule 801(d)(2)(e). However, they were admissible, at least as "reciprocal and integrated utterances," "for the limited purpose of putting the responses of the appellant in context and making them 'intelligible to the jury and recognizable as admissions.'" "Guagliato's statements, then, were not introduced to prove their truth, but rather to prove only that they were uttered" (*U.S. v. Gutierrez-Chavez,* 842 F.2d 77 [5th Cir. 1988]).

Some courts accept proponent's claim that the statement is not being offered to prove the truth of the matter asserted, and go no further. Other courts take a more objective approach, and determine what the evidence is really offered for. All courts, however, ask, "If it isn't being offered for this purpose, then what relevancy does it have?"

TRIAL STRATEGY

In Questioning Purpose for Which Statement Is Being Offered

1. Argue what *real* purpose of evidence is.
2. Argue lack of relevancy if this is *not* real purpose.

There are three basic reasons that evidence is offered for reasons other than to prove the truth of the matter asserted. Though all reasons need not fall into one of these categories, this is an excellent place to start.

TRIAL STRATEGY

Look for Ways Statements Can Be Admitted, Because Not Offered to Prove the Truth of Matter Asserted

1. It is a verbal act.
   EXAMPLE: "John told me Mary is a prostitute" is offered to show that John made the statement, not the truth of whether or not Mary is a prostitute.
2. It shows what declarant was thinking.
   EXAMPLE: "You are going to be my wife," (declared as he gave her a ring), was offered to show declarant intended to give her the ring as a gift, and not to show whether or not she was going to be his wife.
3. It shows what person hearing the declarant was thinking.
   EXAMPLE: "Someone spilled milk in aisle three" was offered to show store manager knew of the spilled milk, not to show whether or not milk had been spilled.

Jurors do not know for what purpose evidence is introduced. What jurors hear is what they consider when arriving at a verdict.

TRIAL STRATEGY

When Evidence Is Admitted for One Purpose, but Jurors May Consider It for Another Purpose

1. Argue the danger inherent in this, not only in the balancing courts use in hearsay, but the balancing courts use under Rule 403 re unfair prejudice, confusing issues, and misleading the jury.
2. If this argument fails, *request an instruction!*

MASTER THE "OFFERED TO PROVE THE TRUTH OF THE MATTER ASSERTED" PART OF THE HEARSAY DEFINITION BY APPLYING IT TO EXAMPLES:

1. *Mailing Letter:* "If letter were submitted to *assert* the implied truth of its *written contents*—that Carlos lived at 600 Wilshire—it would be hearsay and inadmissible. It is, however, admissible nonhearsay because its purpose is to imply from landlord's *behavior*—his mailing a letter to 'Carlos Almaden', 600 Wilshire—that Carlos lived there" (*U.S. v. Singer*, 687 F.2d 1135 [8th Cir. 1982]).

2. *Directive:* "The direction of the decedent to her mother to 'do what was necessary' is not hearsay, since it was not offered in evidence to prove the truth of what was asserted in the statement by Mrs. Harmon" (*Lingham v. Harmon*, 502 F.Supp. 302 [D.C. MD 1980]).

3. *Documents:* Documents were introduced to show "state of mind" of sender, not to show truth of what was in documents, so not hearsay (*Worsham v. A. H. Robins Co.*, 734 F.2d 676 [11th Cir. 1984]).

4. *Subsequent Conduct:* Truth of what was being said was not purpose of testimony; purpose was to show why he later went to the parking lot (*U.S. v. Van Lufkins*, 676 F.2d 1189 [8th Cir. 1982]).

5. *Notice:* Evidence introduced to show that notice had been given, and not to show the truth of what was in the notice, is not hearsay (*U.S. v. Central Gulf Lines, Inc.*, 747 F.2d 315 [5th CA 1984]).

6. *Discrimination Case:* Report of discrimination investigation was admitted, not to show truth of contents, but to show investigation was made, and basis of employer terminating employment (*Crimm v. Missouri Pacific Railway Co.*, 750 F.2d 703 [8th Cir. 1984]).

7. *Quota System:* "Dealers who fell below 50 percent should be replaced" showed policy of company, and not truth as to whether or not a dealer falling under 50 percent should be replaced, hence not hearsay (*Business*

Electronics, Inc. v. Sharp Electronics, Inc., 780 F.2d 1212 [TX CA 5th Cir. 1986]).

8. *Legal Advice:* Evidence showed attorney had advised the client, and was admitted for this purpose, evidence not being offered to show the truth of what attorney had said (*Matter of Patterson,* 70 B.R. 124 [W.D. MO 1986]).

9. *Saudi Memo:* Saudi government memo admitted in action between employer-employee for breach of employment contract, not to show truth of matter asserted, but to show employer's belief that Saudi government was expelling the employee (*Henein v. Saudi Arabian Parsons Ltd.,* 818 F.2d 1508 [9th Cir. 1987]).

10. *Statement to Officer:* In Sec. 1983 civil rights case against officer, what victim said as officer approached him was admitted, not to show truth of matter asserted, but to show officer's state of mind as he approached car, and "to develop context in which incident occurred" (*Nicholson v. Layton,* 747 F.2d 1225 [8th Cir. 1984]).

11. *Complaints:* Evidence was not to show that contents of complaints were true, but that party knew of the complaints, hence admissible (*Mazella v. RCA Global Communications, Inc.,* 642 F.Supp. 1531 [S.D. NY 1986]).

12. *Reports:* Reports that a person was attempting to wrongfully influence votes, admitted to show what a person believed about these activities (*Joyner v. Lancaster,* 553 F.Supp. 809 [W.D. TX 1982]).

13. *Fraud:* Statements by salesmen of fraudulent investment company, admitted to show the statements were made, not that the statements were true (*U.S. v. Hathaway,* 798 F.2d 902 [6th Cir. 1986]).

14. *Relevancy:* Prosecutor argued statement that defendant was a drug smuggler admissible to show why they were investigating defendant; but court held why they were investigating him was not relevant, so statement was hearsay (*U.S. v. Hernandez,* 750 F.2d 1256 [5th Cir. 1985]).

Sec. 8.05 Is It a "Not-Hearsay" Prior Statement?   Rule 801(d)(1) provides that a statement is not hearsay if—

"the declarant testifies at the trial or hearing and is subject to cross-examination concerning the statement, and the statement is

(A) *inconsistent with the declarant's testimony, and was given under oath subject to the penalty of perjury at a trial, hearing, or other proceeding, or in a deposition,* OR

(B) *consistent with the declarant's testimony, and is offered to rebut an express or implied charge against the declarant of recent fabrication or improper influence or motive,* OR

(C) *one of identification of a person made after perceiving the person."*

TRIAL STRATEGY

Be Careful Not to Confuse

1. Prior statement by witness [Rule 801(d)(1)]. Defines such statements as "not hearsay."

2. Prior statements of witnesses [Rule 613]. In examining witness concerning prior statement, contents need not be disclosed to witness but to opposing counsel upon request; and witness must be given opportunity to explain or deny "extrinsic evidence of prior inconsistent statement," and opposing party must be given opportunity to interrogate (does not apply to admissions of party-opponent).

3. Former testimony [Rule 804(b)(1)]. This hearsay exception provides that hearsay does not apply to "testimony given as a witness at another hearing of the same or different proceeding, or in a deposition taken in compliance with law in the course of the same or another proceeding." The rule applies, however, only against the party whom the testimony is now offered, or, in a civil action or proceeding, a predecessor interest who had an opportunity and similar motive to develop the testimony by direct, cross-, or redirect examination.

Grand jury testimony qualifies as "other proceeding," hence not hearsay (*U.S. v. Russell,* 712 F.2d 1258 [8th Cir. 1983]). "Station house" affidavits, such as those obtained by FBI during investigation, are hearsay (*U.S. v. Ragghianti,* 560 F.2d 1376 [9th Cir. 1977]). Sworn statement before postal inspector NOT other proceeding (*U.S. v. Livingston,* 661 F.2d 239 [D.C. Cir. 1981]), but tape-recorded sworn testimony at Border Patrol station WAS found to be other proceeding (*U.S. v. Castro-Ayen,* 537 F.2d 1055 [9th Cir. 1975]).

HISTORICAL NOTE

At common law, prior statements were not admitted as substantive evidence. The Advisory Committee recommended that all prior inconsistent statements be "not hearsay." Rule 801(d)(1) is a compromise of these two views.

A statement may be inconsistent because of what it does NOT say, as well as by what it DOES say (*U.S. v. Williams,* 737 F.2d 594 [7th Cir. 1984]). "Repetition" does not equal "veracity," so you do not rebut a charge of recent fabrication when motive for making both statements was the same (*U.S. v. McPartlin,* 595 F.2d 1321 [7th Cir. 1979]). Some courts, however, admit prior consistent statements made after the motive to fabricate exists (*U.S. v. Pary,* 649 F.2d 1262 [5th Cir. 1981]).

Where defense showed inconsistent statements, the prosecution could then show consistent statements of the witness (*U.S. v. Harris,* 761 F.2d 394 [7th Cir. 1985]). The prosecution cannot, however, put a witness on the stand, knowing he will give adverse testimony, just to have an opportunity to then bring in inconsistent statements not otherwise admissible (*U.S. v. Hogan,* 763 F.2d 697 [5th Cir. 1985]).

TRIAL STRATEGY

Show Oral Understanding Confirmed in Writing

1. Plaintiff and defendant agreed orally.
2. Plaintiff sent letter setting forth terms.
3. Plaintiff sued on oral contract.
4. Defendant implied Plaintiff recently fabricated his testimony.
5. Court admitted the letter to rebut the implication of recent fabrication.

(See *Graybar v. Sawyer,* 485 A.2d 1384 [ME 1985])

What about "Self-Serving" Objection?

"Self-serving" has been a favorite term of courts for centuries, suggesting a need not to admit what the declarant had fabricated to serve his purpose. In this instance, the plaintiff could have written the letter right before trial and brought in a copy. This concept had its beginning with the common law rule that a party was incompetent to testify in his or her own behalf. Courts began using a hearsay test in self-serving situations, and the present law is simple; if it is hearsay, it is not admissible, but the mere fact it may be self-serving does not per se make it hearsay.

CONCLUSION: Object on the basis of hearsay, not on the basis of "self-serving."

Note, inconsistent statements must have been given "*under oath subject to the penalty of perjury at a trial, hearing, or other proceeding, or at a deposition*" [Rule 801(d)(1)(A)]. There is no such requirement for prior consistent statements, Rule 801(d)(1)(B), nor for identifications, Rule 801(d)(1)(C).

It has been suggested that the drafters of FRE meant to include the "under oath subject to penalty of perjury" provision in the consistent-statement rule, but there is no authority for this view. Professor James W. Moore points out:

"Prior consistent statements traditionally have been admissible to rebut charges of recent fabrication or improper influence or motive, but not as substantive evidence. Under the rule 801(d)(1)(B) they are substantive evidence. The prior statement is consistent with the testimony given on the stand, and, if the opposing party wishes to open the door for its admission in evidence, no sound reason is apparent why it should not be received generally" (*Moores Federal Practice,* Rules Pamphlet, 1983, Mathew Bender, p. 243).

For testimony to be inconsistent, it need not be "diametrically opposed or logically incompatible" (*U.S. v. Williams,* 737 F.2d 594 [7th Cir. 1984]). It need be such that a reasonable man would find one statement would help a person's cause, and the other would not. The court will not permit a witness to "forget" only what he wants to forget (*People v. Green,* 479 P.2d 998 [CA 1971]).

TRIAL STRATEGY

Use Prior Inconsistent Statements to Impeach
"I direct your attention to page 32, line 3 of your deposition; did you not at that time tell me . . ."
Use Prior Consistent Statements to Rehabilitate

1. Your witness testifies Jim did it.
2. On cross, opposing counsel suggests the witness is saying this because Jim cursed him at the tavern the night before trial.
3. Your witness can now testify he had told police Jim did it, long before the incident at the tavern. (The statement need not have been under oath.)

Partiality is a form of "improper influence or motive" (*U.S. v. Singer,* 89 N.E. 2d 710 [NY 1940]). It is not an error for the trial court to let the jury hear both statements to evaluate their inconsistency (*U.S. v. Rios,* 611 F.2d 1335 [10th Cir. 1979]).

HISTORICAL NOTE

Courts have always tried to find ways to avoid in-court identifications, on the basis that earlier identifications are more accurate and less sensitive to improper influences (*Gilbert v. California,* 399 U.S. 263 [1967]). Rule 801(d)(1)(C) provides that identification after perception is "not hearsay." The need for the rule arose from witnesses who identified before trial but usually, out of fear of reprisal, would not identify in court (*U.S. v. Jarrard,* 754 F.2d 1451 [9th Cir. 1984]). The rule applies to photos (*U.S. v. Fosher,* 568 F.2d 207 [1st Cir.1978] and sketches (*U.S. v. Moshkowitz,* 581 F.2d 14 [2nd Cir. 1978]). Defendants must be given due process, but courts have leaned toward admitting identifications (*U.S. v. Bubar,* 567 F.2d 192 [2nd

Cir. 1977]). *Jarrard* held that officer who witnessed the identification can testify to it, if he is subject to cross-examination.

Sec. 8.06 Is It a "Not-Hearsay" Admission of Party-Opponent? Rule 801(d)(2) provides an admission of a party opponent is NOT HEARSAY, if

"*The statement is offered AGAINST a party,* and is

(A) *THE PARTY'S OWN STATEMENT, in either an individual* or a *representative capacity* or
(B) *a statement of which the party has* MANIFESTED AN ADOPTION OR BELIEF IN ITS TRUTH, or
(C) a statement by a person AUTHORIZED BY THE PARTY TO MAKE A STATEMENT CONCERNING THE SUBJECT, or
(D) a statement by the PARTY'S AGENT OR SERVANT concerning a matter WITHIN THE SCOPE OF AGENCY OR EMPLOYMENT, made DURING THE EXISTENCE OF THE RELATIONSHIP, or
(E) a statement of a COCONSPIRATOR OF A PARTY DURING THE COURSE AND IN FURTHERANCE OF THE CONSPIRACY."

TRIAL STRATEGY

Be Careful Not to Confuse

1. Admission by party-opponent. Rule 801(d)(2) Defines such statements as "not hearsay."
2. Statement against interest [Rule 804(b)(3)]. Statement is hearsay exception if it was "at the time of its making so far contrary to the declarant's pecuniary or proprietary interest, or so far intended to subject him to civil or criminal liability, or to render invalid a claim by or against another . . ." (If declarant is exposed to criminal liability and offers to exculpate accused, must be corroborated.) Declarant need not be a party, statement must be against interest, and declarant must be unavailable.

The statement must be offered against a party, but need not be against his interest. There is no mental-capacity requirement, and there is no need to show the party had actual knowledge. The party's opinion is admissible, even where it involves a rule of law.

The rule DOES NOT INCLUDE statements by those who have a privity of interest (*Calhoun v. Baylor,* 646 F.2d 1158 [6th Cir. 1981]), since there is no such provision in the rule. Statements attributed to a party by a newspaper reporter, or an unidentified source, are not admission (*Oaks v. City of Fairhope, Alabama,* 515 F.Supp. 1004 [D.C. AL 1981]).

Courts are now holding that admissions of personal representative are admissible against real party in interest, though made in representative capacity (*Estate of Schaefer v. Commissioner,* 749 F.2d 1216 [6th Cir. 1984]). Court may let the jury decide who made the statement, as in one instance where a police officer said, "This is a very hush-hush case," and there was evidence from which jury could find it was the officer, charged with a civil rights violation, who made the statement (*Voutour v. Vitale,* 761 F.2d 812 [1st Cir. 1985]).

TRIAL STRATEGY

Show the Statement Was Made By

1. The party, in his individual or representative capacity.
   EXAMPLE: Partner agrees to pay for an item.
2. Manifesting an adoption or belief in its truth.
   EXAMPLE: When company took false statements about company's finances that appeared in the newspapers and circulated copies, they adopted the statements (*Wagstaff v. Protective Apparel Corporation of America,* 760 F.2d 1074 [10th Cir. 1985]). Silence can be an adoption, but only where declarant understood what was happening and the effect of his silence (*U.S. v. Basic Const. Co.,* 711 F.2d 570 [4th Cir. 1983]).
3. Person authorized to make statement concerning the subject.
   COMMENT: Courts and scholars treat this provision on an agency basis, the same as the following provision, but there is nothing in Rule 801(d)(2)(C) that requires the statement to be made during the existence of the relationship, as there is in Rule 801(d)(2)(D). QUERY: Since there was no need for Rule 801(d)(2)(C), if it has the identical requirements of Rule 801(d)(2)(D), could it not be argued then, that the first provision can apply after the relationship ends, or without the full proof of agency or employment?
4. Party's agent or servant, concerning a matter within the scope of the agency or employment and made during the existence of the relationship.
   EXAMPLES: Letter from attorney was admitted against client, as admission of client (*Contractors Crane Service, Inc. v. Vermont Whey Abatement Authority,* 519 A.2d 1166 [VT 1986]). Translator of foreign language is agent of person whose words are being interpreted (*U.S. v. DaSilva,* 725 F.2d 552 [6th Cir. 1986]). An internal corporate communication can be admission against the corporation (*MCI*

Comm. Corp. v. Am. Tel. & Tel. Co., 708 F.2d 1081 [7th Cir. 1983]).
Whether employees had actual knowledge and whether they were
expressing opinions, the network of inter-corporate communications can be admitted, as in the Dalkon Shield controversy (*In re AH
Robins Co., Inc.,* 575 F. Supp. 718 [D.C. KS 1983]). All in government
can make admission for government (*Corrigan v. U.S.,* 609 F. Supp.
720 [E.D. VA 1985]). When General Westmoreland sued the Colum-
bia Broadcasting System, defendant had the senior executive pro-
ducer make a study and report on the handling of Westmoreland's
war activities, and that report was ruled "not hearsay" (*Westmoreland v. CBS,* 601 F. Supp. 66 [S.D. NY 1984]).

5. A co-conspirator of a party during the course and in furtherance of
   the conspiracy.
   EXAMPLES: Casual admissions to third party were not "in furtherance of" (*U.S. v. Eubanks,* 591 F.2d 513 [9th Cir. 1979]). Joining a
   conspiracy, knowing its unlawful nature, brings with it all admissions ever made by the other conspirators that are admissible (*U.S.
   v. Heater,* 689 F.2d 783 [8th Cir. 1982]).

There are many ways a person can make an admission: Signing a sales slip
for a gun and shells a few months before the accident (*Prince v. Commonwealth,*
324 S.E.2d 660 [VA 1985]). Nudging a friend in the ribs as he is saying something (*U.S. v. Champion,* 813 F.2d 1154 [11th Cir. 1987]). In the Watergate
coverup, even discussion of "past deeds" was actually in furtherance of the
conspiracy, so admitted (*U.S. v. Haldeman,* 559 F.2d 31 [DC Cir. 1976]).

The Government must present substantial independent evidence before using co-conspirator's hearsay (*U.S. v. Austin,* 786 F.2d 986 (10th Cir. 1986]), but
defendant's own statements that he did not want certain people to go to the FBI
were enough (*U.S. v. Sutton,* 732 F.2d 1483 [10th Cir. 1984]). Evidence of conspiracy can be circumstantial (*Glaser v. U.S.,* 315 U.S. 60 [1942], but it must be with
a preponderance of evidence (*In Re Japanese Electronic Products Antitrust Litigation,* 723 F.2d 238 [3rd Cir. 1983]).

A conspiracy is presumed to continue until (1) it is abandoned or (2) its
cause is so frustrated, its goal is no longer plausible (*U.S. v. Ammar,* 714 F.2d 238
[3rd Cir. 1985]). Lawyer's statement that he paid public official is an admission,
and also lays the basis for a conspiracy that makes the public official's words not
hearsay (*U.S. v. Alexander,* 741 F.2d 962 [7th Cir. 1984]). Escaping (*U.S. v. Sears,*
663 F.2d 896 [9th Cir. 1981]) and dividing up the money, *Ammar,* show the
conspiracy does not stop at arrest or after committing the crime, though subsequent "talk" of the crime is not in furtherance (*U.S. v. Silverstein,* 737 F.2d 864
[10th Cir. 1984]).

Sec. 8.07 Hearsay Upon Hearsay   Rule 805 provides:

"Hearsay included within hearsay is not excluded under the hearsay rule if EACH PART OF THE COMBINED STATEMENTS CONFORMS WITH AN EXCEPTION TO THE HEARSAY RULE provided in these rules."

A few courts have dealt with the obvious problem in the wording of Rule 805—it talks about "exceptions" but not "exclusions." This has usually been dealt with realistically by treating the exclusion as an exception (*U.S. v. Lang,* 589 F.2d 92 [2nd Cir. 1978]).

TRIAL STRATEGY

Avoid Multiple Hearsay Problems by Making Each Exception and Exclusion Stand on Its Own

---

Example ———————————————————————————

A Business Record Has the Following Entries:

1. John said, "I did it."
2. Bill said, "John did it."
3. Mary said, "My God, John is stabbing him."

If the business record qualifies under Rule 803(6) it comes in, and (1) can come in as an admission (exclusion), and (3) can come in as an excited utterance (exception), but (2) cannot be admitted, since it is not exclusion or exception, without other circumstances making it one or the other. If the record is offered as a "report" under Rule 803(8), it must satisfy the same requirements.

Sec. 8.08 Attacking or Supporting Hearsay   Rule 806 provides:

"*When a hearsay statement, or a statement defined in Rule 801(d)(2), (C), (D), or (E), has been admitted in evidence, the credibility of the declarant MAY BE ATTACKED, AND IF ATTACKED MAY BE SUPPORTED, by any evidence which would be admissible for those purposes if declarant had testified as a witness. Evidence of a statement or conduct by the declarant at any time, inconsistent with the declarant's hearsay statement, is not subject to any requirement that the declarant may have been afforded an opportunity to deny or explain. If the party against whom a hearsay statement has been admitted calls the declarant as a witness, the party is entitled to examine the declarant on the statement as if under cross-examination.*"

When defense counsel lets his or her client testify through hearsay statements of another person, defense counsel subjects the client to the risks of becoming, in effect, a witness. This may mean that a prior conviction can then be introduced into evidence (*U.S. v. Lawson,* 608 F.2d 1129 [6th Cir. 1979]).

TRIAL STRATEGY

When a Declarant Testifies Through a Witness

    1. Attack him as though he had testified in person.

When Your Declarant's Credibility Has Been Attacked

    1. Rehabilitate his testimony as though he had testified in person.

Since the Declarant was not in court in the hearsay situation, subsequent as well as prior inconsistent statements are available, some courts admit them, while others do not. Rule 613(b) gives a witness an opportunity to "deny or explain," but Rule 806 specifically provides that this does not apply to a hearsay statement.

Statement of co-conspirator was admitted as exception to hearsay rule, and later a second such statement was admitted to support the declarant's credibility (*U.S. v. Bernal,* 719 F.2d 1475 [9th Cir. 1983]). Where hearsay declarant's credibility was attacked, it may be supported with "any evidence which would be admissible for those purposes, if declarant had testified as a witness," including co-defendant's criminal record (*U.S. v. Bovian,* 708 F.2d 606 [11th Cir. 1983]).

HOW TO GET AROUND THE HEARSAY RULE

Sec. 8.09 Use Exceptions and Exclusions In sections 805 and 806 we found ways to keep evidence out through use of exclusions, that is, statements excluded from the hearsay rule by simply defining them as "not hearsay." By arguing the converse of each situation, you can attempt to get around hearsay through use of these exclusions.

This chapter gives you additional ammunition, however, through the use of exceptions to the hearsay rule. It is important to organize these exceptions in a way that you can call upon them during the heat of battle.

TRIAL STRATEGY

Be Able to Recall Immediately the Availability Immaterial Exceptions

    1. Declarant's reaction.
        A. present sense impression
        B. excited utterance
        C. then existing mental, emotional or physical condition
        D. statements for purposes of medical diagnosis or treatment

2. Records.
   A. recorded recollection
   B. records of regularly conducted activity
   C. absence of entry in records kept in accordance with paragraph (6)
   D. public records and reports
   E. records of vital statistics
   F. absence of public records or entry
   G. records of religious organizations
   H. marriage, baptismal and similar certificates
   I. family records
   J. records of documents affecting an interest in property
   K. statements in documents affecting an interest in property
   L. statements in ancient documents
3. Publications.
   A. market reports, commercial publications
   B. learned treatises
4. Reputation.
   A. reputation concerning personal or family history
   B. reputation concerning boundaries or general history
   C. reputation as to character
5. Judgment.
   A. judgment of previous conviction
   B. judgment as to personal, family or general history, or boundaries
6. Residual.
   A. other exceptions

The exceptions that apply whether or not declarant is available are found in Rule 803 (1) through (24). Those that apply only when declarant is unavailable are found in Rule 804 (b) (1) through (5). In Rule 804 (a) are found the five ways to show declarant is unavailable.

TRIAL STRATEGY

Prove Unavailability by Showing

1. Privilege from testifying.
2. Refusing to testify.
3. Lack of memory.
4. Death or then-existing physical or mental illness or infirmity.
5. Unable to procure attendance by process or other reasonable means.

Rule 804 (a) further provides that declarant is NOT unavailable if the foregoing reason for unavailability is "due to the procurement or wrongdoing of the proponent of a statement for the purpose of preventing the witness from attending or testifying." Once availability is shown, counsel must use effectively one of the five exceptions of Rule 804 (b), and that cannot be done until those simple rules are mastered.

TRIAL STRATEGY

Be Able to Recall Immediately the Declarant Unavailable Exceptions

1. Former testimony.
2. Statement under belief of impending death.
3. Statement against interest.
4. Statement of personal or family history.
5. Other exceptions.

Sec. 8.10 "Present Sense Impression" and "Excited Utterance"   Rule 803(1) describes the hearsay exception "Present Sense Impression" as,

"A statement describing or explaining an event or condition made while the declarant was perceiving the event or condition, or immediately thereafter."

The companion to this rule is Rule 803(2), which provides that the "excited utterance" statement is,

"A statement relating to a startling event or condition made while the declarant was under the stress of excitement caused by the event or condition."

HISTORICAL NOTE

WHATEVER HAPPENED TO "RES GESTAE?"
At common law "res gestae" permitted words that were really a part of acts to come in as a hearsay exception, but the term's misuse and abuse prompted Wigmore to call it "not only entirely useless, but even positively harmful" (Six Wigmore Evidence, Sec. 1767). The FRE do not mention "res gestae" but retain some of the concept in hearsay definitions, and in such exceptions as "present sense impression" and "excited utterance."

While a police officer peeked into a window, he talked into a tape recorder, telling what he was observing, and this was admitted as a "present sense impression" (*U.S. v. Andrews*, 765 F.2d 1491 [11th Cir. 1985]). One court held that what the officer said fifteen minutes after defendant handed him heroin, was a "present sense impression" (*U.S. v. Obayarona*, 329 F.Supp. 329 [E.D. NY 1985]). Statement on phone right before murder that defendant was visiting victim (the caller) was admitted (*Booth v. State*, 488 A.2d 195[MD 1985]).

TRIAL STRATEGY

Irving Younger said, "An 'excited utterance' is any statement that begins with "My God," and ends with an exclamation mark." No expert has come up with a better definition, but courts have adopted a few standards.

1. Lapse of time between startling event and statement?
2. Was statement in response to an inquiry?
3. Age of declarant?
4. Physical and mental condition of declarant?
5. The characteristics of event?
6. Subject matter of statement?

(*U.S. v. Iron Shell*, 633 F.2d 77 [8th Cir. 1980])

The fact a startling event occurred, can be shown by the statement, or by the behavior, appearance, or condition of declarant (*U.S. v. Moore*, 791 F.2d 566 [7th Cir. 1986]). Court admitted husband's testimony that wife came downstairs after a phone call and said, "That idiot wants to kill me" (*U.S. v. Vretta*, 790 F.2d 651 [7th Cir. 1986]). Even though sex offense victim was still upset a few hours later, what she told doctor was not "spontaneous" (*State v. Burgess*, 465 A.2d 204 [RI 1983]). HOWEVER, another court held what sex victim told mother three days later was admissible (*State v. Padilla*, 329 N.W. 2d 263 [WI 1982]).

It must be shown that declarant PERCEIVED when shouting, "You set my house on fire" (*State v. Dame*, 488 A.2d 418 [RI 1985]), or "The bastard tried to cut in" (in auto accident case) (*Miller v. Keating*, 754 F.2d 507 [3rd Cir. 1985]) were excluded because of lack of such proof.

"I didn't mean to shoot her," when said by defendant right after shooting, should have been admitted as "excited utterance," with jury deciding weight. "Self-Serving" is not the test, hearsay is the test (*State v. Williams*, 673 F.2d 32 [MO 1984]). Excited utterance of a four-year-old child identifying person charged with abusing her was admitted (*Haggins v. Warden*, 715 F.2d 1050 [6th Cir. 1983]).

When police arrived, since the declarant was still noticeably nervous, there was little chance of fabricating, so admitted as "excited utterance" (*McCurdy v. Greyhound Corporation*, 346 F.2d 224 [3rd Cir. 1965]). In one case, the showing of photograph to victim was enough to elicit an excited utterance (*State v. Napier*, 518 F.2d 316 [9th Cir. 1975]). The court must decide how much "shock" resulted from the circumstances of each case (*David By Berkely v. Pueblo Supermarket,* 740 F.2d 230 [3rd Cir. 1984]).

Sec. 8.11 *"Then Existing Conditions" or "Medical Diagnosis or Treatment"*
Rule 803(3) provides as an exception to the hearsay rule,

> *"A statement of the declarant's then existing state of mind, emotion, sensation, or physical condition (such as intent, plan, motive, design, mental feeling, pain, and bodily health), BUT NOT INCLUDING A STATEMENT OF memory or belief to prove the fact remembered or believed UNLESS IT RELATES TO the execution, revocation, identification, or terms of declarant's will."*

Rule 803(4) provides as an exception to the hearsay rule,

> *"Statements made for purposes of medical diagnosis or treatment and describing medical history, or past or present symptoms, pain, or sensations, or the inception or general character of the cause or external source thereof insofar as reasonably pertinent to diagnosis or treatment."*

Evidence of "intent to meet" must be excluded unless there is other evidence the meeting did occur (*U.S. v. Cicale,* 691 F.2d 95 [2nd Cir. 1982]). Prosecution cannot show intent through statements made two years after crime (*U.S. v. Jackson,* 780 F.2d 1305 [7th Cir. 1980]).

TRIAL STRATEGY

Prove "Medical Diagnosis or Treatment" Exception by Showing

1. Declarant's motive in making statement consistent with purposes of treatment.
2. Content of statement reasonably relied upon by physician in treatment or diagnosis.

(*U.S. v. Iron Shell,* 633 F.2d 77 [8th Cir. 1980])

Courts have extended "diagnosis and treatment" in sex abuse cases, permitting, in one case, the statement by an eleven-year-old child identifying the defendant, to be given by her doctor (*U.S. v. Renville,* 779 F.2d 430 [8th Cir. 1985]) and, in the other case, admitting what a child had told the social worker (*U.S. v. Denoyer,* 811 F.2d 436 [8th Cir. 1987]). The better practice seems to adopt a special rule for child-abuse cases (see Florida Statutes, 90.803(23)).

Where doctor testified, he did not rely upon the statement, and it is not admissible (*Cook v. Hoppin,* 783 F.2d 684 [7th Cir. 1986]).

TRIAL STRATEGY

Have Court Admit:

"The patient said he was hit in head with pipe being swung by John Jones," by having court strike, "being swung by John Jones."

What the doctor tells the patient does not come within the exception (*Bulthuis v. Rexall Drug,* 777 F.2d 1353 [9th Cir. 1985]). That no treatment was anticipated does not matter (*U.S. v. Iron Thunder,* 714 F.2d 765 [8th Cir. 1983]). Nine-year-old's statement that sexual activity occurred was admitted (*State v. Hebert,* 480 A.2d 742 [ME 1984]).

TRIAL STRATEGY

Child's Identification of Abuser May Be Admitted Re "Diagnosis and Treatment"

1. Child abuse involves emotional and psychological problems, as well as physical, and the nature and extent of problems often depends on identifying abuser.
2. Physicians have obligation not to return child to improper environment.

(*U.S. v. Renville,* 779 F.2d 430 [8th Cir. 1985]).
What About Additional Factor of Need to Know If Abuser Has AIDS or Other Disease?

A widow's testimony that she and her husband had talked about his telling his partner he was cancelling the contract and getting out of the partnership, was admitted, to show that he did subsequently act in accordance with this intention (*U.S. v. Calvert,* 523 F.2d 895 [8th Cir. 1975]). The courts have even permitted the statement of declarant can show that he *and another* were going to do something (*Mutual Life Insurance Co. v. Hillmon,* 145 U.S. 285 [1982]). Some courts have held, however, that such testimony cannot be used against "the another."

Sec. 8.12 *"Recorded Recollection" or "Records of Regularly Conducted Activity"* Rule 803(5) provides as an exception to the hearsay rule,

"A memorandum or record concerning a matter about which A WITNESS ONCE HAD KNOWLEDGE BUT NOW HAS INSUFFICIENT RECOLLECTION to enable the witness to testify FULLY AND ACCURATELY, shown to

have been MADE OR ADOPTED by the witness when the matter was fresh in the witness' memory and to reflect that knowledge correctly. If admitted, the memorandum or record MAY BE READ INTO EVIDENCE but MAY NOT itself BE RECEIVED AS AN EXHIBIT, unless offered by an adverse party."

Rule 803(6) provides as an exception to the hearsay rule,

"A memorandum, report, record, or data compilation, in any form, of acts, events, conditions, opinions, or diagnoses, made at or near the time by, or from information transmitted by, a person with knowledge, if kept in the course of A REGULARLY CONDUCTED BUSINESS ACTIVITY, AND if it was THE REGULAR PRACTICE OF THAT BUSINESS ACTIVITY to make the memorandum, report, record, or data compilation, all as shown by the testimony of the custodian or other qualified witness, UNLESS the source of information or the method or circumstances of preparation indicate lack of trustworthiness. The term "business" as used in this paragraph includes business, institution, association, profession, occupation, and calling of every kind, whether or not conducted for profit."

Rule 803(7) provides as an exception to the hearsay rule, "Evidence that a matter is not included in" that which is kept in accordance with 803(6), "*if the matter was of a kind . . .*" that was ". *. . regularly made and preserved, UNLESS the sources of information or other circumstances indicate lack of trustworthiness.*"

Papers sent to accountant with instructions as to how to arrive at costs of borrowing not compiled in normal business (*Slater v. Texaco*, 506 F.Supp. 1099 [D.C. DE 1981]). Appraisals prepared in case of future tax dispute admitted as business record (*Selig v. U.S.*, 740 F.2d 572 [7th Cir. 1984]).

In one trial the following testimony was introduced:

Q. Do you recall giving those answers to those questions back in the June 2nd trial?

A. I believe so.

Q. So apparently now having your recollection refreshed through those transcripts, you do recall Mr. Thompson drove the payloader from the Construction Company?

A. Yeah, probably did. I am not positive, but he could have.

Q. Well, your recollection certainly would have been better back in April or June of this year?

A. Yes, could be.

Q. So your best recollection would be that's the way it happened, is that correct?

A. Yes.

The court held that the prior statement became "present recollection re-vived" (*U.S. v. Thompson,* 708 F.2d 1294 [8th Cir. 1983]).

It is error to accept recorded recollection as an exhibit and let it go to jury (*U.S. v. Ray,* 768 F.2d 991 [8th Cir. 1985]). NOTE, HOWEVER: Where attorney objected on basis of hearsay, *BUT DID NOT OBJECT TO IT BEING ADMIT-TED AS AN EXHIBIT,* admitting the exhibit was not error (*U.S. v. Williams,* 571 F.2d 344 [6th Cir. 1978]).

TRIAL STRATEGY

Offer "Recorded Recollection" Exception (Known at Common Law as "Past Recollection Recorded")

1. Witness once knew the fact or event.
2. Witness made or adopted the fact or event.
3. While it was fresh in his memory.
4. Such recording was accurate.
   A. remembers recording accurately
   B. habitually recorded such matters accurately
5. At trial cannot recall sufficiently to testify "fully and accurately."

Then the Witness Can Read the Recorded Information to the Jury (but the Exhibit Cannot be Admitted).

COMPARE this rule with Rule 612, which permits a writing to be used to refresh memory. In that situation, "present recollection refreshed" or "present recollection revived," the writing is not read to the jury. It is simply used to refresh the memory and then is put away.

TRIAL STRATEGY

Offer Evidence Where Memory Revived

1. Witness cannot recall fact or event.
2. Witness states a certain writing could help recall.
3. Counsel hands the witness the writing.
4. Counsel asks the witness to review the writing silently.
5. Counsel then asks if memory is refreshed.
6. Witness indicates that it is, and testifies with the refreshed mem-ory (putting the writing away).

There is still confusion among trial lawyers as to how Rule 803(5) relates to Recorded Recollection and how Rule 803(6) relates to Records of Regularly Conducted Activity. Through recorded recollection, counsel is trying to admit testimony, but through Records of Regularly Conducted Activity he is trying to admit a written document.

TRIAL STRATEGY

Offer Document of Regularly Conducted Activity

1. Show that it is a "memorandum, report, record or data compilation."
2. Of "acts, events, conditions, opinions, or diagnoses."
3. Made at or near time.
   A. by a person with knowledge *or*
   B. from information transmitted by a person with knowledge
4. Pertains to relevant issue.
5. Kept in course of regularly conducted business activity.
   A. "business" includes business, institution, association, profession, occupation, and calling of every kind, whether or not conducted for profit.
6. Was regular practice of that business activity to make such documents.
7. Witness is
   A. custodian, or
   B. other qualified witness

Opposing Counsel Must Show Lack of "Trustworthiness"

1. As to source of information.
2. As to method used.
3. As to circumstances, or
4. As to preparation of document.

Opinions or conclusions in a business record are admitted only if given by one with required competence (*Clark v. City of Los Angeles*, 650 F.2d 1033 [9th Cir. 1981]). The banking industry is so regulated that its figures were accepted in Cuban takeover, subject to impeachment (*Banco Nacional De Cuba v. Chase Manhattan Bank*, 505 F.Supp. 412 [D.C. NY 1981]).

Proponent has burden of proving "regularity of practice," *In Re Japanese Electronic Products Antitrust Litigation*, 723 F.2d 238 [3rd Cir. 1983]), but other counsel has burden of proving factual finding "untrustworthy" (*U.S. v. Am. Tel.&Tel. Co.*, 498 F.Supp. 353 [D.C. DC 1980]). The trial court has broad discretion in such rulings (*Rosenberg v. Collins*, 624 F.2d 659 [8th Cir. 1980]).

Company records admitted to show truck involved in accident was equipped with air-leaf suspension system, and that it had two broken springs prior to accident (*Farner v. Paccar, Inc.*, 562 F.2d 518 [8th Cir. 1977]). Car dealer's diary admitted to show income and tips in tax dispute of another car dealer (*Keough v. C.I.R.*, 713 F.2d 496 [9th Cir. 1983]).

Court waived custodian requirement where documents showed this testimony not necessary (*In Re Japanese Electric*, above). Testimony of the custodian, or other qualified witness, is, however, usually required (*N.L.R.B. v. First Termite Control Co., Inc.*, 646 F.2d 424 [9th Cir. 1981]). In fact, the witness must be able to explain the procedure under which the records were kept (*Liner v. J.B. Talley and Co., Inc.*, 618 F.2d 327 [5th Cir. 1980]).

Papers prepared regularly for client are business records regularly prepared (*In Re Vaniman International Inc.*, 22 BR. 166 [NY Bky 1982]). Testimony in prior trial about destroyed records was used to refresh witness' memory of the files (*Gryder's Estate v. C.I.R.*, 705 F.2d 336 [8th Cir. 1983]). "PAID," marked on back of check admitted as regularly conducted activity and reliable (*Matter of Richter & Phillips Jewelers & Distributors*, 31 B.R. 512 [Ohio Bky 1983]). In a fee action, a lawyer's calendar was used for whatever purpose relevant, not just to refresh his memory (*Frank v. Bloom*, 634 F.2d 1245 [10th Cir. 1980]).

Admitting business record does not admit all that is in it (*Zenith Radio Corp. v. Matsushita Elec. Ind.*, 505 F.Supp. 1190 [D.C. PA 1980]). Marked-up draft of corporate minutes found not to be reliable (*Lloyd v. Professional Realty Services, Inc.*, 734 F.2d 1428 [11th Cir. 1984]). In personal injury case the medical report of deceased doctor excluded (*Smith v. John Swafford Furniture Co., Inc.*, 614 F.2d 552 [6th Cir. 1980]). Hospital record showing nerve had been severed earlier excluded, since now showing where the information came from, and since it would be misconstrued by jury, as opinion evidence on crucial issue (*Petrocelli v. Gallison*, 679 F.2d 286 [1st Cir. 1982]).

The fact the records are not accurate, or that they were not prepared in the best manner (goes to weight, not admissibility), itself, becomes the primary question in criminal cases. However, the *Oates* line of cases holding law-enforcement reports should not be admitted because of the confrontation clause (*U.S. v. Oates*, 560 F.2d 45 [2nd Cir. 1977]). Courts have held contrary, such as admitting an Internal Revenue Service agent's report (*McGarry v. U.S.*, 388 F.2d 862 [1st Cir. 1967]).

Sec. 8.13 *"Public Records and Reports," or "Records of Vital Statistics," or Lack of Such*   Rule 803(8) provides as an exception to the hearsay rule,

"Records, reports, statements, or data compilations, in any form, of public offices or agencies, setting forth

(A) the activities of the office or agency, or
(B) matters observed pursuant to duty imposed by law as to which matters there was a duty to report, excluding, however, in criminal cases matters observed by police officers and other law enforcement personnel, or

(C) in civil actions and proceedings and against the Government in criminal cases, factual findings resulting from an investigation made pursuant to authority granted by law, unless the sources of information or other circumstances indicate lack of trustworthiness."

Rule 803(9) provides as an exception to the hearsay rule:

"Records or data compilations, in any form, of births, fetal deaths, deaths, or marriages, if the report thereof was made to a public office pursuant to requirements of law."

Rule 803(10) provides that to prove the absence of such record or report *"or the nonoccurrence or nonexistence"* of such a record or report, or such *"was regularly made and preserved by a public office or agency . . ."* such proof can be . . .

"in the form of a certification in accordance with Rule 902," OR "testimony, that diligent search failed to disclose the record, report, statement, or data compilation, or entry".

TRIAL STRATEGY

In Arguing for or Against Admitting Public Agency Report, Consider

1. Timeliness of investigation.
2. Special skill and experience of official.
3. Possible motivation problems (*Ellis v. International Playtex, Inc.,* 745 F.2d 292 [4th Cir. 1984]).
4. Whether hearing was held (*Baker v. Elcona Homes,* 588 F.2d 551 [6th Cir. 1978]).

Ellis took the position the burden is on party opposing admission, to show its lack of reliability. Such a presumption is less popular, however, in admitting congressional reports, which seem to face the question of political motivation (*Pearce v. E.F. Hutton Group, Inc.,* 653 F.Supp. 810 [D.C. DC 1987]), but see (*DeLetelier v. Republic of Chile,* 567 F.Supp. 1490 [S.D. NY 1983]). Generally, reports of judiciary are not admitted (*Trustees of University of Pennsylvania v. Lexington Ins. Co.,* 815 F.2d 890 [3rd Cir. 1987]).

To challenge an FAA report, you must show its untrustworthiness (*Melville v. American Home Assurance Co.,* 584 F.2d 1306 [3rd Cir. 1978]). EEOC report need not be accepted if "sufficient negative factors are present" (*Johnson v. Yellow Freight System, Inc.,* 734 F.2d 1304 [8th Cir. 1984]). Report from Center For

Disease Control re risk period of swine flue vaccinations admitted (*Migliorini v. U.S.*, 521 F.Supp. 1210 [M.D. FL 1981]).

When defendant claimed to be member of CIA, affidavit from CIA director indicating diligent search (though magic words "diligent search failed to disclose" not used) did not reveal defendant as CIA agent, AFFIDAVIT ADMITTED (*U.S. v. Harris*, 551 F.2d 621 [5th Cir. 1977]). Opinions and conclusions need not be excised, but a report of nothing more than opinions and conclusions will not usually be admitted (*Marsee v. U.S. Tobacco Co.*, 639 F.Supp. 46 [W.D. OK 1986]).

Report of Department of Transportation re stopping distances can be used in auto accident case (*Robbins v. Whelan*, 653 F.2d 47 [1st Cir. 1981]). Investigative report showing officer was "a poor police officer" was admitted (*Ward v. Arkansas State Police*, 714 F.2d 62 [8th Cir. 1983]). Workmen's compensation file admitted to show employee had been given notice of asbestos hazards (*In Re Asbestos Cases* 543 F.Supp. 1152 [N.D. CA 1982]). Acceptance of foreign judgment depends upon "civilized jurisprudence" and "clear and formal record" (*Lloyd v. American Export Lines*, 580 F.2d 1179 [3rd Cir. 1978]).

Public records can be used to prove ownership of a car (*U.S. v. King*, 590 F.2d 253 [8th Cir. 1978]), or a survey done by a private surveyor, but under a duty to report to a public official (*U.S. v. Central Gulf Lines*, 747 F.2d 315 [5th Cir. 1984]), or a warrant of deportation (*U.S. v. Bejar-Matrecios*, 618 F.2d 81 [9th Cir. 1980]).

Lack of a public record or statistic can usually be shown by affidavit, and no record of tax return comes within this exception (*U.S. v. Johnson*, 577 F.2d 1304 [5th Cir. 1978]). A diligent search, however, must be made.

Sec. 8.14 *"Records of Religious Organizations," or "Marriage, Baptismal, and Similar Certificates," or "Family Records"* Rule 803(11) provides as an exception to the hearsay rule,

"Statements of births, marriages, divorces, deaths, legitimacy, ancestry, relationship by blood or marriage, or other similar facts of personal or family history, contained in a regularly kept record of a religious organization."

Rule 803(12) provides as an exception to the hearsay rule:

"Statements of fact contained in a certificate that the maker performed a marriage or other ceremony or administered a sacrament, made by a clergyman, public official, or other person authorized by the rules or practices of a religious organization or by law to perform the act certified, purporting to have been issued at the time of the act or within a reasonable time thereafter."

Rule 803(13) provides, as an exception to the hearsay rule:

"Statements of fact concerning personal or family history contained in family Bibles, genealogies, charts, engravings on rings, inscriptions on family portraits, engravings on urns, crypts, or tombstones, or the like."

The provisions of Rule 803(11), Rule 803(12) and Rule 803(13) are clear and have not been the subject of litigation. It is important to study these provisions in connection with Article Nine of the rules relating to authentication and identification.

Sec. 8.15 "Records of Documents Affecting an Interest in Property," or "Statement in Documents Affecting an Interest in Property," or "Statements in Ancient Documents"   Rule 803(14) provides as an exception to the hearsay rule,

> *"The record of a document purporting to establish or effect an interest in property, as proof of the content of the original recorded document and its execution and delivery by each person by whom it purports to have been executed, IF, the record is a record of a public office and an applicable statute authorizes the recording of documents of that kind in that office."*

Rule 803(15) provides as an exception to the hearsay rule,

> *"A statement contained in a document purporting to establish or effect an interest in property if the matter stated was relevant to the purpose of the document, UNLESS dealings with the property since the document was made have been inconsistent with the truth of the statement or the purport of the document."*

Rule 803(16) provides, as an exception to the hearsay rule,

> *"Statements in a document in existence twenty years or more the authenticity of which is established."*

Recitals in two old deeds were used to prove that a marriage between two people existed (*Compton v. Davis Oil Co.*, 607 F.Supp. 1221 [D.C. WY 1985]). The courts stressed the fact there is a NEED for such evidence because other evidence is often not available, and there is a RELIABILITY, since there was no reason to lie about the marriage in the deed.

Ukrainian police employment forms were introduced in a denaturalization proceeding, within the ancient document exception (*U.S. v. Koziy*, 728 F.2d 1314 [11th Cir. 1984]). In the asbestos litigation, many of the documents were more than twenty years old, and admissible under the ancient document exception (*In Re Asbestos Litigation Cases*, 543 F.Supp. 1152 [D.C. CA 1982]). Newspaper articles often come within the ancient document rule (*Ammons v. Dade City, Florida*, 594 F.Supp. 1274 [M.D. FL 1984]). IMPORTANT: Though ancient documents rule was at common law limited to "property interest documents," under FRE contracts, maps, plans, and all other papers can be "ancient."

Sec. 8.16 *"Market Reports, Commercial Publications," or "Learned Treatises"* Rule 803(17) provides, as an exception to the hearsay rule,

"Market quotations, tabulations, lists, directories, or other published compilations, GENERALLY USED AND RELIED UPON by the public or by persons in particular occupations."

Rule 803(18) provides, as an exception to the hearsay rule,

"To the extent called to the attention of an expert witness upon cross-examination or relied upon by the expert witness in direct examination, statements contained in published TREATISES periodicals, or pamphlets on a subject of history, medicine, or other science or art, established as a reliable authority by the testimony or admission of the witness or by other expert testimony or by judicial notice. If admitted, the statements MAY BE READ INTO EVIDENCE, but MAY NOT BE RECEIVED AS EXHIBITS."

Market reports, "blue books" or "red books", newspapers, trade magazines and catalogues have been used to show the value of a stock (*Virginia v. West Virginia*, 238 U.S. 202 [1915]), a cigarette lighter (*U.S. v. Grossman*, 614 F.2d 295 [1st Cir. 1980]), or an automobile (*U.S. v. Johnson*, 515 F.2d 730 [7th Cir. 1975]).

A learned treatise can relate to cattle investments (*Burgess v. Premier Corp.*, 727 F.2d 826 [9th 1984]), or The American Standard Safety Code for Conveyors (*Alexander v. Conveyors & Dumpers, Inc.*, 731 F.2d 1221 [5th Cir. 1984]), or a dictionary to show significance and meaning of words *(WSM Inc. v. Hilton*, 724 F.2d 1320 [8th Cir. 1984]), of driver's handbook given to employee by employer, where truck driver was traveling 65 MPH in a 55 MPH zone (*Marks v. Mobil Oil Corporation*, 562 F.Supp. 759 [D.C. PA 1983]), and copy of the Safety and Health Act Regulations, though the act prohibits their introduction (*Rabon v. Automated Fastners, Inc.*, 672 F.2d 1231 [11th Cir. 1982]).

TRIAL STRATEGY

Introduce Evidence by Market or Commercial Report

1. Show it is a market quotation or other data covered by the rule.
2. Show it is relied upon by
   A. those in the field or
   B. the public

A treatise is "published" when it is in written form and circulated for use by others and includes data or information (*White Industries v. Cessna Aircraft*, 611

F.Supp. 1049 [D.C. MO 1985]). Expert on fire investigation was permitted to read from magazine he said was "somewhat" authoritative in his field (*Allen v. Safeco Ins. Co.,* 782 F.2d 1195 [11th Cir. 1986]). Old Farmer's Almanac admitted to show what time sun set (*Guptill v. Bergman,* 240 A.2d 55 [NH 1968]). A doctor who attempted to introduce treatise he had written, rejected on other basis, not hearsay (*Schneider v. Revici,* 817 F.2d 987 [2nd Cir. 1987]).

TRIAL STRATEGY

Introduce Evidence With Learned Treatise

On Direct Examination

    1. Statement is from learned treatise.
    2. Expert has relied upon the treatise.

On Cross-Examination

    1. Statement if from learned treatise.
    2. Statement called to attention of the expert witness.
    3. The treatise is reliable authority by:
        A. testimony or admission of expert witness
        B. testimony of other expert
        C. judicial notice

Sec. 8.17 "Reputation Concerning Personal or Family History," or "Reputation Concerning Boundaries or General History," or "Reputation As to Character"   Rule 803(19) provides, as an exception to the hearsay rule,

> *"Reputation among members of a person's family by blood, adoption, or marriage, or among a person's associates, or in the community, Concerning a person's birth, adoption, marriage, divorce, death, legitimacy, relationship by blood, adoption, or marriage, ancestry, or other similar fact of his personal or family history."*

Rule 803(20) provides, as an exception to the hearsay rule:

> *"Reputation in a community, arising before the controversy, as to boundaries of or customs affecting lands in the community, and reputation as to events of general history important to the community or State or nation in which located."*

Rule 803(21) provides, as an exception to the hearsay rule:

> *"Reputation of a person's character among associates or in the community."*

HISTORICAL NOTE

Common law limitation that reputation must have been prior to controversy is no longer applicable. ALSO, people now go outside their neighborhood or community and reputation as evidence has expanded accordingly.

Sec. 8.18 "Judgment of Previous Conviction" or "Judgment As to Personal, Family or General History or Boundaries" Rule 803(22) provides, as an exception to the hearsay rule,

"Evidence of a final judgment, entered after a trial or upon a plea of guilty (but not upon a plea of nolo contendere), adjudging a person guilty of a crime punishable by death or imprisonment in excess of one year, to prove any fact essential to sustain the judgment, but not including, when offered by the Government in a criminal prosecution for purposes other than impeachment, judgments against persons other than the accused. The pendency of an appeal may be shown but does not affect admissibility."

Rule 803(23) provides, as an exception to the hearsay rule,

"Judgments as proof of matters of personal family or general history, or boundaries, essential to the judgment, if the same would be provable by evidence of reputation."

Courts have limited use of convictions where confrontation clause would be violated (*Kirby v. U.S.*, 174 U.S. 49 [1899]). When conviction is admitted, its circumstances may be shown in rebuttal (*Lloyd v. American Export Lines, Inc.*, 580 F.2d 1179 [3rd Cir. 1978]). Stock ownership was proven by judgment in another case (*Schwarz v. U.S.*, 582 F.Supp. 224 [D.C. MD 1984]).

A federal court may look to state law to determine effect of its judgment (*Branca by Branca v. Security Benefit Life Ins. Co.*, 773 F.2d 1158 [11th Cir. 1985]). Judgment was used to show act of insured was exception to policy (*Country Mutual Ins. Co. v. Duncan*, 794 F.2d 1211 [7th Cir. 1988]).

Sec. 8.19 "Other Exceptions": The "Residual Exception" Rule 803(24) is the residual exception to the hearsay rule, providing:

"A statement not specifically covered by any of the foregoing exceptions but having EQUIVALENT CIRCUMSTANTIAL GUARANTEES OF TRUSTWORTHINESS, if the court determines that

(A) the statement is offered as evidence of a MATERIAL FACT;
(B) the statement is MORE PROBATIVE on the point for which it is offered than any other evidence which the proponent can procure through reasonable efforts; and

(C) the general purposes of these rules and the interests of justice will best be served by admission of the statement into evidence.

HOWEVER, a statement may not be admitted under this exception UNLESS the proponent of it makes known to the adverse party sufficiently in advance of the trial or hearing to provide the adverse party with a fair opportunity to prepare to meet it, the proponent's intention to offer the statement and the particulars of it, including the name and address of the declarant."

TRIAL STRATEGY

Remember Five "Residual" Exception Requirements

1. Trustworthiness.
2. Materiality.
3. Probative value (no better evidence).
4. Interest of justice.
5. Notice.

(*Moffett v. McCauley*, 724 F.2d 581 [7th Cir. 1984])

COURTS *ARE* REQUIRING THE NOTICE CALLED FOR BY RULE 803(24) and Rule 804(b)(5), unless there is good reason. Notice given a few days before trial was sufficient, under the circumstances (*U.S. v. Iaconetti*, 540 F.2d 574 [2nd Cir. 1976]). Where need for the evidence did not arise until trial, and other party did not request a continuance, "latitude" given proponent of the evidence (*Iaconetti,* Supra). One court held lack of notice is not fatal, unless opposing counsel shows "did not have a fair opportunity to meet it" (*U.S. v. Obayagbona*, 627 F.2d 329 [E.D. NY 1985]). In business record exception opponent has burden of showing trustworthiness, but in residual exception that burden is with proponent (*Zenith Radio Corp. v. Matsushita Electric Industry Co. Ltd.,* 05 F.Supp. 1190 [E.D. PA 1980]). In fact, one court said if hearsay rule is to be preserved at all, proponent must show "special trustworthiness" to have residual exception admitted (*Wolfson v. Mutual Life Ins. Co. of New York*, 455 F.Supp. 82 [D.C. PA 1978]). There must be a balancing of need and trustworthiness (*Herdman v. Smith*, 707 F.2d 839 [5th Cir. 1983]). Another court said, Congress intended the residual exception be used "very rarely" and only in "exceptional circumstances" (*Huff v. White Motor Corp.*, 609 F.2d 286 [7th Cir. 1979]).

The view that failing to meet requirements of another exception could keep proponent from succeeding under residual exception has not survived. In fact, courts have held failing to meet one exception is the kind of "other" that qualifies for the residual (*Zenith Radio Corp. v. Matsushita Electric Industry Co. Ltd.*, 505 F.Supp. 1190 [E.D. PA 1980]). Where business records were accepted, court said it could have been admitted under "residual exception" anyway (*U.S. v. Pfeiffer,* 539 F.2d 668 [8th Cir. 1976]).

MASTER RULES 803(24) AND 804(b)(5) BY APPLYING THEM TO EXAMPLES:

1. *Doctor's Records:* Eye-exam records of deceased doctor admitted, including even a deposition of a doctor in a different case, where reliability not really in question (*Dartez v. Fireboard Corp.,* 765 F.2d 456 [5th Cir. 1985]). Statements to manufacturer of birth-control device giving report of patient's problems admitted (*In Re A.H. Robins Co.,* 575 F.Supp. 718 [D.C. KS 1983]).

2. *Newspapers:* What reporter tells party about interview with mayor was clearly hearsay (*Oaks v. City of Fairhope, AL,* 515 F.Supp. 1004 [D.C. AL 1981]).

HISTORICAL NOTE

Irving Younger called the *Dallas County* case the most important evidence case ever decided, and all other experts join in citing it as authority. A fire that occurred years earlier had become the key point of the trial, since this would relieve the insurance company of a duty to pay under the policy. When no witness could be found (since they were dead) and no records were available in this rural area, the ONLY evidence available was a fifty-eight-year-old newspaper article found at the historical society. It was admitted because of its RELIABILITY, and this became the "granddaddy" of all residual exceptions. READ IT! (*Dallas County v. Commercial Union Assurance Co.,* 286 F.2d 388 [5th Cir. 1961]). ALSO, while you are at the library look at the *Zenith Radio* cases that contain one hundred fifty-five pages of good discussion on the law of evidence (*Zenith Radio Corp. v. Matsushita Electric Industry Co.,* 505 F.Supp. 1190 [D.C. PA 1980]).

Copies of newspaper articles attached to summary judgment motion is hearsay (*De La Cruz v. DuFresne,* 533 F.Supp. 145 [D.C. NV 1982]). Press reports hearsay (*Democratic Party of U.S. v. National Conservative Political Action Committee,* 578 F.Supp. 797 [D.C. PA 1983]). Statement in newspaper attributed to defendant not admissible (*Ray v. Edwards,* 557 F.Supp. 664 [D.C. GA 1982]). Newspaper article offered to show information was available admitted, but to show public opposition, not admitted (*Grossman v. Waste Management, Inc.,* 589 F.Supp. 395 [D.C. IL 1984]).

3. *Statements by Children:* What an eleven-year-old child told deputy sheriff admitted, though child changed her testimony at trial (*U.S. v. Renville,* 779 F.2d 430 [8th Cir. 1985]). What a four-year-old child told FBI agent and social worker was admitted under residual exception (*U.S. v. Cree,* 778 F.2d 474 [8th Cir. 1985]).

4. *Statements by Attorneys:* Court should have admitted affidavit from attorney taking blame for the tax evasion (*U.S. v. Popenas*, 780 F.2d 545 [6th Cir. 1985]).

5. *Statements by Employees:* Documents authored by employees were admitted (*U.S. v. Am. Tel. & Tel. Co.*, 516 F.Supp. 1237 [D.C. DC 1981]). Employees "valuable input concerning performance of intrauterine device" admitted (*In Re A.H. Robins, Inc.*, 575 F.Supp. 718 [D.C. KA 1983]). Manager's report as to what company's employees had learned through investigation admitted (*Navel Orange Administration Committee v. Exeter Orange Co., Inc.*, 722 F.2d 449 [9th Cir. 1983]).

6. *Seizure:* Hearsay can be used to establish reasonable belief as to probable cause for seizure, but cannot be used to support a permanent taking (*Flores v. U.S.*, 551 F.2d 1169 [9th Cir. 1977]).

7. *Damages:* Plaintiff's statement that at time of accident she was about to take a job paying sixty dollars a day admitted (*O'Shea v. Riverway Towing Co.*, 677 F.2d 1194 [7th Cir. 1982]).

8. *Construction:* Witness who had been on job from beginning could tell what he remembers (*Westminister Elec. Corp. v. Salem Engineering & Const.*, 712 F.2d 720 [1st Cir. 1983]).

9. *Polls & Surveys:* Survey of members of club not scientifically conducted not admitted, to show how much of its business was with nonmembers (*Pittsburgh Press Club v. U.S.*, 579 F.2d 751 [3rd Cir. 1978]). Customer questionnaires admitted where no reason to fabricate (*Weiner King, Inc. v. Weiner King Corp.*, 407 F.Supp. 1274 [D.C. NJ 1976]). Surveys are generally admitted, if properly conducted, and proof of such is shown the court (*Scott Paper Co. v. Scott's Liquid Gold, Inc.*, 439 F.Supp. 1022 [D.C. DE 1977]).

10. *Securities:* In securities litigation, hearsay in records admitted because they were "inherently trustworthy" (*Securities Exchange Commission v. Musella*, 578 F.Supp. 425 [D.C. NY 1984]). In securities matter, statement by chief executive officer not admitted, because no guarantee of trustworthiness (*Securities Exchange Commission v. Scott*, 565 F.Supp. 1513 [D.C. NY 1983]); admitted, however, where trustworthiness found (*Sherrell Perfumers, Inc. v. Revlon, Inc.*, 524 F.Supp. 302 [D.C. NY 1980]).

11. *Self-Serving:* Where it is obvious the report or other form of statement (such as how an accident happened) is suspect, not admitted (*Land v. American Mutual Insurance Co.*, 582 F.Supp. 1484 (D.C. MI 1984).

12. *Rating:* Rating of commercial paper as "prime" admitted (*Alton Box Board Co. v. Goldman, Sachs, & Co.*, 418 F.Supp. 1149 [D.C. MO 1976]).

13. *Documents:* Documents and data sent accountant were not made in ordinary course of business and did not qualify under residual exception (*Slater v. Texaco,* 506 F.Supp. 1099 [D.C. DE 1981]).

14. *Grand Jury:* Grand jury testimony should not be admitted as residual exception (*U.S. v. Vigoa,* 656 F.Supp. 1499 [D.C. NJ 1987]).

15. *Letters:* Letters from a corporate file that did not qualify as business record, did qualify as residual exception (*Attorney General of U.S. v. The Irish People, Inc.,* 595 F.Supp. 114 (D.C. DC 1984]).

16. *Affidavits:* Court admitted fifteen affidavits where court's finding of trustworthiness was based largely on fact affidavits agreed with oral testimony (*Federal Trade Commission v. Kitco of Nevada,* 612 F.Supp. 1282 (D.C. MN 1985]).

17. *Multiple Hearsay:* Triple hearsay was admitted where some levels were exceptions, and entire testimony seemed trustworthy (*U.S. v. Medico,* 557 F.2d 309 [2nd Cir. 1977]).

18. *Confrontation:* Court refused to admit statement of defendant's companion made while both were in custody, as barred by confrontation clause. Since companion was never subject to cross-examination, the self-serving statement was not reliable, and companion could have been made available to defendant had companion been given use of immunity (*U.S. v. Yates,* 524 F.2d 1282 [D.C. Cir. 1975]). However, certificate showing blood sample taken of defendant charged with DWI was admitted (*Kay v. U.S.,* 255 F.2d 476 [4th Cir. 1958]).

Sec. 8.20 *Proving Unavailability of Declarant*   Rule 804(a) sets forth the following methods of proving the unavailability of the declarant:

"(1) is exempted by ruling of the court on the ground of PRIVILEGE FROM TESTIFYING concerning the subject matter of the declarant's statement; or

(2) persists in REFUSING TO TESTIFY concerning the subject matter of the declarant's statement despite an order of the court to do so; or

(3) testifies to a LACK OF MEMORY of the subject matter of the declarant's statement; or

(4) is unable to be present or to testify at the hearing because of DEATH OR THEN EXISTING PHYSICAL OR MENTAL ILLNESS OR IN-FIRMITY; or

(5) is absent from the hearing and the proponent of statement has been UN-ABLE TO PROCURE the declarant's ATTENDANCE (or in the case of a hearsay exception under subdivision (b)(2), (3), or (4), the declarant's attendance or testimony) BY PROCESS OR OTHER REASONABLE MEANS.

A declarant is NOT UNAVAILABLE as a witness if exemption, refusal, claim of lack of memory, inability, or absence is due to the PROCUREMENT OR WRONGDOING OF THE PROPONENT of a statement for the purpose of preventing the witness from attending to testify."

TRIAL STRATEGY

REMEMBER, it is the STATEMENT that is not available, NOT the WITNESS. A witness may be sitting on the witness stand, yet "unavailable" due to privilege, refusal to testify, or lack of memory.

Unavailability need not be proven if caused by party against whom it is being used (*Steele v. Taylor*, 684 F.2d 1193 [6th Cir. 1982]). Continuance should have been granted where temporary physical infirmity caused prior testimony rather than live testimony to be used (*U.S. v. Faison*, 67 F.2d 292 [3rd Cir. 1982]).

TRIAL STRATEGY

In Proving Unavailability Show

1. Privilege.
   A. privilege must be claimed
   B. privilege must be ordered
2. Refusal to testify.
   A. judge must order that witness testify
   B. judge must warn of contempt
3. Lack of memory.

(*U.S. v. Zappola*, 646 F.2d 48 [2nd Cir. 1981])

   A. must show lack of memory as to "material portion" of the former testimony (*McDonnell v. U.S.*, 472 F.2d 1153 [8th Cir. 1973]).
4. Death or illness.
   Court may try part of case outside district to accommodate sick witness and avoid need for use of "former testimony" (*In Re Application To Take Testimony In Criminal Case Outside District*, 102 F.R.D. 521 (E.D. NY 1985]).
5. Lack of process.
   The courts have broad subpoena powers (Federal Rules of Civil Procedure Rule 45) that must be exhausted.

REMEMBER: The same "unavailable" rule applies to all five unavailable exceptions. At common law, each exception had its own unavailability test.

Counsel has a duty to take depositions where witness cannot be brought to court (*Zenith Radio Corp. v. Matsushita Electric Industry Co. Ltd.,* 505 F.Supp. 1190 [E.D. PA 1980]). Depositions can be used if witness is in hospital, and cause not continued (*M.S.D. v. U.S.,* 434 F.Supp. 85 [D.C. OH 1977]).

Sec. 8.21 "Former Testimony" Rule 804(b)(1) provides as a hearsay exception, IF DECLARANT UNAVAILABLE,

"Testimony given as a witness at another hearing of the same or a different proceeding, or in a deposition taken in compliance with law in the course of the same or another proceeding, IF the party against whom the testimony is now offered, OR, in a civil action or proceeding, A PREDECESSOR IN INTEREST, had an OPPORTUNITY AND SIMILAR MOTIVE to develop the testimony by direct, cross, or redirect examination."

HISTORICAL NOTE

At early common law "Former Testimony" was admitted only where identical parties were involved in a subsequent suit. This concept was extended to include "one in privity." The Advisory Committee recommended an extremely liberal approach, but Congress did not want counsel to be strapped with all the shortcomings of counsel in previous litigation. Federal Rules of Evidence require the "predecessor in interest" to have had "an opportunity and similar motive."

In a criminal case, the statement was offered against the same party, such as in a preliminary hearing where right to cross-examine satisfies constitutional requirements (*California v. Green,* 399 U.S. 149 [1970]). The confrontation clause is satisfied through cross-examination or a substitute (*Ohio v. Roberts,* 448 U.S. 56 [1980]). Grand jury testimony can be used where witness not available (*State v. Driscoll,* 445 F.2d 864 [D.C. Cir. 1978]).

TRIAL STRATEGY

Prove with Former Testimony

1. Prove unavailability.
   A. be sure to issue process, even if sheriff may not be able to find him.
2. Show deposition or hearing was conducted properly.
   A. testimony was under oath
   B. opportunity to cross-examine by party with similar motive
   C. right to counsel in criminal case where right guaranteed

3. Show identity of issues.
4. Show predecessor in interest.
5. Show opportunity and similar motive.

Where state trooper testified at bail hearing, but died before trial, his testimony was admitted (*State v. Caouette,* 462 A.2d 1171 [ME 1983]). Court refused testimony from civil trial where Government did not have right to cross-examine, though similar motive (*U.S. v. Kapnison,* 743 F.2d 1450 [10th Cir. 1984]).

In an asbestos case, testimony in a trial years earlier was admitted on basis the defendant in the earlier case had a similar motive to cross-examine (*Clay v. Johns-Mansville Sales Corp.,* 722 F.2d 1289 [6th Cir. 1983]).

The court will usually accept counsel's statement as to what he did to obtain presence of witness (*U.S. v. Johnson,* 735 F.2d 1200 [9th Cir. 1984]). However, an expert's unwillingness to testify does not suffice (*State v. Aillon,* 521 A.2d 555 [CT 1987]).

Sec. 8.22 *"Statement Under Belief of Impending Death*   Rule 804(b)(2) provides, as a hearsay rule exception, IF DECLARANT UNAVAILABLE:

> *"In a prosecution for homicide OR in a civil action or proceeding, a statement made by a declarant while believing that the declarant's death was imminent, concerning the cause or circumstances of what the declarant believed to be his impending death."*

HISTORICAL NOTE

At common law, "dying declaration" was limited to use in the homicide case of the death described and for the sole purpose of convicting the person accused, and it didn't apply if declarant recovered. Federal Rules of Evidence expanded to "homicide" or "civil action" re statements concerning "the causes or circumstances of which he believes to be his impending death." Some states have extended the rule even further, seeing no need to limit the kind of criminal case in which the exception applies.

There must be a "settled hopeless expectation" that death is near (*Shepard v. U.S.,* 290 U.S. 96 [1933]). This may be done with circumstantial evidence (see *Shepard*) or by declarant's own statement (*U.S. v. Kearney,* 420 F.2d 170 [D.C. Cir. 1969]). The extent of wounds could establish impending death, even if declarant expressed no awareness of his condition (*U.S. v. Mobley,* 421 F.2d 345 [5th Cir. 1970]).

Sec. 8.23 *"Statement Against Interest"*   Rule 804(b)(3) provides, as a hearsay exception, IF DECLARANT UNAVAILABLE,

> "A statement which was at the time of its making so far contrary to the declarant's pecuniary or proprietary interest, OR so far tended to subject the

declarant to civil or criminal liability, OR to render invalid a claim by the declarant against another, that a reasonable person in the declarant's position would not have made the statement unless believing it to be true. A statement tending to EXPOSE THE DECLARANT TO CRIMINAL LIABILITY and offered to exculpate the accused is NOT ADMISSIBLE unless CORROBORATING CIRCUMSTANCES clearly indicate the trustworthiness of the statement."

Declarant must have "understanding" of incriminating nature of his statement (*Pink Supply Corp. v. Hiebert, Inc.,* 612 F.Supp. 1334 [D.C. MN 1985]). Where declarant knew he was going to prison, court felt he was just helping a friend and excluded the statement (*U.S. v. Tovar,* 687 F.2d 1210 [8th Cir. 1982]).

Where statement was to avoid physical harm, statement made to avoid police brutality was not admitted, though against interest (*U.S. v. Manshaw,* 714 F.2d 785 (8th Cir. 1983]). Statement he was drinking with defendant prior to robbery may incriminate him, but not such that "a reasonable man would not have made it unless he believed it to be true" (*U.S. v. Chalan,* 812 F.2d 1302 [10th Cir. 1987]).

The employee's statement, to qualify as an exception, must be against employee's interest, not employer's interest (*Zenith Radio Corp. v. Matsushita Electric Industry Co. Ltd.,* 505 F.Supp. 1190 [E.D. PA 1980]). Where federal prisoner said he was not afraid of state prosecution, his statements were not against interest (*State v. Woodman,* 480 A.2d 169 [NH 1984]).

Statements by deceased that she forgave a loan could be used against her personal representative who was trying to collect on the loan (*Guardian State Bank & Trust Co. v. Jacobson,* 369 N.W. 2d 80 [NB 1985]). Though statement subjected declarant to theft charge, it cleared him of more serious crime so not against penal interest. (Also, exculpatory statement offered by accused must have corroborating evidence of trustworthiness; *U.S. v. Williams,* 738 F.2d 173 [7th Cir. 1984]).

TRIAL STRATEGY

Qualify Statement Against Interest by

1. Showing declarant not available.
2. Showing declarant *believed* the statement against interest.
3. Showing the interest is one recognized by the courts.
   A. "pecuniary or propriety interest"
   B. "civil or criminal liability"
   C. "render invalid a claim"
   D. some states expand this, even to "social interest"
4. Where accused offers as exculpatory, showing trustworthiness with other evidence.

Sec. 8.24 "Statement of Personal or Family History"   Rule 804(b)(4) provides, as an exception to the hearsay rule, when declarant unavailable:

"(A) A statement concerning the declarant's own birth, adoption, marriage, divorce, legitimacy, relationship by blood, adoption, or marriage, ancestry, or other similar fact of personal or family history, even though declarant had no means of acquiring personal knowledge of the matter stated; OR (B) a statement concerning the foregoing matters, and death also, of another person, if the declarant was related to the other by blood, adoption, or marriage OR was so intimately associated with the other's family as to be likely to have accurate information concerning the matter declared."

HISTORICAL NOTE

Rule 803(b)(4) extends the common law "Pedigree" hearsay exception:

1. Includes entire area of family history.
2. Eliminates *ante litem motem* requirement (only death established unavailability for this exception at common law).
3. Nonfamily members "intimately associated" can now be declarant.
4. Statement need not have been made before controversy (now goes to weight only).
5. No longer required that when relationship is between two parties, declarant must qualify as to both.

Sec. 8.25 "Other Exceptions" Where Declarant Not Available   The "residual exception" in Rule 804(b)(5) is the same as it is in Rule 803(24). It merely applies when declarant is not available.

Section 8.19 of this book contains the law that pertains to both of these sections. REMEMBER, this exception requires argument from counsel on either side. The court does exercise discretion, and it is up to counsel to convince the court of his or her position.

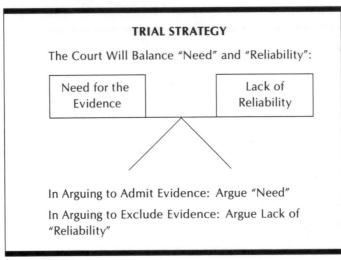

TRIAL STRATEGY

The Court Will Balance "Need" and "Reliability":

| Need for the Evidence | Lack of Reliability |

In Arguing to Admit Evidence: Argue "Need"

In Arguing to Exclude Evidence: Argue Lack of "Reliability"

The following tables show whether or not states adopting the Federal Rules of Evidence adopted substantially same provisions relative to the rules discussed in this chapter:

	Rule 801a-c	Rule 801d	Rule 802	Rule 803-1	Rule 803-2	Rule 803-3	Rule 803-4	Rule 803-5
ALASKA	Yes	Yes	Yes	Yes	Yes	Yes	Yes	Yes
ARIZONA	Yes	Yes	Yes	Yes	Yes	Yes	Yes	Yes
ARKANSAS	Yes	No	Yes	Yes	Yes	Yes	Yes	Yes
COLORADO	Yes	Yes	Yes	Yes	Yes	Yes	Yes	No
DELAWARE	Yes	Yes	No	Yes	Yes	Yes	Yes	No
FLORIDA	Yes	Mod	Yes	No	Yes	Yes	Yes	Yes
HAWAII	Yes	Yes	Yes	Yes	Yes	Yes	Yes	Yes
IDAHO	Yes	Yes	Yes	Yes	Yes	Yes	Yes	Yes
IOWA	Yes	Yes	Yes	Yes	Yes	Yes	Yes	Yes
MAINE	Yes	Yes	Yes	Yes	Yes	Yes	Yes	Yes
MICHIGAN	Yes	No	Yes	Yes	Yes	Yes	Mod	Yes
MINNESOTA	Yes	Yes	Yes	No	Yes	Yes	Yes	Yes
MISSISSIPPI	Yes	Yes	Yes	Yes	Yes	Yes	Yes	Yes
MONTANA	Yes	Yes	Yes	Yes	Yes	No	Yes	Yes
NEBRASKA	Yes	Yes	Yes	Yes	Yes	Yes	Yes	No
NEVADA	Yes	Yes	Yes	Yes	Yes	Yes	Yes	Yes
NEW HAMPSHIRE	Yes	Yes	Yes	Yes	Yes	Yes	Yes	Yes
NEW MEXICO	Yes	Yes	Yes	Yes	Yes	Yes	Yes	Yes
NORTH CAROLINA	Yes	No	Yes	Yes	Yes	Yes	Yes	Yes
NORTH DAKOTA	Yes	plus	Yes	Yes	Yes	Yes	Yes	Yes
OHIO	Yes	Yes	Yes	Yes	Yes	Yes	Yes	Yes
OKLAHOMA	Yes	Yes	Yes	Yes	Yes	Yes	Yes	Yes
OREGON	Yes	Yes	Yes	No	Yes	Yes	Yes	Yes
RHODE ISLAND	Yes	Yes	Yes	Yes	Yes	Yes	Yes	Yes
SOUTH DAKOTA	Yes	Yes	Yes	Yes	Yes	Yes	Yes	Yes
TEXAS	Yes	Yes	Yes	Yes	Yes	Yes	Yes	Yes
UTAH	Yes	Yes	Yes	Yes	Yes	Yes	Yes	Yes
VERMONT	Yes	Yes	Yes	Yes	Yes	Yes	Yes	Yes
WASHINGTON	Yes	Yes	Yes	Yes	Yes	Yes	Yes	Yes
WEST VIRGINIA	Yes	Yes	Yes	Yes	Yes	Yes	Yes	Yes
WISCONSIN	Yes	Yes	Yes	Yes	Yes	Yes	Yes	Yes
WYOMING	Yes	plus	Yes	Yes	Yes	Yes	Yes	Yes

Rule	Subject
801a-c	Hearsay Definition
801d	Not Hearsay
802	Hearsay Rule
803-1	Present Sense Impression
803-2	Excited Utterance
803-3	Then Existing Mental, Emotional or Physical Condition
803-4	Statements for Purpose of Medical Diagnosis or Treatment
803-5	Recorded Recollection

	Rule 803-6	Rule 803-7	Rule 803-8	Rule 803-9	Rule 803-10	Rule 803-11	Rule 803-12	Rule 803-13
ALASKA	Yes	Yes	No	Yes	Yes	Yes	Yes	Yes
ARIZONA	No	Yes	Yes	Yes	Yes	Yes	Yes	Yes
ARKANSAS	Yes	Yes	No	Yes	Yes	Yes	Yes	Yes
COLORADO	Yes	Yes	Yes	Yes	Yes	Yes	Yes	Yes
DELAWARE	Yes	Yes	Mod	Yes	Yes	Yes	Yes	Yes
FLORIDA	Yes	Yes	Mod	Mod	Yes	Yes	Yes	Yes
HAWAII	Mod	Yes	Yes	Yes	Yes	Yes	Yes	Yes
IDAHO	Yes	Yes	Yes	Yes	Yes	Yes	Yes	Yes
IOWA	Yes	Yes	No	No	Yes	Yes	Yes	Yes
MAINE	Yes	Yes	No	Yes	Yes	Yes	Yes	Yes
MICHIGAN	Yes	Yes	Mod	Yes	Yes	Yes	Yes	Yes
MINNESOTA	Yes	Yes	Yes	Yes	Yes	Yes	Yes	Yes
MISSISSIPPI	Yes	Yes	Yes	Yes	Yes	Yes	Yes	Yes
MONTANA	Mod	Yes	No	Yes	Yes	Yes	Yes	Yes
NEBRASKA	Yes	Yes	Yes	Yes	Yes	Yes	Yes	Yes
NEVADA	Yes	Yes	Yes	Yes	Yes	Yes	Yes	Yes
NEW HAMPSHIRE	Yes	Yes	Yes	Yes	Yes	Yes	Yes	Yes
NEW MEXICO	Yes	Yes	Yes	Yes	Yes	Yes	Yes	Yes
NORTH CAROLINA	Yes	Yes	Yes	Yes	Yes	Yes	Yes	Yes
NORTH DAKOTA	Yes	Yes	plus	Yes	Yes	Yes	Yes	Yes
OHIO	Yes	Yes	Mod	Yes	Yes	Yes	Yes	Yes
OKLAHOMA	Yes	Yes	Mod	Yes	Yes	Yes	Yes	Yes
OREGON	Yes	Yes	Yes	Yes	Yes	Yes	Yes	Yes
RHODE ISLAND	Yes	Yes	Yes	Yes	Yes	Yes	Yes	Yes
SOUTH DAKOTA	Yes	Yes	Yes	Yes	Yes	Yes	Yes	Yes
TEXAS	Yes	Yes	Yes	Yes	Yes	Yes	Yes	Yes
UTAH	Yes	Yes	Yes	Yes	Yes	Yes	Yes	Yes
VERMONT	Yes	Yes	No	Yes	Yes	Yes	Yes	Yes
WASHINGTON	Yes	Yes	Yes	Yes	Yes	Yes	Yes	Yes
WEST VIRGINIA	Yes	Yes	Yes	Yes	Yes	Yes	Yes	Yes
WISCONSIN	Yes	Yes	Yes	Yes	Yes	Yes	Yes	Yes
WYOMING	Yes	Yes	Yes	Yes	Yes	Yes	Yes	Yes

Rule	Subject
803-6	Records of Regularly Conducted Activity
803-7	Absence of Records
803-8	Public Records and Reports
803-9	Records of Vital Statistics
803-10	Absence of Public Record of Entry
803-11	Record of Religious Organizations
803-12	Marriage, Baptismal and Similar Certificates
803-13	Family Records

	Rule 803-14	Rule 803-15	Rule 803-16	Rule 803-17	Rule 803-18	Rule 803-19	Rule 803-20	Rule 803-21
ALASKA	Yes	Yes	Yes	Yes	Yes	Yes	Yes	Yes
ARIZONA	Yes	Yes	Yes	Yes	Yes	Yes	Yes	Yes
ARKANSAS	Yes	Yes	Yes	Yes	Yes	Yes	Yes	Yes
COLORADO	Yes	Yes	Yes	Yes	Yes	Yes	Yes	Yes
DELAWARE	Yes	Yes	Yes	Yes	Yes	Yes	Yes	Yes
FLORIDA	Yes	Yes	Yes	Yes	No	Yes	Yes	Yes
HAWAII	Yes	Yes	Yes	Yes	Yes	Yes	Yes	Yes
IDAHO	Yes	Yes	Yes	Yes	Yes	Yes	Yes	Yes
IOWA	Yes	Yes	No	Yes	No	Yes	Yes	Yes
MAINE	Yes	Yes	Yes	Yes	Mod	Yes	Yes	Yes
MICHIGAN	Yes	Yes	Yes	Yes	Yes	Yes	Yes	Mod
MINNESOTA	Yes	Yes	Yes	Yes	Yes	Yes	Yes	Yes
MISSISSIPPI	Yes	Yes	Yes	Yes	Yes	Yes	Yes	Yes
MONTANA	Yes	Yes	Yes	Yes	Yes	Yes	Yes	Yes
NEBRASKA	Yes	Yes	Yes	Yes	Yes	Yes	Yes	Yes
NEVADA	Yes	Yes	Yes	Yes	Yes	Yes	Yes	Yes
NEW HAMPSHIRE	Yes	Yes	Yes	Yes	Mod	Yes	Yes	Yes
NEW MEXICO	Yes	Yes	Yes	Yes	Yes	Yes	Yes	Yes
NORTH CAROLINA	Yes	Yes	Yes	Yes	Yes	Yes	Yes	Yes
NORTH DAKOTA	Yes	Yes	Yes	Yes	Yes	Yes	Yes	Yes
OHIO	Yes	Yes	Yes	Yes	No	Yes	Yes	Yes
OKLAHOMA	Yes	Yes	Yes	Yes	Yes	Yes	Yes	Yes
OREGON	Yes	Yes	Yes	Yes	No	Yes	Yes	Yes
RHODE ISLAND	Yes	Yes	Yes	Yes	Yes	Yes	Yes	Yes
SOUTH DAKOTA	Yes	Yes	Yes	Yes	Yes	Yes	Yes	Yes
TEXAS	Yes	Yes	Yes	Yes	Yes	Yes	Yes	Yes
UTAH	Yes	Yes	Yes	Yes	Yes	Yes	Yes	Yes
VERMONT	Yes	Yes	Yes	Yes	Mod	Yes	Yes	Yes
WASHINGTON	Yes	Yes	Yes	Yes	Yes	Yes	Yes	Yes
WEST VIRGINIA	Yes	Yes	Yes	Yes	Yes	Yes	Yes	Yes
WISCONSIN	Yes	Yes	Yes	Yes	Yes	Yes	Yes	Yes
WYOMING	Yes	Yes	Yes	Yes	Yes	Yes	Yes	Yes

Rule	Subject
803-14	Records of Documents Affecting an Interest in Property
803-15	Statements in Documents Affecting an Interest in Property
803-16	Statements in Ancient Documents
803-17	Market Reports, Commercial Publications
803-18	Learned Treatises
803-19	Reputation Concerning Personal or Family History
803-20	Reputation Concerning Boundaries or General History
803-21	Reputation As To Character
803-22	Judgment of Previous Conviction

	Rule 803-22	Rule 803-23	Rule 803-24	Rule 804(a)	Rule 804b1	Rule 804b2	Rule 804b3	Rule 804b4	Rule 805	Rule 806
ALASKA	Yes	Yes	Yes	Yes	Yes	Yes	Yes	Yes	Yes	Yes
ARIZONA	Yes	Yes	Yes	Yes	Yes	Yes	Yes	Yes	Yes	Yes
ARKANSAS	Yes	Yes	Yes	Yes	Yes	plus	Yes	Yes	Yes	Yes
COLORADO	No	Yes	Yes	Yes	Yes	Yes	Yes	Yes	Yes	Yes
DELAWARE	No	Yes	Yes	Yes	Mod	Mod	Yes	Yes	Yes	Yes
FLORIDA	No	No	No	Yes	Yes	Yes	Yes	Yes	Yes	Yes
HAWAII	Yes	Yes	Yes	Yes	Yes	plus	Yes	Yes	Yes	Yes
IDAHO	Yes	Yes	Yes	Yes	Yes	Yes	Yes	Yes	Yes	Yes
IOWA	Yes	Yes	Yes	Yes	Yes	Mod	Yes	Yes	Yes	Yes
MAINE	Yes	Yes	Yes	Yes	Yes	Yes	Yes	Yes	Yes	Yes
MICHIGAN	Yes	Yes	No	Yes	Yes	Yes	Yes	Yes	Yes	Yes
MINNESOTA	No	Yes	Yes	Yes	No	Yes	Yes	Yes	Yes	Yes
MISSISSIPPI	Yes	Yes	Yes	Yes	Yes	Yes	Yes	Yes	Yes	Yes
MONTANA	No	Yes	No	Yes	No	Yes	Mod	Yes	Yes	Yes
NEBRASKA	No	Yes	No	Yes	Yes	Yes	Yes	Yes	Yes	Yes
NEVADA	Yes	Yes	Yes	Yes	Yes	Yes	Yes	Yes	Yes	Yes
NEW HAMPSHIRE	Yes	Yes	Yes	Yes	Yes	Yes	Yes	Yes	Yes	Yes
NEW MEXICO	Yes	Yes	Yes	Yes	Yes	Yes	Yes	Yes	Yes	Yes
NORTH CAROLINA	Yes	Yes	Yes	Yes	Yes	Yes	Yes	Yes	Yes	Yes
NORTH DAKOTA	No	Yes	No	Yes	Yes	Yes	Yes	Yes	Yes	Yes
OHIO	Yes	Yes	No	Yes	Yes	Yes	Yes	Yes	Yes	Yes
OKLAHOMA	Yes	Yes	Yes	Yes	Yes	Yes	Yes	Yes	Yes	Yes
OREGON	Yes	Yes	Yes	Yes	Yes	plus	Yes	Yes	Yes	No
RHODE ISLAND	Yes	Yes	Yes	Yes	Yes	Yes	Yes	Yes	Yes	Yes
SOUTH DAKOTA	Yes	Yes	Yes	Yes	Yes	Yes	Yes	Yes	Yes	Yes
TEXAS	Yes	Yes	Yes	Yes	Yes	Yes	Yes	Yes	Yes	Yes
UTAH	Yes	Yes	Yes	Yes	Yes	Yes	Yes	Yes	Yes	Yes
VERMONT	No	Yes	No	Yes	Yes	Yes	No	Yes	Yes	Yes
WASHINGTON	Yes	Yes	No	Yes	Yes	Yes	Yes	Yes	Yes	Yes
WEST VIRGINIA	Yes	Yes	Yes	Yes	Yes	Yes	Yes	Yes	Yes	Yes
WISCONSIN	Yes	Yes	Yes	Yes	Yes	Yes	Yes	Yes	Yes	Yes
WYOMING	Yes	Yes	Yes	Yes	Yes	Yes	Yes	Yes	Yes	Yes

Rule	*Subject*
803-22	Judgment of Previous Conviction
803-23	Judgment as to Personal, Family or General History
803-24	Other Exceptions
804-a	Definition of Unavailability
804-b-1	Former Testimony
804-b-2	Statement under Belief of Impending Death
804-b-3	Statement against Interest
804-b-4	Statement of Personal or Family History
805	Hearsay Within Hearsay
806	Attacking and Supporting Credibility of Declarant

See Sec. 12.06 for Discussion of the Law in Non-FRE States Relative to the Rules Discussed in This Chapter.

9

AUTHENTICATION AND IDENTIFICATION OF EVIDENCE

See Federal Rules of Evidence
Article Nine: Authentication And Identification

Sec. 9.01 Show That "The Matter in Question Is What Its Proponent Claims"   Rule 901(a) provides:

"The requirement of authentication or identification as a condition precedent to admissibility is satisfied by evidence sufficient to support a finding that THE MATTER IN QUESTION IS WHAT ITS PROPONENT CLAIMS."

TRIAL STRATEGY

In Presenting An Exhibit You Must

1. Have the exhibit marked.
   "Please mark this as plaintiff's Exhibit One for identification." (Some courts require "this," others permit "this letter," none permit, "this letter which defendant claims . . .")
2. Show to opposing counsel (even if not required in your jurisdiction; it shows jury fairness and causes less interruption later).
3. Have it authenticated by:
   A. witness
      "Does this photo show fairly and accurately the scene of the accident at the time of the accident?" or
   B. certificate, if permitted
4. Offer it into evidence.
5. Give opposing counsel an opportunity to voir dire the witness.
6. Obtain court ruling.
7. Pass it among jurors.
   A. at that time, or
   B. later (depending on dramatic considerations and court policy)

Whether a document is "authentic," or whether it "identifies" a person or thing is to be decided by the jury, and with only a prima facie showing, the evidence will be admitted for the jury's consideration (*U.S. v. Cuesta,* 597 F.2d 903 [5th Cir. 1979]). Exhibits should be admitted freely after discovery and pretrial stipulation, unless there is a genuine question as to their reliability, or if a 403 question as to prejudice has been raised.

Rule 901 sets forth the basic requirements for admitting an exhibit—IT IS WHAT THE PROPONENT CLAIMS.

Examples ————————————————————————

1. Proponent offers letter to show what defendant wrote, so he must show it was written by defendant.
2. Proponent offers photo of scene of accident to show physical facts of the intersection, so he must show that photo fairly and accurately represents the scene.

3. Proponent offers contract to show what parties agreed to, so he must show that this is, indeed, the contract they signed.

IMPORTANT: IF THE EXHIBIT IS NOT WHAT PROPONENT CLAIMS IT TO BE, IT IS PROBABLY NOT RELEVANT ANYWAY.

Rule 901(b) "by way of illustration only . . ." gives the following examples of authentication or identification:

1. Testimony that a matter is what it is claimed to be.

   EXAMPLE: Witness can tell what he sees, hears, feels, tastes and smells (*Fox v. United Commercial Travellers of America,* 192 F.2d 844 [5th Cir. 1951]), but chain of custody must be shown (*U.S. v. McKinney,* 631 F.2d 569 [8th Cir. 1980]).

2. Nonexpert familiarity with handwriting prior to litigation.

   EXAMPLE: Officer could testify signature was same as on statement signed by defendant (*U.S. v. Standing Soldier,* 538 F.2d 196 [8th Cir. 1975]).

3. Comparison of specimens which have been authenticated.

   HOWEVER, "other known and less prejudicial specimens should have been used" (*U.S. v. Turquitt,* 557 F.2d 464 [5th Cir. 1977]).

4. Appearance, contents, substance, internal patterns, or other distinctive characteristics.

   EXAMPLE: Clerk testified bill was in form "customarily used" (*U.S. v. Grande,* 620 F.2d 1026 [4th Cir. 1988]).

5. Identification of voice based on hearing the voice under similar circumstances.

   HOWEVER: Identity of speaker must be "satisfactorily established" (*U.S. v. Alberto,* 539 F.2d 860 [2nd Cir. 1976]).

6. Telephone conversation with "number assigned at the time by the telephone company."

   HELD: "Unlikely anyone else would have answered" (*U.S. v. Sawyer,* 607 F.2d 1190 [7th Cir. 1979]).

7. Public records and reports in "PUBLIC OFFICE" (authorized by law to be kept).

   EXAMPLE: "Certified affidavit" can be used to admit public records (*Bury v. Dodge,* 692 F.2d 1335 [11th Cir. 1982]).

8. Ancient document or data

   A. in condition creating no concern about authenticity

   B. in place where, if authentic, would likely be, and

   C. in existence at least twenty years when offered.

9. "Evidence describing a *process or system used to produce a result and showing that the process or system produces an accurate result.*"

EXAMPLE: Film authenticated by showing how cameras used during bank robbery (*U.S. v. Taylor*, 530 F.2d 639 [5th Cir. 1976]).

10. Method of authentication or identification provided by law.

These examples of authentication and identification are merely illustrative. Whatever is "WHAT IT CLAIMS TO BE" should be stipulated to prior to trial.

TRIAL STRATEGY

Learn the Language of Authentication and Identification

1. "Does this photo fairly and accurately represent . . ."
2. "I show you what has been marked plaintiff's Exhibit One for identification . . ."
3. "I offer plaintiff's Exhibit One into evidence, your Honor."
4. "May I approach the witness, your Honor." (where required)
5. "I hand you Exhibit Two, what is it?"
6. "May I pass this exhibit among the jurors, your Honor?"
7. "Do you recognize this signature?" "Why?"
8. "Where did you get defendant's address?"
9. "How often have you . . ."
10. "Why are you familiar with this exhibit?"
11. "Would you please read this to the jury?"
12. "What are your duties at this office?"
13. "How do you compare this with . . ."
14. "When did you last test this machine before the incident we have been discussing?"
15. "How thoroughly did you examine . . ."
16. "How do you know this is the same . . ."
17. "Your Honor, let the record show . . ."
18. "Please tell the jury what this means . . ."
19. "Can you translate that into terms we can understand?"
20. "Your Honor, the certificate states this is a true and accurate copy of the official record . . ."
21. "Are you familiar with his voice?" "Why?"
22. "What is the procedure you used . . ."
23. "How does this instrument work?"
24. "What experience have you had in . . ."
25. "What is the quality of the tape recording?"
26. "How accurate is this chart?"
27. "Please put your initials at that point on the diagram."
28. "What experiment, if any, have you conducted relative to . . ."

Rule 903 provides that testimony of a subscribing witness is not necessary to authenticate a writing unless required by law. The state law on execution will come into play only where the validity of the document is questioned.

Sec. 9.02 Determine If The Document Is Self-Authenticated   Rule 902 provides *"extrinsic evidence of authenticity as a condition precedent to admissibility is not required with respect to the following*:

1. *Domestic Public Documents Under Seal.*

   EXAMPLE: Certification from postal service (*U.S. v. Trotter,* 538 F.2d 217 [8th Cir. 1975]).

2. *Domestic Public Documents Not Under Seal.*

   EXAMPLE: Affidavit attested to by counsel for CIA (*U.S. v. Wilson,* 732 F.2d 404 [5th Cir. 1983]).

3. *Foreign Public Documents.* "FINAL CERTIFICATION as to genuineness (by secretary of embassy, etc.) that document was executed by person "authorized by laws of a foreign country" to do so. HOWEVER, where there has been reasonable opportunity to investigate authenticity and accuracy, court may order document "presumptively authentic." (GIVING OPPOSING COUNSEL THAT NOTICE MAY MAKE YOUR JOB EASIER.)

   EXAMPLES: Court admitted records of Hungarian state-run taxi company (*U.S. v. Regner,* 677 F.2d 754 [9th Cir. 1981]). Where forum officer refused to appear before American embassy, document admitted, since counsel had opportunity to investigate its authenticity (*U.S. v. Leal,* 509 F.2d 122 [9th Cir. 1975]).

   NOTE: Treaty with several countries making public documents (court records, administrative documents, notarial acts, or private documents bearing official certification) admitted if it has certification known as an "aspostile."

4. *Certified copies of public records* OR *"document authorized by law to be recorded or filed and actually recorded or filed in a public office . . ."* if *". . . certified as correct by custodian or person authorized to make the certification."*

   EXAMPLE: Authenticating affidavit need only state position of authority and that copy is correct, extraneous portions will be stricken (*U.S. v. Stone,* 604 F.2d 922 [5th Cir. 1979]).

5. *Official publications.* "Books, pamphlets, or other publications purporting to be issued by public authority."

EXAMPLE: Agency's facsimile of its seal on cover of its report was self-authenticating (*California Assn. of Bioanalysts v. Rank,* 588 F.Supp. 1342 [D.C. CA 1983]).

6. *Newspapers and periodicals.* "Printed materials purporting to be newspapers or periodicals."

NOTE: Chance of forging newspaper is so unlikely, the courts accept them.

7. *Trade inscriptions and the like.* "Inscriptions, signs, tags, or labels purporting to have been affixed in the course of business and indicating ownership, control, or origin."

NOTE: 19 USC Section 1615(2) provides marks and labels upon or accompanying merchandise indicating its foreign origin is prima facie evidence of the same.

8. *Acknowledged documents.* "Documents accompanied by a certificate of acknowledgment executed in the manner provided by law by a notary public or other officer authorized by law to take acknowledgments."

9. *Commercial paper and related documents.* "Commercial paper, signatures thereon, and documents relating thereto to the extent provided by general commercial law."

NOTE: Section 3.307 of the Uniform Commercial Code makes mere production of a note prima facie evidence of validity of holder's right to recover.

10. *Presumptions under acts of Congress.* "Any signature, document, or other matter declared by Act of Congress to be *presumptively or prima facie genuine or authentic.*"

EXAMPLE: Individual's signature on a tax return is prima facie evidence of his authority to sign the return (26 USC Section 6062).

The following table shows whether or not states adopting the Federal Rules of Evidence adopted substantially same provisions relative to the rules discussed in this chapter:

	Rule 901	Rule 902	Rule 903
ALASKA	No	Yes	No
ARIZONA	Yes	Yes	Yes
ARKANSAS	Yes	Yes	Yes
COLORADO	Yes	Yes	Yes
DELAWARE	No	No	Yes
FLORIDA	Yes	Mod	Yes

	Rule 901	Rule 902	Rule 903
HAWAII	Yes	Yes	Yes
IDAHO	Yes	Yes	Yes
IOWA	Yes	Yes	Yes
MAINE	Yes	Yes	Yes
MICHIGAN	Yes	Yes	Yes
MINNESOTA	Yes	Yes	Yes
MISSISSIPPI	Yes	Yes	Yes
MONTANA	Yes	Yes	Yes
NEBRASKA	Yes	Yes	Yes
NEVADA	Yes	Yes	Yes
NEW HAMPSHIRE	Yes	Yes	Yes
NEW MEXICO	Yes	Yes	Yes
NORTH CAROLINA	Yes	Yes	Yes
NORTH DAKOTA	Yes	Yes	Yes
OHIO	Yes	Yes	Yes
OKLAHOMA	Yes	Yes	Yes
OREGON	Yes	Yes	Yes
RHODE ISLAND	Yes	Yes	Yes
SOUTH DAKOTA	Yes	Yes	Yes
TEXAS	Yes	No	Yes
UTAH	Yes	Yes	Yes
VERMONT	Yes	No	Yes
WASHINGTON	Yes	Yes	Yes
WEST VIRGINIA	Yes	Yes	Yes
WISCONSIN	Yes	Yes	Yes
WYOMING	Yes	No	Yes

Rule   Subject

901   Requirement of Authentication or Identification
902   Self-Authentication
903   Subscribing Witness's Testimony Unnecessary

See Sec. 12.07 for Discussion of the Law in Non-FRE
States Relative to the Rules Discussed in This Chapter.

10

ADMITTING AND EXCLUDING WRITINGS, RECORDINGS AND PHOTOGRAPHS

See Federal Rules of Evidence
Article Ten: Contents of Writings, Recordings, and Photographs

Sec. 10.01 What Is a "Writing, Recording or Photograph?" Rule 1001(1) provides that "writings" and "recordings" consist of

> "Letters, words, or numbers, or their equivalent, set down by handwriting, typewriting, printing, photostating, photographing, magnetic impulse, mechanical or electrical recording, or other form of data compilation."

Rule 1001(2) provides that "photographs" include:

> "still photographs, X-ray films, video tapes, and motion pictures."

Rule 1001(3) defines an "original" as a

> "writing or recording itself or any counterpart intended to have the same effect by a person executing or issuing it. An 'original' of a photograph includes the negative or any print therefrom. If data are storage in a computer or similar device, any printout or other output readable by sight, shown to reflect the data accurately, is an 'original'."

Rule 1001(4) defines "duplicate" as

> "a counterpart produced by the same impression as the original, or from the same matrix, or by means of photography, including enlargements and miniatures, or by mechanical or electronic re-recordings, or by chemical reproduction, or by other equivalent technique which accurately reproduces the original."

HISTORICAL NOTE

The Advisory Committee did not even include the term *best evidence* in the proposed Federal Rules of Evidence, and the term doesn't appear in the final draft adopted by Congress. This finalized a trend that recognized a world of photocopy machines, videocameras, and computers. There is simply no longer anything secondary about that which is identical, or equally reliable.

Where writer of letter writes "second copy," whichever copy is not sent is a duplicate (*McDonald v. Hanks,* 113 S.W. 604 [TX app. 1908]). Where several copies of a contract are executed, parties intend those copies to be "originals" or "duplicate originals." Though the cases are not consistent on what constitutes an original, there is less need today to update a document from duplicate to original.

Sec. 10.02 How to Get Duplicates Admitted Rule 1002 provides:

> "To prove the content of a writing, recording, or photograph, *the original writing, recording, or photograph is required,* except as otherwise provided in these rules or by Act of Congress."

Rule 1003, however, provides that:

"A duplicate is admissible to the same extent as an original UNLESS (1) a genuine question is raised as to the authenticity of the original OR (2) in the circumstances it would be UNFAIR to admit the duplicate in lieu of the original."

Rule 1004 makes the further provision that:

"The ORIGINAL IS NOT REQUIRED, and other evidence of the contents of a writing, recording, or photograph is admissible if—

(1) *All originals are lost or have been destroyed, unless the proponent lost or destroyed them in bad faith; or*
(2) *No original can be obtained* by any available judicial process or procedure; or
(3) *At a time when an original was under the control of the party against whom offered, That party was PUT ON NOTICE, by the pleadings or otherwise, that the contents would be a subject of proof at the hearing, and that party does not produce the original at the hearing; or*
(4) *The writing, recording, or photograph is NOT closely related to a controlling issue.*

TRIAL STRATEGY

Beat the "Best Evidence" Rule by

1. Showing it is not a "writing, recording or photograph" that is being introduced, or
2. The terms ("content") of the document are not in issue, or
3. If in issue, *only collaterally* in issue, or
4. Evidence being offered is an original or "duplicate original," or
5. If all of above fails:
   A. good reason original cannot be produced or
   B. secondary evidence being offered is reliable

Article Ten is applicable only when the writing, recording, or photograph is being used to prove an event or transaction. "I paid the bill" or "I saw them get married" is admissible, though such could also be proven with documentary evidence.

A witness could testify to having a conversation, though a tape recording of that conversation could have been produced. The court said, "The rule does not set up an order of preferred admissibility which must be followed to prove a fact," instead it is a rule that applies "only when one seeks to prove the contents of documents or recordings" (*U.S. v. Gonzales-Benitez*, 537 F.2d 1051 [9th Cir. 1976]).

TRIAL STRATEGY

Keep in mind that "contents" or "terms" of document must be what is being offered for the "best evidence" rule to apply.

EXAMPLE: Defendant told officer, "I stole the money." The statement was heard by the officer while tape recording was being made. Recording was then transcribed, and officer signed the confession.

1. Officer can testify, "I heard Defendant say 'I stole the money'."
2. Officer cannot say, "We have a written confession in which defendant said, 'I stole the money'."

Under the "best evidence" rule, a witness can testify, "I heard defendant say . . ." at a previous trial or at deposition. If a transcript of the previous trial or deposition is available, the court may require that to be used, but if it is also available to opposing counsel, the court should let proponent present his proof in either form, and let opposing counsel use the transcript on cross-examination.

TRIAL STRATEGY

When witness is about to read to jury the content of a document that has been admitted into evidence, opposing counsel rises and says

"I object, your Honor. The document speaks for itself."

There is no "best evidence" reason this cannot be read to the jury, so, you need only assure the judge that no part of the exhibit will be unduly emphasized through voice or editing.

Where prosecutor offered tape of a recording of the original tape, it was admitted as "exact recording" (*U.S. v. DiMatteo*, 716 F.2d 1361 [11th Cir. 1983]). Even where entire transcript of original recording was not included on the tape offered into evidence, all portions offered to defense counsel prior to trial were admitted, because "it was not even intimated the erasure was intentional" (*U.S. v. Conway*, 507 F.2d 1047 [5th Cir. 1975]). RELIABILITY is extremely important in determining such matters as hearsay, and is equally important in determining "best evidence."

TRIAL STRATEGY

Where you will be called upon to show an attempt to obtain the original, ISSUE A SUBPOENA!

(*U.S. v. Taylor*, 648 F.2d 565 [9th Cir. 1979])

Where the Internal Revenue Service destroyed taxpayer's waiver of statute of limitations, testimony was admitted, showing procedure for destroying records (*U.S. v. Conry,* 631 F.2d 599 [9th Cir. 1980]). You can prove the fact there is insurance orally, but you must show the contents of the policy with the policy (*U.S. v. Sliker,* 751 F.2d 477 [2nd Cir. 1984]).

One court permitted jury to read transcripts while listening to a tape recording (*U. S. v. Gordon,* 688 F.2d 42 [8th Cir. 1982]). Personal property does not come within the rule, so a photograph of stolen jewelry admitted over "best evidence" objection (*Territory of Guam v. Ojeda,* 758 F.2d 403 [9th Cir. 1985]).

TRIAL STRATEGY

When Arguing "Best Evidence" Rule, Remember

1. Secondary evidence may be admissible,
   BUT
2. "Best evidence" may be more persuasive.

Sec. 10.03 How to Get Public Records Admitted   Rule 1005 provides that official record *"or a document authorized to be recorded or filed and actually recorded or filed"* may be proved by copy . . .

"certified as correct in accordance with Rule 902 OR testified to be correct by a witness who has compared it with the original."

Rule 1005 further provides that if such copy cannot be obtained ". . . by the exercize of reasonable diligence, then other evidence of the contents may be given."

This rule refers to the public record, such as the microfilm of the recorded deed, not the original deed that was returned to the client (*Amoco Production Co. v. U.S.,* 619 F.2d 1383 [10th Cir. 1980]). In this case the original deed was lost, so Rule 1004 instead of Rule 1005 should have been relied upon.

TRIAL STRATEGY

Offer Public Record into Evidence by Showing

1. Contents are otherwise admissible, and are
   A. official record or
   B. authorized to be recorded or filed
2. Actually is recorded or filed.

---

3. You are offering
   A. copy certified per Rule 902 or
   B. testified to be correct by witness who compared it with original

However, if Such Copy Cannot be Obtained

1. Show you exercised due diligence.
2. Introduce other evidence of contents.

Sec. 10.04 How to Use Summaries Effectively   Rule 1006 provides:

"The contents of voluminous writings, recordings, or photographs which cannot conveniently be examined in court may be presented in the form of a chart, summary, or calculation."

This rule further provides that originals or duplicates shall be made available for "examination or copying" at a reasonable time and place, and the court may order that they be produced in court. The need for convenience and moving the trial along that prompted Rule 1005 was also a factor in adopting Rule 1006.

The court should be assured as to the accuracy of the charts, summaries, or calculations (see *U.S. v. Citron*, 783 F.2d 307 [2nd Cir. 1986]). Also, jury should be told that the underlying documents are the real evidence (*U. S. v. Stephens*, 779 F.2d 232 [5th Cir. 1985]).

TRIAL STRATEGY

When You Use Chart, Summary or Calculation

1. Make sure it is based on admissible evidence.
   EXAMPLE: Error to admit evidence based on inadmissible hearsay (*Hackett v. Housing Authority of City of San Antonio*, 750 F.2d 1308 [5th Cir. 1985]).
2. Make sure it is accurate.
   EXAMPLE: Summary of more than 100 phone calls accurately reflected records (*U.S. v. Drough*, 748 F.2d 8 [1st Cir. 1984]).
3. Make the underlying data available far in advance of trial.
   EXAMPLE: Court excluded summaries made available "right before trial" (*Davis and Cox v. Summa Corp.*, 751 F.2d 1507 [9th Cir. 1985]).
4. Have the underlying data ready to present to the court.
   EXAMPLE: Error to admit summary where underlying data had not been made available to court (*Hackett v. Housing Authority of City of San Antonio*, 750 F.2d 1308 [5th Cir. 1985]).

If summary is prepared for trial it is secondary evidence, but if it is prepared in ordinary course of business it is primary evidence (*U.S. v. Drainman*, 784 F.2d 248 [7th Cir. 1986]). If it can be presented in a form of an opinion, that is best approach.

For charts or summaries to be admitted as evidence, key words are *fairly represent, underlying documentary proof, too voluminous for in-court examination, accurate,* and *non prejudicial* (*U.S. v. Scales*, 594 F.2d 558 [6th Cir. 1978]). The court will probably give limiting instruction giving purpose of summary and stating that the summary, itself, is not evidence (*U.S. v. Seelig*, 622 F.2d 207 [6th Cir. 1980]).

Summaries can summarize past experience, but cannot summarize future experience, except as used by an expert (*Teed-Ed, Inc. v. Kimball International, Inc.*, 620 F.2d 399 [3rd Cir. 1980]). Where witness has prepared them, charts can summarize evidence already introduced (*U.S. v. Nelson*, 735 F.2d 1070 [8th Cir. 1984]).

IMPORTANT: Where charts or summaries are used pedagogically to explain evidence, a limiting instruction should be given, telling the jury this is not evidence (*Gomez v. Great Lakes Steel Div., National Steel Corp.*, 803 F.2d 250 [6th Cir. 1986]). It was error to let counsel use charts during final argument to explain his theory of the case, where chart had not been properly presented during trial and no limiting instruction had been given. Also, pedagogical charts should not go to the jury (*U.S. V. Gardner*, 611 F.2d 770 [9th Cir. 1980]).

Sec. 10.05 How to Get Admissions Admitted   Rule 1007 provides:

"Contents of writings, recordings, or photographs may be PROVED BY THE TESTIMONY OR DEPOSITION OF THE PARTY AGAINST WHOM OFFERED or by that party's written admission, without accounting for the nonproduction of the original."

HISTORICAL DATA

The English rule at common law permitted contents of a document to be proved by an oral admission. A witness's inability to remember or ability to fabricate caused American courts to not follow that rule. The Federal Rules of Evidence expressly provide that, except as otherwise admitted, contents of a document will not be admitted as an admission unless it is in writing.

Formal proof is not necessary where a fact is not in issue (*Click v. U.S.*, 614 F.2d 748 [U.S. Court of Claims 1980]). Secondary materials can be used to show contents of written admission (*U.S. v. Johnson*, 594 F.2d 1253 [9th Cir. 1979]).

```
                        TRIAL STRATEGY

    Prove Contents of Writing, Recording or Photograph with Admission

            1.  From deposition or
            2.  Trial testimony or
            3.  Written statement.
```

Sec. 10.06 Functions of Court and Jury   Rule 1008 provides that:

"When the *admissibility of other evidence of contents of writings, recordings, or photographs* under these rules depends upon fulfillment of a condition of fact, the question whether the condition has been fulfilled is ordinarily for the court to determine." (Under Rule 104 which permits court to use inadmissible evidence.)

HOWEVER, this rule further provides the trier of fact is to decide:

"(a) whether the asserted writing ever existed, or

(b) whether another writing, recording, or photograph produced at the trial is the original, or

(c) whether other evidence of contents correctly reflects the contents . . ."

The court is to decide whether a sufficient foundation has been laid so "a reasonable juror could be convinced that the secondary evidence correctly reflects the contents of the original" (*U.S. v. Gerhart*, 538 F.2d 807 [8th Cir. 1976]).

The rule calls upon the court to decide where the document is, prior to the jury finding that a document did exist. This is done by the court assuming if a document existed, there is, or is not, proof as to who has it.

The following table shows whether or not states adopting the Federal Rules of Evidence adopted substantially same provisions relative to the rules discussed in this chapter:

	Rule 1001	Rule 1002	Rule 1003	Rule 1004	Rule 1005	Rule 1006	Rule 1007	Rule 1008
ALASKA	Yes	Yes	Yes	Yes	Yes	Yes	No	Yes
ARIZONA	Yes	Yes	Yes	Yes	Yes	Yes	Yes	Yes
ARKANSAS	Yes	Yes	Yes	Yes	Yes	Yes	Yes	Yes
COLORADO	Yes	Yes	Yes	Yes	Yes	Yes	Yes	Yes
DELAWARE	Yes	Yes	Yes	Yes	Yes	Yes	Yes	Yes
FLORIDA	Yes	Yes	Yes	Yes	Yes	Yes	Yes	Yes

	Rule 1001	Rule 1002	Rule 1003	Rule 1004	Rule 1005	Rule 1006	Rule 1007	Rule 1008
HAWAII	Yes	Yes	Yes	Yes	Yes	Yes	Yes	Yes
IDAHO	Yes	Yes	Yes	Yes	Yes	Yes	Yes	Yes
IOWA	Yes	Yes	Yes	Yes	Yes	Yes	Yes	Yes
MAINE	Yes	Yes	Yes	Yes	Yes	Yes	Yes	Yes
MICHIGAN	Yes	Yes	Yes	Yes	Yes	Yes	Yes	Yes
MINNESOTA	Yes	Yes	Yes	Yes	Yes	Yes	Yes	Yes
MISSISSIPPI	Yes	Yes	Yes	Yes	Yes	Yes	Yes	Yes
MONTANA	Yes	Yes	No	Yes	Yes	Yes	Yes	Yes
NEBRASKA	Yes	Yes	Yes	Yes	Yes	Yes	Yes	Yes
NEVADA	Yes	Yes	Yes	Yes	Yes	Yes	Yes	Yes
NEW HAMPSHIRE	Yes	Yes	Yes	Yes	Yes	Yes	Yes	Yes
NEW MEXICO	Yes	Yes	Yes	Yes	Yes	Yes	Yes	Yes
NORTH CAROLINA	Yes	Yes	Yes	Yes	Yes	Yes	Yes	Yes
NORTH DAKOTA	Yes	Yes	Yes	Yes	Yes	Yes	Yes	Yes
OHIO	Yes	Yes	Yes	Yes	Yes	Yes	Yes	Yes
OKLAHOMA	Yes	Yes	Yes	Yes	Yes	Yes	Yes	Yes
OREGON	Yes	Yes	Yes	Yes	Yes	Yes	Yes	Yes
RHODE ISLAND	Yes	Yes	Yes	Yes	Yes	Yes	Yes	Yes
SOUTH DAKOTA	Yes	Yes	Yes	Yes	Yes	Yes	Yes	Yes
TEXAS	Yes	Yes	Yes	No	Yes	plus	Yes	Yes
UTAH	Yes	Yes	Yes	Yes	Yes	Yes	Yes	Yes
VERMONT	Yes	Yes	Yes	Yes	Yes	Yes	Yes	Yes
WASHINGTON	Yes	Yes	Yes	Yes	Yes	Yes	Yes	Yes
WEST VIRGINIA	Yes	Yes	Yes	Yes	Yes	Yes	Yes	Yes
WISCONSIN	Yes	Yes	Yes	Yes	Yes	Yes	Yes	Yes
WYOMING	plus	Yes	plus	Yes	Yes	Yes	Yes	Yes

Rule	Subject
1001	Definitions (Contents) of Writings, Recordings, and Photographs
1002	Requirement of Original
1003	Admissibility of Originals
1004	Admissibility of Other Evidence of Contents
1005	Public Records
1006	Summaries
1007	Testimony or Written Admission of Party
1008	Functions of Court and Jury

See Sec. 12.07 for Discussion of the Law in Non-FRE States Relative to the Rules Discussed in This Chapter.

11

MISCELLANEOUS RULES
HOW TO LAY A PROPER FOUNDATION
AVOIDING AND MAKING OBJECTIONS
THE RULES CAN HELP YOU CROSS-EXAMINE

See Federal Rules of Evidence
Article Eleven: Miscellaneous Rules

MISCELLANEOUS RULES

Sec. 11.01 Miscellaneous Rules The Federal Rules of Evidence (FRE) may be amended as provided for in Sec. 2076, Title 28 of the United States Code. They apply to federal courts, including claims court, bankruptcy and magistrate proceedings (Rule 11.01).

They apply to civil, criminal and maritime cases, but not where Court can act summarily or under Title 11. The rules are not applicable in determining "preliminary questions of fact," grand jury proceedings, or miscellaneous proceedings such as extradition, rendition, criminal preliminary hearings, and hearings re bail, warrants, search warrants, probation and sentencing.

HOW TO LAY A PROPER FOUNDATION

Sec. 11.02 The Need to Lay a Foundation There are three reasons why LAYING A FOUNDATION IS EXTREMELY IMPORTANT:

1. *It Brings Life And Understanding To The Process Of Applying Rules.*

2. *It Brings Dramatic Impact To Other Evidence That Is About To Be Introduced.*

3. *The Judge Will Simply Not Let You Do "B" Until You Do "A."*

Every rule of evidence has its own special requirements. Rule 801(4) (B) makes a statement of a party opponent admissible as "not hearsay." Before you can offer the statement as evidence, however, you must show that the statement was made by a party opponent. The foundation must be laid and in laying it, the rule becomes meaningful.

Example _____

Q. Did you approach the man standing next to his car?
A. Yes.
Q. Do you know the name of that man?
A. Yes. He is David Jones, the defendant.
Q. Did he make a statement in your presence?
A. Yes. He said he did not see the other car.

If an expert is to give an opinion, he must be qualified under Rule 702. While satisfying this foundation requirement, the trial lawyer can dramatize the doctor's testimony.

Example ————————————————————————————

Q. Doctor, will you tell the jury your educational background?
A. I graduated from Johns Hopkins University Medical School.
Q. Where did you do your internship?
A. Fitzsimmons General Hospital in Denver.
Q. How many years have you been practicing medicine?
A. Twenty-three years.
Q. Have you specialized in any special area of medicine?
A. Yes. I am an orthopedic surgeon.
Q. Have you written articles for medical journals?
A. Yes. My article on "Back Trauma" appeared in the AMA Journal of Medicine.

Keep Going As Long As You Are IMPRESSING The Jurors, but STOP, BEFORE You Bore Them

Part of laying the foundation relates specifically to the law of evidence. Even if the judge permits you to lay the foundation later, you simply MUST satisfy all elements of PROOF, and if there is an element that depends upon a foundation, MEET THAT REQUIREMENT.

Example ————————————————————————————

Proponent wants to introduce photocopy of document.

Q. Mr. Smith, I now show you what has been marked Plaintiff's Exhibit One.
A. Yes, it is a copy of the document I have been talking about.
Q. Do you know where the original is?
A. Yes. Last week I saw the defendant take it from his pocket, tear it to bits, and throw it into the fire.

Sec. 11.03 Methods of Laying Foundations   The method of laying a foundation can be as important as the evidence being introduced. It gives the trial lawyer another opportunity to think about WINNING WHILE PROVING.

TRIAL STRATEGY

While Laying a Foundation

1. *Increase credibility of witness laying foundation through questions that display witness's perception (or expert's opinion).*
2. *Add drama to the evidence about to be introduced, by highlighting it.*
3. *Avoid objections by following rules, even if court may permit inadmissible evidence under Rule 104(a).*
4. *Let your witness testify in his or her own words (detailed evidence is believed and remembered).*

5. *Blend leading and nonleading questions.*
   A. *leading questions make sure the witness lays the foundation*
   B. *open-ended questions beginning with "who," "what," "where," "why," and "when" let your witness testify*

The method of laying the foundation will vary with each requirement. You may want to "show off" an expert witness by prolonging the qualifying process, yet you may want merely to meet the requirements if you are introducing a photocopy to replace the original.

Special consideration should be given to the laying of a foundation for a diagram.

TRIAL STRATEGY

Lay Foundation for a Diagram

1. Witness is familiar with what diagram shows.
2. Diagram shows it "accurately and fairly."
3. Diagram will help understand what it shows.

EXAMPLE _____

Q. I show you what has been marked Plaintiff's Exhibit Six, do you recognize it?
A. Yes, it is a diagram of the intersection where the accident occurred.
Q. Are you familiar with that intersection?
A. Yes. I pass there several times a day.
Q. Were you familiar with that intersection at the time of the accident.
A. Yes. It hasn't changed in any way.
Q. Does this diagram fairly and accurately represent that intersection the way it was at the time of the accident?
A. Yes. It does.
Q. You have testified that you saw the car run into the lady, will you show me where she was on the diagram at the time of the car hitting her?
A. She was right here on the curb. (pointing)
Q. I am handing you a red pencil, will you mark that spot on the diagram?
A. Of course. (and she does.)

Since many jurors are in awe of computers, special attention should be given to this form of foundation. Meet the requirements, but do it with an educational process.

TRIAL STRATEGY

When Laying the Foundation for a Computer Readout, the Witness Should

1. *Tell how his company uses the computer.*
2. *Explain why the computer being used is reliable.*
3. *Explain the procedure for feeding data into the computer.*
4. *Explain what safeguards and procedures guarantee accuracy.*
5. *Tell how he knows computer was in proper working condition.*
6. *Testify that he obtained a readout from the computer.*
7. *Testify that at such time computer was working accurately.*
8. *Testify that the witness obtained the readout properly.*
9. *Properly mark and identify the readout.*
10. *Explain exactly the meaning of the contents of the readout in lay terms.*

Sec. 11.04 Qualifying a Witness   The witness is competent to testify if he or she has perceived an occurrence (Rule 601) or if he or she has an admissible opinion not based on perception (Rule 702). This competency is not automatic, however. The trial lawyer must lay a foundation.

TRIAL STRATEGY

Show Perception of Witness

1. Show witness was capable of perceiving the event.
2. Show witness did perceive the event.
3. Show what witness perceived.

Example ————————————————————————————

Q. Were you at the scene when the accident occurred?
A. Yes. I was ten feet from where the lady was standing.
Q. Where were you looking at the time?
A. At the lady.
Q. What did you see?
A. I saw the car come up on the curb and hit the lady.

Special requirements must be met when introducing opinion evidence. (See Sec. 7.02 for qualifying the expert. The federal rules specifically provide for lay opinion evidence.)

TRIAL STRATEGY

Introduce Lay Opinion by Showing

1. Witness perceived an occurrence or condition.
2. Based on that perception, witness could form an opinion.
3. Opinion is on a subject accepted by the courts.
4. The opinion would be useful in deciding the case.
5. Witness can then give that opinion.

Example _____

Q. Did you observe the car as it passed you?
A. Yes.
Q. Could you, based on what you observed, form an opinion as to the approximate speed of the car?
A. Yes.
Q. What is that opinion?
A. It was going between fifty and sixty miles an hour.

(Witness can give an estimate of speed, but cannot make a guess.)

Sec. 11.05 Qualifying Evidence   Two types of evidence require special attention. The trial lawyer must qualify oral testimony and physical evidence.

Counsel often has a statement that is necessary to the proving of the lawsuit. The foundation must be laid for the introduction of that statement as evidence.

TRIAL STRATEGY

Introducing Statement by Defendant's Employee

1. Show declarant was employee of defendant.
2. Show statement "concerned a matter within the scope of his employment."
3. Show statement was made "during the relationship."

[Rule 801(d)(2)(D)]

Example _____

Q. Where do you work?
A. At Jones and Company.
Q. What are your duties for that company?
A. I handle health and accident claims.

Q. Among your duties, do you decide under what circumstances a claim will be paid?

A. Yes.

Q. Did you make a statement to my client January thirty-first of this year?

A. Yes.

Q. At that time were you so employed by Defendant?

A. Yes.

Q. And at that time did you have the duties you have described?

A. Yes.

Q. What was the statement you made?

A. I said the company will not pay this claim unless suit is filed.

Counsel's challenge in introducing exhibits is equally important. Laying the foundation for this process can give the exhibit dramatic impact.

TRIAL STRATEGY

Introduce Letter As Evidence with Non-Expert Opinion by Showing

1. Witness has examined the letter.
2. Witness has formed an opinion as to who wrote the letter.
3. Opinion is based on "familiarity not acquired for purposes of litigation."

[Rule 901(b)(2)]

Sec. 11.06 Foundations and Rules of Evidence Many rules of evidence make the laying of the foundation absolutely necessary. The trial lawyer must look at each rule with the foundation requirement in mind.

Examples ───────────────────────────────

1. Rule 803(24) provides for overall hearsay exception where declarant available. It further provides, however, that prior to use of the statement, the proponent must have given notice "sufficiently in advance of the trial or hearing to provide the adverse party with a fair opportunity to prepare to meet it, his intention to offer the statement, and the particulars of it, including the name and address of declarant." LAY THE FOUNDATION BY SHOWING SUCH NOTICE.

2. Counsel offers evidence that a business call was made to defendant's company and that the conversation related to business reasonably transacted over the telephone. Rule 901(6) requires proof that the number called was the number assigned at the time to the company by the telephone company. LAY THE FOUNDATION BY OFFERING SUCH PROOF.

3. Counsel introduced a stock report as evidence. Rule 803(17) requires that such a report be one "generally used and relied upon by the public or persons in particular occupations." LAY THE FOUNDATION BY OFFERING SUCH PROOF.

Throughout this book, you will find rules of evidence that require foundations. Developing a habit of laying foundations within rule requirements will prepare you for doing same in the courtroom under the stress of battle.

AVOIDING AND MAKING OBJECTIONS

Sec. 11.07 How to Avoid Objections   When a trial lawyer presents his courtroom drama, he should do so with as few interruptions as possible. He or she should, therefore, conduct examination in a way that avoids objections that are proper, and if possible, in a way that avoids all objections.

TRIAL STRATEGY

1. Make sure the form of the question is not subject to attack.
2. Do not lead the witness, except as permitted.
3. Do not argue with the witness.
4. Don't get ahead of yourself; lay the foundation.
5. Don't misquote the evidence.
6. Don't turn the witness loose.
7. Include all essential facts in your hypothetical.
8. Follow the rules of evidence.
9. Prepare your witness.
10. Don't go outside your pleadings.
11. Follow pretrial stipulation and in limine rulings.
12. Do not go beyond discovery.
13. Prepare for introduction of exhibits.
14. Don't waste the court's time, which slows down your courtroom drama.
15. Remember, it is the jury who must hear and accept your story.
16. Get the facts from the witness to the jury.

Sec. 11.08 The Need to Object   Whether or not to object depends upon trial strategy, as well as the rules of evidence. A mastery of the rules should be used to advance counsel's cause but never to harm it.

Trial judges enjoy presiding over trials involving experienced trial lawyers, because of the few objections. Objections are like sour notes in a symphony; you should not expect to hear them. Beginning lawyers make the mistake of objecting, merely because the objection may be sustained.

In determining whether or not to object, the old risk-benefit ratio used by economists and others must be applied. If the benefit of objecting does not outweigh the risk, DO NOT OBJECT! If it is a tie, DO NOT OBJECT!

TRIAL STRATEGY

Before Objecting, Ask Yourself

1. How important is it that the evidence be excluded?
2. How will objecting affect the jury's perception of the objecting lawyer, his client, and his lawsuit?
3. Will objecting bring special attention to evidence unfavorable to the objecting party?
4. Will the trial be slowed down by objections that are really not necessary?

Too often, a lawyer is not concerned with a slowing down caused by or concurred in by opposing counsel. This ignores the fact that any slowing down of the trial makes the courtroom drama less dramatic and makes your telling of your story less effective.

Deciding whether to object challenges the trial lawyer most when opposing counsel leads a witness. He must know

1. Which leading questions CAN be objected to and

2. Which leading questions SHOULD be objected to.

Examples

Leading questions on preliminary matters are not objectionable: "Are you the wife of Plaintiff?" The same is true as to laying foundations: "Does this photo fairly and accurately represent the scene of the accident at the time of the accident?"

HOWEVER, as soon as opposing counsel says, "Isn't it true . . ." (or such), let the jury know opposing counsel is trying to testify. "The Defendant was drunk when you arrived, wasn't he, officer?" is the kind of leading question that shouts for OBJECTION.

"What color?" NOT "Was it red?"; "Below or above?" NOT "Below?"; "Tell me WHETHER OR NOT . . ." AVOID OBJECTIONS.

Object to leading questions, when necessary, and avoid jury criticism by letting the jury know of the fairness and common sense involved in your objection.

OBJECT if questioning is repetitious or where the question calls for a narrative answer.

Examples ——

"Your Honor, we have been through this several times" tells the jury it is opposing counsel who is boring them and wasting their time.

WARNING When a lawyer lets opposing counsel ask, "What happened next?" he is inviting the witness to say, "A man standing there said the light was red." This could have been avoided by merely saying, "Your Honor, I object for the reason the question calls for a narrative answer," thus forcing opposing counsel to break the question into parts that would signal your need to object ("and, what did the man say?" "I object, your Honor, on grounds of hearsay").

The need to object at trial, AND AT DEPOSITION, to questions assuming facts not in evidence is EXTREMELY IMPORTANT. If a lawyer asks, "When you filed this frivolous lawsuit, . . ." you know to jump to object, but a trial lawyer must be just as alert when opposing counsel asks, "Did you notice this before or after the officer struck you . . ." (where the testimony was the officer HELD him, or there was no testimony on the subject).

IMPORTANT: LISTEN to testimony, OBJECT when necessary, and COMMUNICATE to the jury that you are protecting your client from unfair treatment.

"Your Honor, counsel is arguing with the witness" is often heard in the courtroom, and such an objection should be made if the witness is being called upon to comment, evaluate, or respond to the interrogator's position.

Examples ——

1. "Are you trying to tell this jury . . ."
2. "Do you honestly believe . . ."
3. "If this really happened the way you said it did . . ."

(ALL OF THESE ARE INVITATIONS FOR COUNSEL TO OBJECT.)

Objections based on such basic areas of the law as relevancy and hearsay are discussed in other parts of this book. Suffice it to say

1. There is a need to object.

2. There is a need to know when to object.

3. There is a need to know how to object.

Sec. 11.09 The Art of Objecting The art of objecting begins with learning to object in time. In most circumstances, not objecting in time is the same as not objecting at all.

To object in time, the trial lawyer must listen carefully to the QUESTION AND THE ANSWER. Listen at the very beginning, and listen to each word.

Examples _____

1. "In your opinion . . ." tells counsel by this time to object, if the witness is not permitted to give an opinion.
2. "Did you notice anything unusual about the dress?" "Yes, in my opinion, it had been ripped off her." Here you are not alerted to object until the answer.

Object as soon as possible, and if anything improper has reached the ears of the jury, move to strike, and ask that the jury be instructed to disregard the evidence. If substantial damage has been done, request a mistrial.

TRIAL STRATEGY

How to "Stop the Clock" If You Need a Few Moments to Present an Objection Properly

1. "Your Honor . . ." notifies the Court you wish to make an objection. You have, in effect, called a TIME OUT!
2. Your request for a "time out" lasts for only a moment, and you must immediately follow up, and explain why you are entitled to halt the proceedings ("I am trying to think of the proper objection" will not do). "Your Honor, I wish to object to this question," gives you a few more seconds.
3. "Your Honor, I wish to object to this question because it obviously calls for hearsay," will pass the ball to opposing counsel and has given you time to group your thoughts. You are now ready to explain why the answer would be hearsay.

IMPORTANT: The objection process should be crisp and to the point. It is only when time is needed to gather thoughts that time should be used generously. MASTERING THE RULES WILL AVOID THE NEED FOR THOSE "THOUGHT-PROCESSING" SECONDS.

The second most important art in objecting is that of communicating with the jury. Timeliness protects you from improper evidence and preserves an appeal, but next comes the art of causing the jury to perceive all of this in your client's favor.

TRIAL STRATEGY

Remember, the Jurors Are Asking Themselves

1. Is the objection necessary, or just a waste of time?
2. Is counsel being overly technical?

3. Is counsel trying to hide something from the jury?
4. What is this objection all about?
5. What will the judge have to say about this objection?
6. Will the objection backfire on objecting counsel?
7. Can the jury consider the subject of the objection, even if the objection is overruled?

A trial lawyer must think about these questions, in deciding whether to object, and how to object. How he handles this problem must be such an integral part of his style, that he does not consciously think about it.

TRIAL STRATEGY

WARNING: For a hundred years, lawyers tried to impress juries by shouting, "I object, your Honor, this statement is irrelevant, immaterial and has no direct bearing upon any issue in this case. It is inflammatory and highly prejudicial, and I demand a mistrial." Judges no longer look with favor on such objections.

SUGGESTION: The better practice is to be concise, but specific. "I object, your Honor, this exhibit has no probative value and is offered only to inflame the jury."

IMPORTANT: Each judge has his own demands upon lawyers, and each trial lawyer has his own style. "Objection" will often take the place of, "I object, your Honor, the statement is . . ." as long as the court is put on notice as to the specifics of the objection, and appeal rights are protected.

COMMUNICATE to the jury by letting them know what is unfair. To keep opposing counsel from communicating improperly ask, "Your Honor, may we approach the bench?" COMMUNICATE with the judge by using HIS WORDS: "Asked and answered," "Repetitious," "Inflammatory," "Waste of time" (a nonlegal term that is found in FRE [Rule 403]), and others.

Objecting is an art, just as not objecting is an art. Trying a case without objections requires two good trial lawyers, working at it. When this does occur, it is like a beautiful drama that is not interrupted with commercials.

Sec. 11.10 Objections During Direct Examination
It is impossible to object during opposing counsel's direct examination, unless thoroughly familiar with the various grounds for objecting. The following grounds must be so much a part of the trial lawyer's thinking that any question or answer that violates a rule will trigger the objection process:

1. Is the statement hearsay?

    A. Does it assert anything?

    B. Is it offered to prove the matter asserted.

    C. Is it defined as "not hearsay" because of former testimony or admission?

    D. Is it an exception to the hearsay rule?

2. Is the statement relevant?

    A. Even if it makes a fact more or less likely, should it be excluded because of prejudice or delay?

    B. Even if relevant, should it be excluded because of offer of settlement, plea discussion, remedial measures, liability insurance, or the like?

3. Is the statement an opinion?

    A. Is witness an expert by knowledge, skill, experience, training or education?

    B. If a lay witness, is the statement rationally based on perception of witness AND helpful to understand his testimony or explain a fact?

    C. Is opinion within expert opinion's expertise, based on proper data and reliable principle, and does evidence support the conclusion?

4. Is it the *best evidence?*

    A. Is it the CONTENT of the writing, recording, or photograph that is being proved?

5. Has a proper foundation been laid?

    A. Does the evidence being offered depend upon other evidence that has not been offered?

6. Is the statement outside the pleading, or contrary to stipulation, admission, discovery, or order in limine?

    A. Does the evidence violate order, agreement, or fairness?

7. Is witness competent to give the statement?

    A. Does he have actual knowledge?

    B. Is the statement privileged?

    C. Has witness given oath and not been disqualified as being attorney, judge, juror, or unable to perceive, comprehend, or communicate?

8. Does statement violate dead man's statute?

   A. Is witness the claimant?

   B. Is the statement that of deceased or incompetent?

   C. Has the statute been waived?

9. Is counsel leading the witness?

   A. Is there legal cause for objecting?

   B. Does trial strategy warrant objecting?

10. Is it "asked and answered" or otherwise a waste of time?

11. Does question assume a fact not in evidence?

12. Is question in proper form, in that it is not

   A. Argumentative?

   B. Ambiguous?

   C. Call for narrative answer?

   D. Needs to be broken down?

   E. Overly broad?

   F. Confusing?

   G. Fails to include essentials of hypothetical?

13. Is the answer unresponsive, narrative in form, or inaudible?

14. Is there improper use of notes by witness?

15. Is there improper communication between counsel and witness?

16. Is there improper communication or action by judge?

17. Is there improper introduction or use of exhibits?

   IMPORTANT: If you do not object, you probably cannot appeal!

Sec. 11.11 Objections Throughout Trial Trial lawyers must be ready to object during every part of the trial. KNOWING the following situations for objection enables the trial lawyer to object in a timely and professional manner:

1. Is cross-examination being conducted properly?

   A. Does it go beyond direct? (Not proper objection if for a purpose such as impeachment)

   B. Is counsel arguing or bickering?

    C. Is counsel not letting witness answer?

    D. Is counsel's conduct unfair or improper?

    E. Is counsel repetitive, or otherwise delaying the trial?

    F. Is it improper impeachment?

    G. Is counsel asking more than one question at a time, or making improper assumptions?

    H. Does the interrogation enter prohibited areas?

    I. Is witness properly responding to questions?

    J. Is evidence inadmissible? (Leeway granted on cross, especially where door opened on direct, but rules still apply as to introduction of substantive evidence.)

    K. Does question involve privilege, or rule as to self-incrimination?

    L. Does question violate special rule as to prior conduct of rape victim?

2. Is voir dire being conducted properly?

    A. Is counsel's conduct unfair or improper?

    B. Is counsel asking prospective juror to prejudge the case or promise a certain verdict?

    C. Is counsel arguing the case by telling more of the facts than necessary for voir dire, or telling them in an argumentative manner?

    D. Is counsel repetitive, or otherwise delaying the trial?

    E. Is counsel presenting his voir dire in a prejudicial or inflammatory manner?

    F. Is voir dire entering prohibited areas (privilege, liability insurance, remedial measures, in limine orders, etc.)?

    G. Is questioning in proper form?

    H. Does question improperly embarrass the witness?

    I. Does question relate to possible challenge for cause?

    J. Is counsel misstating the law?

    K. Is counsel trying improperly to gain favor with a juror?

    L. Is counsel violating the purpose of voir dire?

        IMPORTANT: The trial judge has wide discretion in the conduct of voir dire. The trial lawyer who makes effective objections during voir dire can obtain favorable rulings which will help his voir dire and impress prospective jurors.

3. Is the opening statement being conducted properly?

   A. Is counsel arguing his case, and not just telling what he is going to prove?

   B. Is conduct of counsel unfair or improper?

   C. Is counsel introducing evidence he knows will not be presented and admitted?

   D. Is opening statement entering prohibited areas (liability insurance, privilege in limine order, stipulation, remedial measures, and the like)?

   E. Is counsel instructing on law, or misstating the law?

   F. Is opening statement inflammatory or prejudicial?

   G. Is counsel making statements that are immaterial and not for purpose of showing what he will prove?

4. Is closing argument being conducted improperly?

   A. Is counsel's conduct improper or unfair?

   B. Is counsel using an improper approach, such as Golden Rule argument considered improper in many states? ("What would you feel entitled to if you lost a leg?")

   C. Is counsel misquoting the evidence?

   D. Is counsel misquoting the law?

   E. Is final argument entering prohibited areas (liability insurance, privilege, in limine order, stipulation, remedial measures, and the like)?

   F. Is counsel being inflammatory, attacking personally, expressing personal view, or citing wealth or poverty where not permitted?

   G. Is counsel misusing charts, exhibits, or any form of demonstrative evidence?

   H. Is counsel stressing facts or issues improperly, or referring to excluded matters?

   I. Is counsel improperly seeking favor of a juror by using his name, etc.?

   J. Is counsel improperly referring to failure of opposing counsel to call witness?

Sec. 11.12 Objecting Is Not Enough   Objecting in a timely and adequate manner is important, but often it will not suffice. A trial lawyer must constantly keep in mind additional steps he must take.

TRIAL STRATEGY

In Addition to Objecting

1. Move to strike, if the answer has been given.
2. Move to instruct the jury to disregard prejudicial testimony.
3. Move for mistrial, where prejudice warrants it.
4. Require a "yes" or "no" answer where appropriate.
5. Move to admonish the witness or counsel, where they may repeat prejudicial conduct.
6. Request a ruling from the court, where necessary to protect your appeal.
7. Do all of the above outside the hearing of the jury, OR WITHIN THE HEARING OF THE JURY, if permitted, as dictated by trial strategy.

Trial counsel must make one determination, every time an objection is made. HAS THE JURY HEARD WHAT IT SHOULD NOT HAVE HEARD?

TRIAL STRATEGY

Objecting Counsel Must Consider One of Two Courses

If Answer Was NOT Given:
    "I object, your Honor, the question calls for hearsay."
If the Answer HAS Been Given:
    "The answer is hearsay, your Honor, and I move that it be stricken and the jury instructed to disregard it."

THE RULES CAN HELP YOU CROSS-EXAMINE

Sec. 11.13 Develop on Cross, What the Rules Would Not Let You Introduce on Direct   The Federal Rules of Evidence seldom even mention cross-examination, but throughout the rules there are provisions that you must constantly keep in mind while opposing counsel's witness is on the stand:

Rule 102— Argue purpose of the rules is to "secure fairness" and promote the "law of evidence to the end that the truth may be ascertained."

Rule 104(a)—Court is not bound by rules of evidence in deciding admissibility.

Rule 104(d)—By testifying upon preliminary matter accused does not subject himself to cross as in other issues.

Rule 105— Can require that jury be instructed as to the limited purpose of certain evidence.

Rule 106— Can require that related writing be submitted where it "it ought in fairness be considered contemporaneously."

Rule 201— Permits use of judicial notice of adjudicative fact in cross.

Rule 301— Permits use of a presumption to force opposing counsel to go forward with the evidence.

Rule 403— Permits exclusion of evidence that causes (a) "unfair prejudice," (b) "confusion of issues," (c) "misleading the jury," (d) "undue delay," (e) "waste of time," or (f) "needless presentation of cumulative evidence."

Rule 404— Character evidence not admitted to show he acted "in conformity therewith on a particular occasion." EXCEPT "Pertinent trait of his character offered by an accused" or by the prosecution to rebut "peacefulness" or to rebut "first aggressor." "Character of a witness" re Rule 607, Rule 608, or Rule 609. OTHER CRIMES not admitted to show acting in conformity, but "as proof of motive, opportunity, intent, preparation plan knowledge, identity or absence of mistake or accident."

Rule 405— Proving character with "testimony as to reputation or by testimony in the form of an opinion," and with "relevant specific instances" on cross-examination or where "a trait of character is an essential element of a charge, claim or defense."

Rule 406— "Habit" of an individual or "routine practice" of an organization can be used to show conduct was in conformity.

Rule 407— Subsequent remedial measure CAN be used to show such things as "ownership control, or feasibility of precautionary measures, if controverted, or impeachment."

Rule 408— Evidence re negotiations not admitted unless offered for purpose other than showing liability, such as "proving bias or prejudice of a witness, negativing a contention of undue delay, or proving an effort to obstruct a criminal investigation or prosecution." Does NOT exclude "evidence otherwise discoverable, just because it is presented in the course of compromise negotiations."

Rule 410— Plea of guilty later withdrawn, plea of nolo contendere, statement under Rule 11, or statement to prosecutor in plea discussions where plea withdrawn, cannot be used in CRIMINAL

OR CIVIL case. HOWEVER, plea of guilty can be admitted if another statement during negotiations is admitted and this should in fairness be admitted, or re perjury or false statement.

Rule 411— Insurance CAN be admitted if "offered for another purpose, such as proof of agency, ownership or control, or bias or prejudice of a witness."

Rule 412— "Past sexual behavior of alleged victim" not admissible in case of rape or intent to commit rape, through reputation or opinion. Specific instances admitted where constitutionally required and where there was proper notice and ruling as to need and propriety, also where necessary as to "source of semen or injury" or as to "whether the alleged victim consented to the sexual behavior with respect to which rape or assault is alleged."

Rule 501— Privilege is determined under state law in civil actions where "state law supplies the rule of decision;" otherwise under common law "as they may be interpreted by the courts of the United States in the light of reason and experience."

Rule 601— "Every person is competent to be a witness except as otherwise provided in these rules."

Rule 602— Testimony must be based on PERCEPTION, except expert opinions.

Rule 607— "THE CREDIBILITY OF A WITNESS MAY BE ATTACKED BY ANY PARTY, INCLUDING THE PARTY CALLING HIM."

Rule 608— CREDIBILITY OF WITNESS may be attacked or supported by opinion or reputation, to show "character for truthfulness or untruthfulness" AFTER character of witness for truthfulness has been attacked. "Specific instances of conduct of a witness," except as to conviction of crime under Rule 609, may not be proven by intrinsic evidence UNLESS by court's discretion, if "probative of truthfulness, be inquired into on cross-examination of the witness (1) concerning his character for truthfulness or untruthfulness, or (2) concerning the character for truthfulness or untruthfulness of another witness as to which character the witness being cross-examined has testified."

Rule 609— Conviction of crime can be used during cross-examination if (1) crime was punishable by death or imprisonment for more than a year and court determines probative value outweighs prejudicial effect, or (2) involved dishonesty or false statement, regardless of punishment. Not admitted if more than ten years since conviction or upon release whichever is later, unless judge decides probative value outweighs prejudice.

However, no ten-year conviction can be used without notice (written and sufficiently in advance to give opportunity to oppose). Conviction not admissible if pardon, etc., and no subsequent crime of death or more than one year of punishment, or pardon, etc. based on finding of innocence. Juvenile adjudications not generally admissible, but admissible against a witness if offense would be admitted against an adult witness (if judge decides the evidence necessary for fair determination). If appeal is pending conviction and evidence of the appeal can be admitted.

Rule 610—   "Beliefs or opinions of a witness on matters of religion" are not admissible.

Rule 611—   The court controls order of interrogation and presentation, and provides, "CROSS-EXAMINATION SHOULD BE LIMITED TO THE SUBJECT MATTER OF THE DIRECT EXAMINATION AND MATTERS AFFECTING CREDIBILITY OF THE WITNESS. THE COURT MAY, IN THE EXERCISE OF DISCRETION, PERMIT INQUIRY INTO ADDITIONAL MATTERS AS IF ON DIRECT." ALSO, "ORDINARILY LEADING QUESTIONS SHOULD BE PERMITTED ON CROSS-EXAMINATION."

Rule 612—   THE RULE 612 QUESTION FORCES WITNESS TO PRODUCE WRITINGS HE RELIED UPON IN PREPARING TO TESTIFY. (See Sec. 14.06 for effective use of this rule.)

Rule 613—   This rule provides a prior oral or written statement "NEED NOT BE SHOWN NOR ITS CONTENTS DISCLOSED TO THE WITNESS," but on request shall be shown to opposing counsel. The rule further provides extrinsic evidence of a prior inconsistent statement is not admissible "UNLESS THE WITNESS IS AFFORDED AN OPPORTUNITY TO EXPLAIN OR DENY THE SAME," and opposite party can interrogate witness. (This rule does not apply to party opponent admissions.)

Rule 614—   The court can call and interrogate witnesses.

Rule 701—   Lay opinion must be based on perception and "helpful to a clear understanding of the witness' testimony or the determination of a fact in issue."

Rule 702—   Expert can "assist the trier of fact" with opinion.

Rule 703—   Basis of expert opinion can be that "perceived or made known to him "at or before the hearing," and even inadmissible evidence can be used if "of a type reasonably relied upon by experts in the particular field."

Rule 704—   REMEMBER, an opinion can now be given on the "ULTIMATE ISSUE."

Rule 705— Expert need not give prior disclosure of underlying data, unless required by court, but, "THE EXPERT MAY IN ANY EVENT BE REQUIRED TO DISCLOSE THE UNDERLYING FACTS OR DATA ON CROSS-EXAMINATION."

Rule 706(a)—Court-appointed experts "SHALL BE SUBJECT TO CROSS-EXAMINATION BY EACH PARTY, INCLUDING A PARTY CALLING THE WITNESS."

Rule 801— The cross-examiner must know what is or is not hearsay, by definition.

Rule 803 and 804— The cross-examiner must know the exceptions to the hearsay rule.

Rule 805— The cross-examiner must know when there is hearsay within hearsay.

Rule 806— Credibility of declarant can be attacked, even if declarant did not testify directly.

Rule 901— The cross-examiner must know the rule on authentication.

Rule 902— Even where documents are self-authenticated, they must satisfy the rule.

Rule 1002— The cross-examiner must force opponent to comply with best evidence rule.

Rule 1003— Duplicate can be admitted to same extent as original, unless "genuine question is raised as to its authenticity" or "it would be unfair to admit the duplicate in lieu of the original."

Rule 1004— There are other ways to get evidence without the original.

Rule 1005— It is easy to get public records admitted, and their admittance should usually be stipulated.

Rule 1006— "THE CONTENTS OF VOLUMINOUS WRITINGS, RECORDINGS, OR PHOTOGRAPHS WHICH CANNOT CONVENIENTLY BE EXAMINED IN COURT MAY BE PRESENTED IN THE FORM OF A CHART, SUMMARY OR CALCULATION." Originals must be made available, and produced in court, if judge requires it.

TRIAL STRATEGY

Use the Federal Rules of Evidence to Get Evidence Before the Jury

EXAMPLES

1. Use leading questions that could not be used on direct. "Was this the only . . ."
2. Credibility includes many issues that could never be used on direct.
3. "Personalities" so important to the jury, but not to the rules of evidence, can be explored on cross-examination.

4. The same evidence presented during cross may have a more dramatic impact than if presented on direct. "I show you Exhibit Two, isn't that in your own handwriting?"
5. Where opposing counsel has "opened the door" on direct, even privileged evidence may reach the jury on cross.

Court has considerable discretion during cross-examination, but must accord accused constitutional rights (*U.S. v. Summers,* 598 F.2d 450 [5th Cir. 1979]). The court should, in fact, give counsel "wide latitude" during cross-examination (*U.S. v. Bleckner,* 601 F.2d 382 [9th Cir. 1979]).

HISTORICAL NOTE

At common law, cross-examination was limited to restricted rule of matters covered on direct, plus attack on credibility. In 1968 the Advisory Committee recommended this rule, but the final draft suggested a more wide-open rule. The Supreme Court recommended that cross-examination be permitted to include "any matter relevant to any issue in the case." Congress adopted the restrictive rule provided for in Rule 611(b) that cross should be limited to the subject matter of direct, and any matters affecting the credibility of the witness, adding that the court may permit "inquiry into additional matters as if on direct examination."

Sec. 11.14 Attack Those Areas of Direct Where the Direct Damaged You

The most important role of cross-examination is to undo damage done on direct examination. In fact, if no damage has been done on direct, it is very possible you should not even cross-examine the witness.

TRIAL STRATEGY

Before Beginning Cross-Examination, Ask Yourself

1. How do the jurors perceive this witness?
2. Do they believe his testimony?

If They Like the Witness or His or Her Testimony, Then Ask

1. How far will the jury let me go in changing this image, and
2. How can I best accomplish correcting any damage that has been done?

Avoid the negative aspects of cross-examination. Rule 611(a) warns that you must "avoid needless consumption of time," and you must not subject the witness to "harassment or undue embarrassment." (DUE embarrassment may be a proper objective of cross-examination where the witness's conduct prior to or during trial prompts the embarrassment.)

The most devastating means of attacking credibility is through prior inconsistent statements. You are, in effect saying, "If what you said before is true, you are now lying under oath." REMEMBER: Where prior inconsistent statement is under oath and subject to penalties of perjury, it can be used as substantive evidence.

TRIAL STRATEGY

Use the Prior Inconsistent Statement Effectively

1. Pin the witness down by having him or her repeat on cross what he or she had said on direct.
    "On direct examination you said, you never met John, is that right?"
2. Remind witness of circumstances surrounding the prior statement.
    "You remember giving a deposition in my office on May first, don't you?"
3. Establish time sequence.
    "That was a few months after the accident, wasn't it?" "Yes." "The facts were fresher in your mind then than today, isn't that right?" "Yes, I guess so."
4. Establish truthfulness of prior statement.
    "You understood what we were talking about, didn't you?" "Yes." "You had no reason to lie about this, did you?" "No." "You were telling the truth, weren't you?" "Yes."
5. Have witness confirm prior statement.
    "You told me, and I am referring to page eight, line two of your deposition, and I am reading your answer, 'I met John Henderson at a football game and told him I was sorry.' Do you remember making that statement?" "Yes."

WARNING: If witness denies making the prior inconsistent statement or fails to admit it, you must show evidence of the alleged statement (*Robertson v. M/S Sanyao Marv,* 374 F.2d 463 [5th Cir. 1967]). Where witness fails to admit, good faith basis for question needed, but if admitted, extrinsic evidence need not and, according to some courts, cannot be made.

HISTORICAL NOTE

QUEEN CAROLINE'S CASE required counsel to show witness the witness's own prior written statement before cross-examining on it (*Queen Caroline's*

Case, 2 Brod. & Bing 284, 129 Eng. Rep. 976 [1820]). Though the rule lasted only 34 years in England, it was embraced by most courts in the United States. This restriction on cross-examination was losing favor with the courts in the United States, however, especially the federal courts, and was completely rejected by Rule 613(a), which provides, "The statement need not be shown nor its contents disclosed to him at that time, but ON REQUEST, the same shall be shown or disclosed to opposing counsel."

Rule 609(a) and (b) provides means of impeaching by evidence of conviction of a crime. The details of this procedure have been discussed in a previous section, but should be kept ready as an effective impeachment.

Beginning with the *Luck* decision, courts were given latitude in weighing the need for prior conviction evidence and danger of unfair prejudice (*Luck v. U.S.,* 348 F.2d 763 [DC App. 1965]). This view has been clarified, with use of such factors as the nature of the crime, remoteness in time, subsequent life of defendant, and similarity with crime in question (*Gordon v. U.S.,* 383 F.2d 936 [DC Cir. 1967]).

Rule 608 provides for use of character evidence, as discussed in prior sections. This can be an effective means of impeachment, especially the use of specific instances under Rule 608(b).

The law of relevancy excludes much evidence where offered to show liability (such as subsequent remedial measures, liability insurance, or payment of medical bills). On cross, take another look and see if this evidence can be admitted for another purpose, such as ownership, control, or bias.

Example _____

"Tell the jury, Mr. Brown, weren't you there as a representative of the insurance company?"

Sec. 11.15 Discredit to the Limit the Jury Will Let You Discredit

Rule 611(b) provides that you CAN cross-examine relative to "matters affecting the credibility of the witness." The right to attack credibility is explicit, and the manner and degree of attack should be determined by trial strategy.

The first task of the trial lawyer is to establish clearly what aspects of the witness and testimony you are going to attack. Authorities on evidence have their favorite lists, but I suggest you make your own list, and that you make it a simple list.

TRIAL STRATEGY

Aim Your Attack on Cross-Examination at

1. Sincerity.
   Oath, bias, and whether the witness is intentionally lying.

2. Perception.
   What did the five senses really tell the witness?
3. Recollection.
   Does the witness really remember?
4. Communication.
   Is the witness telling the jury what he believes to be true, what he has perceived, or what he remembers?

Cross-examination is a basic right that is "not to be lightly curtailed" (error where cross-examination of witness who administered breathalyzer test was curtailed) (*Keel v. State,* 609 P.2d 555 (AK 1980]). Cross-examination cannot (and should not) be used as a "fishing expedition" (*State v. Clayton,* 658 P.2d 621 [UT 1983]).

Cross-examination as to whether defendant was making car payments, though offered to show motive for burning her own car, was rejected as improper cross-examination, upheld on appeal since question merely injected "suspicion, innuendo, and insinuation" (*State v. McCon,* 645 S.W.2d 67 [MO App. 1982]). Confrontation clause was violated where court restricted inquiry of a felon turned informant, where it could have been shown other than defendant could have been source of drugs (*State v. Pritchett,* 699 F.2d 317 [6th Cir. 1982]).

Court permitted cross-examination of witness in criminal case as to fact witness had a civil case arising from the occurrence to show bias (*State v. Kellog,* 350 So. 2d 656, 98 ALR3rd 1055, [LA 1977]). Fact police officer testifying and defendant had disagreements prior to occurrence is proper area of cross-examination (*Coleman v. State,* 545 S.W. 2d 831 [TX Crim. 1977]).

Psychiatric reports re witness have been admitted to show "intellectual grasp" of witness (*State v. Wright,* 225 S.E.2d 645 [NC App 1976]). Witness' association with those selling drugs was admitted to show bias (*U.S. v. Hodnett,* 537 F.2d 828 [5th Cir. 1976]). Fact witness is a drug addict has been held proper inquiry on credibility (*People v. Adams,* 485 N.E. 2d 339 [IL 1985]). Fact victim previously propositioned armed robbery defendant for homosexual act was proper subject of cross-examination (*State v. Becraft,* 236 S.E.2d 850 (NC App. 1976]).

The U.S. Supreme Court has made it clear that the FRE's failure to expressly refer to "bias and prejudice" did not impeach this basic factor in cross-examination, holding that witness's membership in gang dedicated to perjury, and other crimes, was proper subject of cross (*U.S. v. Abel,* 469 U.S. 45 [1984]).

It has been held that credibility can be attacked by showing:

1. Mental disease (*State v. Giglio,* 441 A.2d 303 [ME 1982]).

2. Drug use (*People v. Di Maso,* 426 N.E. 2d 972 [IL app 1981]).

3. Use of alcohol before incident (*Padgett v. General Motors*, 544 F.2d 704 [4th Cir. 1976]) BUT, NOT ALCOHOLISM UNLESS SHOWN AS RELEVANT.

4. History of blacking out (*Barnes v. Jones*, 665 F.2d 427 [2nd Cir. 1981]).

5. Physical condition, where relevance shown (mere showing of epilepsy was not enough) *Sturdevant v. State*, 181 N.W.2d 523,44 ALR3rd 1196 (WI 1970).

6. Bad psychological problem for telling lies (*Gamble v. State*, 492 So.2d 1132 [FL App. 1986]).

7. Long history of psychiatric problems (*People v. Knowell*, 512 N.Y.S. 190 [NY App. 1987]).

8. Ability to separate dreams from reality (*State v. Hall*, 727 F.2d 1255 [ID 1986]).

Sec. 11.16 Prepare Cross During Direct   While listening to opponent's direct examination, you must listen with an attentive ear to make timely objection, plan strategy, and prepare for cross-examination. By keeping certain evidence out, the task of cross-examination is made easier.

TRIAL STRATEGY

During Opponent's Direct, Prepare for Cross by

1. Noting areas in which opponent has "opened the door."
2. Defining the perimeters of direct that will limit your cross.
3. Listing under "questions" areas in which you will inquire, and under "testimony" a synopsis of the entire testimony, including areas in which you may not inquire.
4. Objecting to testimony and exhibits that should be excluded.
5. Applying the "probability" test to everything the witness says (if something "probably" did not happen exactly as witness is testifying, red lights should be flashing).
6. Observing the jurors and analyzing their reaction to the witness and his or her testimony.
7. Comparing testimony with depositions and other trial preparation.

By making proper objections, you prepare for cross-examination. You force opponent to give purpose of what you allege is hearsay. You force opponent to show relevancy; you force opponent to give basis of expert opinions; and you force the court to say the objection goes to the weight and not the admissibility of the evidence.

Anything that goes to "weight" suggests cross-examination. The judge, in effect, is saying, "I expect you to cover this on cross." The jury, as well as the judge, may wonder why you do not cover it on cross.

REMEMBER: There is a low threshold for admission under most rules of evidence. Rule 401 speaks of "having a tendency" to make "more probable or less probable." Rule 601 makes the most incompetent witness competent, until counsel files a proper objection on direct and attacks the incompetency on cross. Rule 702 merely requires that an expert "assist the trier of fact."

These and other rules shout out for proper cross-examination! Before cross, however, there must be an objection on direct. Often before an objection, there must be a voir dire of the witness by counsel, who will eventually cross-examine the witness.

TRIAL STRATEGY

Voir Dire the witness ("Your Honor, I would like to voir dire the witness before you make a ruling") to

1. Determine relevancy.
   "Does the photo fairly and accurately represent the scene at the time of the accident?" (If answer is "no" his answer is irrelevant.)
2. Determine other admissibility.
   "How soon after the occurrence did she make the statement?" (If too distant in time, it is not an excited utterance and not admissible.)

Sec. 11.17 The "New" Rule for Experts Can Offer "New" Opportunities for Cross-Examiners
Cross-examining experts presents a special challenge to the trial lawyer because of its unlimited opportunities and unlimited risks. Waiving cross-examination of an expert should occur only when waiver of any other witness would logically occur. Waiver of any witness should occur only when trial strategy suggests the waiver.

Pretrial preparation is important for any cross-examination but it is absolutely necessary for effective cross-examination of an expert. This preparation will necessarily include depositions, medical (and other) professional records, writings, or lectures of the expert, and a thorough knowledge of the expert and his subject.

TRIAL STRATEGY

Some Questions Must Be a Part of the Trial Lawyer's Vocabulary

1. "Medicine is not an exact science, is it, Doctor?"
2. "In the many opinions you have given, have you ever been wrong?"
3. "Experts in this field are not in complete agreement on this, are they?"
4. "You can't really be sure about this, can you?"
5. "If . . . was true, would that not change your opinion?"
6. "You are familiar with the doctor who testified here this morning, aren't you, Doctor?"
7. "Is it your opinion then, Doctor, that all of these other doctors are lying under oath?"
8. "My client cooperated with you in every way possible, didn't he?"
9. "What risk was involved in this operation?"
10. "How certain can you be about this, Mr. Jones?"
    IMPORTANT: Know how certain the witness must be under the law of your jurisdiction. Though "can you tell me with a reasonable degree of medical certainty . . ." is usually an accepted method. One court held evidence hair "could have come from" defendant admitted for what help it would be to jury (*U.S. v. Cyphers,* 553 F.2d 1064 [7th Cir. 1977]); but another court held words "possible factor" and "was extremely likely" did not make a submissible case (*Kineally v. Southwestern Bell Telephone Co.,* 368 S.W. 2d 400 [MO 1963]).
11. "How much time did you actually spend with my client, Doctor?"
12. "You really don't specialize in this area of medicine, do you, Doctor?"
13. "You base this opinion on your classroom experience, and not on experience of actually treating patients, isn't that a fair statement, Doctor?"
14. "With whom have you consulted on this matter?"
15. "Do you think these medical costs incurred by my client are reasonable?"
16. "How much is it costing for you to testify here today?"
17. "Would you please explain that so we who are not doctors can understand it?"
18. "Do you think my client's doctor was right in telling my client not to return to work under these circumstances?"
19. "Doctor, let me show you what you wrote on May first of this year . . ."
20. "Mrs. Jones, would it be fair to say . . ."

REMEMBER: The rule does permit an opinion to be based on inadmissible evidence. On cross-examination the credibility of that evidence must be attacked. The test under Rule 703 is:

> *"Is the type of data reasonably relied upon by experts in this field in forming opinions?"*

If that test is met, you must then follow up with, "You don't really know of your own knowledge, though, do you Doctor?"

A hypothetical question is not needed under the new rule, but if used, it must be attacked. Choose the weakest point or points. "But if this factor were NOT present, then your opinion would be different, would it not?"

Rule 702 permits the expert to merely give an opinion, but Rule 705 requires the expert to "disclose the underlying facts or data on cross-examination." Through discovery and other pretrial preparation you will be ready to cross-examine thoroughly on the facts and data.

Sec. 11.18 Use The "612 Question"   Rule 612 provides that, except as otherwise provided for in criminal proceedings, . . . *"If a witness uses a writing to refresh his memory for the purpose of testifying either—*

(1) *while testifying, or*

(2) *before testifying, if the court in its discretion determines it is necessary in the interests of justice, an adverse party is entitled to have the writing produced at the hearing, to inspect it, to cross-examine the witness thereon, and to introduce in evidence those portions which relate to the testimony of the witness."*

The court may examine "in camera" and excise unrelated portions and make orders to enforce the rule.

TRIAL STRATEGY

How to Use the "612 Question" on Cross-Examination

Judge Frederick Lacey, a well-known Federal Judge and lecturer, warns trial lawyers to always ask the 612 Question on cross-examination, which is done by simply asking:

> "Prior to testifying here today, did you use any papers or documents to refresh your memory?"

If the witness answers, "Yes," you have a right to see those documents and use them during cross-examination. If counsel objects, the judge can examine in camera and determine what you can use.

WARNING: When your own witness uses documents to refresh memory, make sure you are not giving opposing counsel documents he could not otherwise obtain, or opening the door to inquiry re the documents that may not otherwise be admissible.

The trial court has broad discretion in matters pertaining to refreshing memory (*U.S. v. Boyd*, 606 F.2d 792 [8th Cir. 1979]). The practice is, however, to permit broad use of notes and other data—though the court warned the whole adversary system would fall if we permit the previously written statement to substitute for oral testimony (*Goings v. U. S.*, 377 F.2d 753 [8th Cir. 1967]). The court must not, however, permit unreliable evidence incorporated in a memorandum to reach the jury (*Parliament Insurance Co. v. Hanson*, 676 F.2d 1069 [5th Cir. 1982]).

The cross-examiner must be careful not to "open the door" and not to permit additional evidence under Rule 106 (Rule of Completeness). In one case a court held a cross-examination could mislead the jury and permitted Prosecution to answer impression of inconsistencies (*U.S. v. Rubin*, 609 F.2d 51 [2nd Cir. 1979]).

TRIAL STRATEGY

When Opposing Witness Uses Writing to Refresh Memory

1. Mark the exhibit.
2. Examine the exhibit.
3. Do not let witness read from it (have witness read, then testify).
4. Note any difference between the exhibit and the testimony.
5. Cross-examine!

The possibility of waiving a privilege must also be considered. It has been held that attorney's work product is not privileged where it was used by expert in preparing for trial (*Boring v. Keller*, 97 FRD 404 [D.C. CO 1983]).

The attorney's "mental impressions," however, should be protected (*James Julian, Inc. v. Raytheon Co.*, FRD 138 [D.C. DE 1982]). The Supreme Court of the United States has warned against the dangers of subjecting privileged evidence to exposure (*Hickman v. Taylor*, 329 U.S. 495 [1947]).

HISTORICAL NOTE

The Supreme Court recommended pretrial refreshing of memory be treated the same as during trial, but Congress kept the common law rule of court discretion as to pretrial refreshing. Report of House Committee intended Rule 612 to protect privilege, but that is not a part of Rule 612, and some courts hold there is a waiver when privileged evidence is used to refresh memory.

Sec. 11.19 *Avoid Common Cross-Examination Mistakes*   The trial attorney must remain in control of his cross-examination at all times. He loses control, however, when he fails to understand or fails to properly apply the rules of evidence.

The most common error is that of "arguing with the witness." This can be avoided by not giving opposing counsel grounds to object.

TRIAL STRATEGY

Avoid the "Arguing with Witness" Objection by

1. NEVER start a question with "You testified earlier that . . ." (Don't repeat.)
2. NEVER start a question with "Are you trying to tell this jury . . ." (Don't question credibility so obviously.)
3. NEVER start a sentence with "Since you have already testified that . . ." (Don't summarize.)
4. NEVER start a sentence with "If you had not been . . ." (Don't try to persuade with the question.)
5. NEVER say, "You did this just because you are a nice guy, right?" (Don't invite argument from witness.) HOWEVER, some courts permit: "Your testimony today is in conflict with your deposition, isn't it?" (Though you may want to save this for summation.)
6. NEVER ask, "The truth is, you did . . ." (Don't ask a question that merely asks witness to agree with your inferences.)
7. NEVER say, "What did you do when this drunk plowed into . . ." (Don't characterize people or evidence in a question.)

EXCEPTIONS: *During depositions,* you may occasionally find a reason to "argue" with a witness for strategic reasons. *During trial* you may bend the "arguing" rule a little IF (a) you think the judge will permit it, (b) you think the jury will approve of it, and (c) it does not interfere with a professional and effective cross-examination.

The scope of this chapter is limited to cross-examination strategy as affected by the rules of evidence. A broader approach can be found in books dealing specifically with trial strategy. (See *Cross-Examination: The Mosaic Art,* John Nicholas Iannuzzi, Prentice-Hall, 1982; *How To Use Courtroom Drama To Win Cases,* Edward T. Wright, Prentice-Hall, 1987.)

Such common mistakes as "asking one question too many" have been covered thoroughly in law books and lectures. The most common, and commonly ignored, mistake is "FAILURE TO ANALYZE HOW THE JURY PERCEIVES THE WITNESS YOU ARE ABOUT TO CROSS-EXAMINE, AND HOW FAR THE JURY WILL LET YOU GO IN CHANGING THAT PERCEPTION."

It is your job to prove the witness a liar, not merely CALL him a liar. If at the beginning of cross, the jury thinks the witness is telling the truth, you must decide what you can do to cause the jury to change its mind. The stronger their perception, the more damaging the evidence or questioning must be, yet the stronger the resistance is that must be overcome.

Example ————————————————————————————————

The jury thinks witness was telling the truth on direct, and you can tell the jury likes the witness. If you beat the witness with a slight discrepancy in his story, they will hate you for it.

We learned a lot about "jury perception" from the Iran-Contra hearings before the United States in the summer of 1987. A witness named Oliver North testified that he took it upon himself to change the foreign policy of his country on the questions of sending arms to a staunch enemy (Iran), and dealing with terrorists for hostages, both positions being directly opposed to the announced position of the President, Congress and the Secretary of State.

The jury in this case was the American people who were glued to their television sets, watching the proceedings. You might think this "jury" would be outraged at such "un-American" activities, and at the "criminal" conduct of shredding the evidence.

Not so! This witness proved that wrapped in the American flag he could violate the basic concept of American democracy. If the "jury" likes the appearance and demeanor of the witness, and likes the idea of a colonel in the basement of the White House exercising authority constitutionally given to others, it will conclude the whole thing was a "neat idea," and not take lightly the task of trying to show otherwise during the brief period of a cross-examination.

TRIAL STRATEGY

A Few "Rule-Related" Mistakes on Cross-Examination

1. Don't ignore the "scope" of cross.
   Rule 611(b) sets forth the perimeter and to go too far beyond it will not gain favor with the judge or the jury.
2. Lead the witness.
   Rule 611(c) provides, "Ordinarily leading questions should be permitted on cross-examination." Ordinarily, that is the way to go!
3. Don't open the door.
   The courts have added to nearly every rule the "HOWEVER, you opened the door . . ." Avoid this pitfall by
   A. knowing in advance what doors you are opening,
   B. finding a way to present the same evidence or ask the same question in a way that will *not* open the door, and
   C. determining if this cannot be avoided, whether it may not be best to just give up the evidence or question as a poor trade-off for what will happen when the door is opened.

4. Use the exceptions to relevancy exceptions.

   Rule 402 states "all relevant evidence is admissible, except as otherwise provided, . . ." but then the rules set forth exceptions relative to character (Rule 404), subsequent remedial measures (Rule 407), compromise and offers to compromise (Rule 408), payment of medical and similar expenses (Rule 409), pleas, plea discussions and related statements (Rule 410), liability insurance (Rule 411), and rape victim's past behavior (Rule 12).

   EXAMPLE: In cross-examining in case where subsequent remedial measure was made, FIND OUT WHO MADE THE REPAIR OR CHANGE IN PROCEDURE. If the repair was made by the landlord and you are suing the tenant, you can proceed as an exception to the exception.

5. Don't "cave-in" on question of privilege.

   Maybe a third person was present, or any of the other exceptions exist. REMEMBER, Rule 5.01 provides that the courts are to interpret the common law principles of privilege "in light of reason and experience." This is a green light for the cross-examiner to proceed, and may even make "new law."

6. Remember the new broad rule on competency.

   What the law giveth, the law taketh away. When Rule 601 made everyone a competent witness, it also made every witness subject to more rigorous cross-examination. USE IT!

7. Make reasonable requests.

   Rule 611(a) gives the court "reasonable control over the mode and order of interrogating witnesses and presenting evidence." While conducting your cross-examination, call upon the court to postpone till morning; take a ten minute recess; let you voir dire the witness during direct; introduce an exhibit out of order; have the witness come down from the witness stand; approach the witness, or ANYTHING REASONABLE.

8. Attack underlying data of expert.

   Rule 705 provides that on cross-examination the expert may be required to "disclose the underlying facts or data." Too often counsel lets the expert get by without really demanding this disclosure.

9. Cross-examine the "hearsay declarant."

   If a declarant testifies in court through a hearsay witness, and not in person, Rule 806 provides that you may attack the "credibility of the declarant," and do so "by any evidence which would be admissible for those purposes if declarant had testified as a witness."

10. Don't forget the "612 question."

    Rule 612 gives you the right to writings used to refresh memory. (See Section 14.06 as to how this rule can be used effectively during cross-examination.)

12

DISTINGUISHING FEDERAL RULES FROM COMMON LAW AND STATE LAW

Sec. 12.01 Federal Rules and the Law of Evidence The previous chapters enable every trial lawyer to walk into a federal court and feel comfortable with the Rules of Evidence, and every student to pass the evidence section of the bar exam. With this chapter, the lawyer and law student can adapt to the law of a particular state.

Table One of this chapter gives the reader the background of the adoption of the Federal Rules of Evidence of those states that have adopted the rules. The law is not spelled out for each rule in each state, but the basic concept and source is given, from which the trial lawyer can decide whether further research is needed.

It is imperative that lawyers practicing in a state that has adopted the FRE, have a basic concept of which rules were not adopted in substantially the same form as the federal rule. It is also important that a trial lawyer be able to obtain a quick review of the law of other states in which he may have a matter pending.

Example ───

Trial lawyer has an accident case pending in another state. His only way of proving liability is through an "excited utterance." He knows such evidence is admitted under the FRE but may want to file in the state court (especially with the increased diversity amount) if he knows the law of that state also accepts "excited utterances."

By studying the tables at the end of each chapter, you can get a feel of what is happening in those states that adopted the FRE. It is easy to see that some states are "purists," adopting all, or nearly all, of the federal provisions, whereas other states have been reluctant to go that far.

It is interesting to note that many states refused to change their common law in such areas as past behavior of rape victims (Rule 412), privilege (Rule 501), presuming every witness competent (Rule 601), impeaching with conviction of crime (Rule 609), writing used to refresh memory (Rule 612), court-appointed experts (Rule 706), that part of public reports that may let in hearsay (Rule 803-8), and the general exception for hearsay (Rule 803-24).

On the other hand, all other rules have generally been accepted in the FRE states, and the concept of all FRE rules is being accepted in non-FRE states by case law. Mastering the Federal Rules of Evidence, the laws interpreting those rules, and the trial strategy that turns rules into winning lawsuits is now an absolute must for every trial lawyer.

Sec. 12.02 Non-FRE States—General—Judicial Notice—Presumptions The evidence law of the states that have not adopted the Federal Rules of Evidence can be found in certain statutes, case decisions, codes, and rules of the various states. Table Two at the end of this chapter gives the reader the sources of this great body of law.

A review of the law of all states, including those that have not adopted the federal rules, shows a modern approach that each year lessens any gap between states that have adopted the FRE and those which have not. It also shows that some of the new concepts have been around for a long time.

The following are a few cases on JUDICIAL NOTICE:

ALABAMA: "Pickups are commonly used as passenger vehicles" (*Berdeau v. Gamble Alden,* 338 So. 2d 403 [1975]).

CALIFORNIA: Method of operation of crematories (*Abbey Land & Improvement Co. v. San Mateo County,* 139 P 1068 (CA [1914]).

CONNECTICUT: General rule (see *Miller v. Poli's New England Theatre,* 7 A. 2d 845 [1939]).

GEORGIA: General rule (see *Savannah v. Jordon,* 83 S.E. 109 [1921]).

ILLINOIS: "Cannot be used to evade proof" (*National Aircraft Leasing v. American Airlines,* 394 N.E. 2d 470 [1979]).

INDIANA: General rule (*State v. Louisville & N. R.,* 96 N.E. 340 [1911]).

KANSAS: General rule (see *State v. Finch,* 280 P. 910 [1929]).

KENTUCKY: "Spinal fusion operations are often dangerous" (*Ratliff v. Celebrezze,* 338 F. 2d 677 [1964]).

LOUISIANA: Judicial notice of "quality of homemade whisky" (*State v. McClinton,* 94 So. 141 [1922]).

MASSACHUSETTS: General rule (see *Commonwealth v. Pear,* 66 N.E. 719 [1903]).

MARYLAND: Can't take judicial notice of contract provision, because it is "not self-evident and not a notorious fact" (*Ranover Insurance Co. v. Nationwide Mutual,* 365 A. 2d 352 [1977]).

MISSOURI: "Common knowledge of every person of ordinary understanding and intelligence" (*Endicott v. St. Regis Investment Co.,* 443 S.W. 2d 122 [MO 1969]).

NEW JERSEY: "Such facts as are generally known or of such common knowledge in the area" (Rule 9, *New Jersey Rules of Evidence*).

NEW YORK: General rule (see *Rowland v. Miller,* 39 N.E. 765 [1893]).

PENNSYLVANIA: SPCA means "Society For Prevention of Cruelty to Animals" (*Sieman's Estate,* 31 A. 2d 280 [1943]).

SOUTH CAROLINA: General Rule (see *Fleishman v. Southern Railroad Co.,* 56 S.E. 974 [1907]).

TENNESSEE: "Laws of physics" (*Gordon's Transport v. Bailey,* 294 S.W. 2d 313 [1956]).

VIRGINIA: "Rule of necessity and public policy" (*Williams v. Commonwealth,* 56 S.E. 2d 537 [1949]).

The Federal Rules of Evidence adopted the "bursting bubble" theory of presumptions under which presumptions are merely procedural devices that have no substantive effect, and once rebutted return the burden to its original place. The use of this approach is followed in many states, and presumptions, generally, have become a part of a court's saving time by avoiding presentation of evidence.

ALABAMA: Presumption merely procedural (*Louisville and NR v. Marbury Lumber Co.*, 28 So. 458 [1900]).

CALIFORNIA: Presumption merely procedural (*Lane & Pryal, Inc. v. Gibbs*, 71 Cal. Rep. 817 [1916]).

CONNECTICUT: Presumption merely procedural (*O'Dea v. Amodeo*, 170 A. 486 [1934]).

GEORGIA: "Presumption must give way to reality" when rebutted (*Floyd v. Colonial Stores*, 176 S.E. 2nd 14 [1970]).

ILLINOIS: Presumption merely procedural (*Hendrick v. Uptown Safe Deposit Co.*, 159 N.E. 2d 58 [1959]).

INDIANA: Presumption merely procedural (*Hibbard v. Hibbard*, 73 N.E. 2d 181 [1947]).

KANSAS: Presumption merely procedural (*Blakeman v. Lofland*, 252 P. 2d 852 [1953]).

KENTUCKY: Presumption is evidence (*Mills v. Bailey*, 130 S.W. 1077 [1910]).

LOUISIANA: Presumption is evidence (*New Orleans Canal & Bkg. Co. v. Templeton*, 20 La. Ann. 141).

MASSACHUSETTS: Presumption merely procedural (*Commonwealth v. De Francesco*, 142 N.E. 749 [1924]).

MARYLAND: Presumption is evidence (*Maryland use of Geils v. Baltimore Transit Co.*, 329 F. 2d 738 [1963]).

MISSOURI: Presumptions merely procedural (*Michler v. Krey Packing Co.*, 253 S.W. 2nd 707 [MO 1952]); presumed that a death was accidental (*Hendrix v. Metropolitan Life*, 250 S.W. 2d 300 [MO 1956]); a child was born in wedlock, *J.D. v. M.D.*, 453 S.W. 2d 661 [MO App. 1970]); and testator was of sound mind (*Detrick v. Mercantile Trust Co.*, 250 S.W. 2nd 518 [MO App 1952]).

NEW JERSEY: Presumption merely procedural (*Kirshbaum v. Metropolitan Life Ins.*, 42 A. 2d 257 [1945]).

NEW YORK: Presumption merely procedural. (Whether defendant had knowledge of the tampering of the meter must still be proven beyond a reasonable doubt.) (*People v. Castenada*, 400 N.Y.S. 2d 702 [1977]).

PENNSYLVANIA: Presumption merely procedural (*Watkins v. Prudential Ins. Co.*, 173 A. 644 [1934]).

SOUTH CAROLINA: Presumption merely procedural (*Strawhorne v. Atlantic Coast Life Insurance Co.*, 119 S.E. 2d 101 [1961]).

TENNESSEE: Presumption merely procedural (*Marie v. State*, 319 S.W. 2d 86 [1958]).

VIRGINIA: "An inference cannot be drawn from a presumption and it must be founded on some legally proven fact." *(Foster v. Willhite*, 172 S.E. 2d 745 [1970]).

Sec. 12.03 Non-FRE States—Relevancy   The Federal Rules of Evidence established a low threshold for admitting evidence on the basis of relevancy. Rule 401 provides that evidence is relevant if it has "any tendency to make the existence of any fact that is of consequence to the determination of the action more probable or less probable than it would be without the evidence."

A review of the non-FRE states shows a modern trend toward an equally low threshold:

ALABAMA: Relevancy is "largely within discretion of the trial court" (*State Farm v. Humprhies*, 304 So. 2d 573 [1974]).

CALIFORNIA: "Which may have a tendency" (*Mercado v. Hoefler*, 190 C. App. 12 [1961]).

CONNECTICUT: "Conduces to any reasonable degree to establishment . . . of the fact in issue" (*National Broadcasting Co. v. Rose*, 215 A. 2d 123 [1965]).

GEORGIA: "Elucidates or throws light on" (*Ackerman/Adair Realty v. Coppedge*, 273 S.E. 2d 645 [1980]).

ILLINOIS: Court talks of "need" for the evidence (*Heggert Nat. Bank v. Johnson*, 316 N.E. 2d 191 [1974]).

INDIANA: Not admitted where of little probative value (*France v. State*, 387 N.E. 2d 66 [1979]). Test is its value "in the particular case" (*State v. Lee*, 83 N.E. 2d 778 [IND. 1949]).

KANSAS: Admitted if it "has a tendency" (*Dawson v. Asso. Fin. Services*, 529 P. 2d 104 [1974]).

KENTUCKY: "Renders probable or improbable" . . . "relationship of facts offered and fact in issue" (*Glen Falls Ins. v. Ogden*, 310 S.W. 2d 547 [KY App. 1958]).

LOUISIANA: "Accused can use *all* evidence which is available to his defense, even though such evidence in itself be insufficient to establish the whole or any definite portion of defendant's contention" (*State v. Kelly*, 146 So. 2d 368 [1933]).

MASSACHUSETTS: Basically the federal rule (*Edgarton v. H. P. Welch Co.*, 74 N.E. 2d 674 [1947]).

MARYLAND: General rule (see *Worthington v. State*, 381 A. 2d 712 [1978]).

MISSOURI: "More probable or less probable" (*McIlroy v. Hamilton*, 539 S.W. 2d 669 [MO App. 1976]).

NEW JERSEY: "Renders the desired inference more probable" (*Hagopian v. Fuchs*, 169 App. 2d 172 [1961]).

NEW YORK: "Logically tends to prove or disprove" (*Oliver v. England*, 264 N.Y.S. 2nd 999 [Fam. Ct. 1965]).

PENNSYLVANIA: "Makes the desired inference more probable" (*Commonwealth v. Stewart*, 336 App. 2d 232 [1975]).

SOUTH CAROLINA: "Legally tend to establish or make more or less probable" (*Winburn v. Minn Mutual*, 201 S.E. 2d 372 [1973]).

TENNESSEE: "Sound discretion of the trial court" (*Strickland v. Lawrenceburg*, 611 S.W. 2d 832 [TN App. 1980]).

VIRGINIA: "Tending to prove or disprove" (*Barnette v. Dickens*, 135 S.E. 2d 109 [1964]).

Sec. 12.04 Non-FRE States—Privilege—Witnesses

Rule 501 provides that the law of privilege is to be interpreted "in the light of reason and experience," suggesting a case-by-case consideration. A review of a few privilege cases in states that have not adopted FRE shows the following:

ALABAMA: Spouse can testify as to what other spouse told third party (*Arnold v. State*, 353 So. 2d 524 [1977]).

CALIFORNIA: Privilege cannot be claimed until witness sworn and person calling him begins examination (*People v. Harris*, 155 CA Rep. 472 [1979]); cannot just refuse to testify, must claim Fifth Amendment privilege with "specific reference to particular question" (*Warford v. Medeiros*, 207 CA Rep. 94 [1984]).

CONNECTICUT: General rule re attorney/client privilege (*Rienzo v. Sanatansel*, 279 A. 2d 565 [1971]).

GEORGIA: Testifying waives the privilege and subjects defendant to cross-examination on "all proper and relevant questions" (*Dickey v. State*, 242 S.E. 2d 55 [1973]).

ILLINOIS: In testifying at motion to suppress, privilege waived only as to that issue (*People v. Williams*, 185 N.E. 2d 686 [1962]).

INDIANA: Where wife helped husband commit burglary, husband's testimony as to her acts not admissible (*Shepard v. State*, 277 N.E. 2d 165 [1971]).

KANSAS: News media has limited privilege that must yield to fair trial (*State v. Sandstrom*, 581 P2d 812 [KA 1978]).

KENTUCKY: Where accused took stand to defend as to homicide, he had to answer questions as to concealed weapon, since possession of weapon was part of res gestae (*Rose v. Commonwealth*, 422 S.W. 2d 130 [1967]).

LOUISIANA: Accused can refuse to take stand, but witness must claim privilege as to particular questions *(State v. Wilson*, 394 So. 2d 254 [1981]). No error in letting accused claim his privilege outside hearing of jury *(State v. Berry*, 324 So. 2d 822 [1975]).

MASSACHUSETTS: Privilege extended to social worker *(Massachusetts General Laws Ann.* CH 112 Sec. 135 [West 1983]).

MARYLAND: Where defendant, on cross, told of conversations with his former counsel, former counsel could not testify that defendant did not so tell him (*Harrison v. State*, 345 App. 2d 830 [1975]).

MISSOURI: Missouri adds privilege to (a) syphilis blood tests, *MO Rev. Stat.* Sec. 210.040, (b) employment security records, *MO Rev. Stat.* Sec. 288.250, (c) juvenile proceedings matters, *MO Rev. Stat.* Sec. 211.271(3), and (d) anything doctor "obtains through his observation, inspection, examination and treatment" (*F. v. F.*, 333 S.W. 2nd 320 [1960]).

NEW JERSEY: Privilege extends to religious beliefs (Rule 30), political vote (Rule 31), and the news media (Rule 27) (*New Jersey Rules of Evidence*).

NEW YORK: Whether witness must claim a privilege in the presence of the jury is "within the sound discretion of the trial court" (*People v. Thomas*, 434 N.Y.S. 2d 941 [1980]).

PENNSYLVANIA: Witness who testified at preliminary can invoke privilege at trial and refuse to testify (*Commonwealth v. Reese*, 354 A. 2d 573

[1976]). In custody case, refusing to give client's address and telephone number was within privilege and such did not operate to "permit or continue a crime or fraud" (*Brennan v. Brennan*, 422 A. 2d 510 [1980]).

SOUTH CAROLINA: Cannot impeach own witness (*State v. Richburg*, 158 S.E. 2d 769 [1968]).

TENNESSEE: If it appears to court witness intends to claim privilege as to essentially all questions, trial court may excuse witness from taking stand (*State v. Dicks*, 615 S.W. 2d 126 [1980]).

VIRGINIA: In disciplinary action, Defendant lost privilege by communications to attorney that were "made in the futherance of the commission of an intended fraud on the committee" (*Seventh District Committee Of The Virginia State Bar v. Gunter*, 183 S.E. 2d 713 [1971]).

The federal rules broaden the concept of competency and clarify other rules relating to witnesses. A review of a few cases on this subject from non-FRE states show:

ALABAMA: Confinement to mental hospital does not disqualify witness (*Moore v. State*, 469 So. 2d 1308 [1985]).

CALIFORNIA: Trial court could force plaintiff's law firm to withdraw where member of firm needed by Plaintiff as witness, and such could not prejudice Plaintiff (*Comden v. Superior Court of Los Angeles County*, 576 P. 2d 971 [1978]).

CONNECTICUT: Cannot impeach own witness, even where "hostility, surprise or deceit" without permission of judge (*State v. Esposito*, 353 A. 2d 746 [1974]).

GEORGIA: Attorney for plaintiff who served as attorney and accountant for plaintiff could not be disqualified on basis defendant wanted to call him as witness, since he was not even competent to testify against his client (*Southern Shipping Co. v. Oceans International Corp.*, 329 S.E. 2d 263 [1985]).

ILLINOIS: Defense counsel could not impeach witness with testimony of pretrial conversation with the witness, if counsel refuses to withdraw, and such refusal would not work a hardship (*People v. Attaway*, 354 N.E. 2d 448 [ILL 1976]).

INDIANA: Accused has no right to have sexual assault victim given mental exam where no evidence of mental illness, though relative of victim called her "born liar." (*Stanton v. State*, 428 N.E. 2d 1203 [1981]).

KANSAS: To be competent, a witness must be conscious of his duty to tell the truth (*Lee v. Missouri Pacific Railroad Co.*, 73 P 110 [KA 1903]).

KENTUCKY: Mistake in spelling of Christian name of witness does not disqualify him as witness, where no harm done (*Evans v. Commonwealth,* 19 S.W. 2d 1091 [1929]).

LOUISIANA: Testimony of witness with "permanent reduction of intellectual power" should be admitted and jury decide weight of evidence (*Carollo v. Wilson,* 353 So. 2d 249 [1977]).

MASSACHUSETTS: Court erred in forcing law firm to withdraw because member of firm "ought" to be witness re financial statements that could be filed without testimony (*Borman v. Borman,* 393 N.E. 2d 847 [1979]).

MARYLAND: Trial court abused discretion in refusing to conduct examination of five and a half-year-old witness, in open court or chambers, in custody battle (*Brandau v. Webster,* 382 A. 2d 1103 [1978]).

MISSOURI: Child under ten presumed incompetent (*MO Rev. Stat.* Sec. 491.060(2); to overcome the presumption, there must be "present understanding of, or intelligence to understand on instruction" (*State v. Starks,* 472 S.W. 2d 407 [1971]); understanding of "truth and falsity" *(State v. Sanders,* 553 S.W. 2nd 632 [1971]); and "capacity to translate into words the memory of such obligation" (*State v. Ball,* 529 S.W. 2d 901 [1976]); cannot impeach own witness (*State v. Kinne,* 372 S.W. 2d 62 [1963]); however, no risk in calling adverse party (*Wells v. Goforth,* 443 S.W. 2d 155 [1969]); if witness testimony is inconsistent with prior statements, and such is not known in advance (*State v. Ruff,* 589 S.W. 2d 322 [1979]); and party calling the witness is damaged (*State v. Woodard,* 499 S.W. 2d 553 [1973]). Missouri has not adopted the FRE 613 concept (*Missouri Evidence Restated* Sec. 613).

NEW JERSEY: Witness is disqualified if "incapable of expressing himself concerning the matter" or is incapable of understanding the duty of a witness to tell the truth" (Rule 17), and must either have personal knowledge, or experience, training or education (Rule 19) (*New Jersey Rules of Evidence*).

NEW YORK: Each case must consider facts relative to infant testimony and once admitted, jury can decide weight to be given testimony (*Bergren v. Reilly,* 407 N.Y.S. 2d 960 [1978]).

PENNSYLVANIA: Judge could let ninety-four-year-old testify (*Commonwealth v. Short,* 420 A. 2d 694 [1980]).

SOUTH CAROLINA: Cannot impeach own witness (*State v. Richburg,* 158 S.E. 2d 769 [1968]).

TENNESSEE: Statute providing person can be compelled to testify against spouse in criminal action is not invalid (*McCormick v. State,* 186 S.W. 95 [TENN. 1916]).

VIRGINIA: Divorced person can testify against former spouse for grand larceny of her property (*Stewart v. Commonwealth,* 252 S.E. 2d 329 [1979]).

Sec. 12.05 Non-FRE States—Opinions Admitting opinions that help the trier of the fact, "in the form of an opinion or otherwise" (Rule 702); permitting the expert to use hearsay if it is "type reasonably relied upon" (Rule 703); and admitting opinion on the ultimate fact to be decided, exemplify the federal concept on expert opinions. A review of a few "expert opinion" cases from states that have not adopted the federal rules is very helpful:

ALABAMA: Expert could tell jury point of impact of auto collision if he details the facts (*Dyer v. Traeger,* 357 So. 2d 328 [1978]).

CALIFORNIA: Expert cannot testify on issue if jury could draw conclusion "as easily and as intelligently" as expert (*Westbrooks v. State,* 219 CA Rep. 674 [1985]).

CONNECTICUT: "Peculiar knowledge or experience" required (*State v. Hanna,* 460 A. 2d 124 [1963]).

GEORGIA: Expert can testify on ultimate issue (*King v. Browning,* 268 S.E. 2d 653 [1980]). Expert can testify as to what benefits person entitled, if regulations given to jury (*Stewart v. State,* 268 S.E. 2d 906 [1980]).

ILLINOIS: Can testify "at the central hub of the controversy" (*Arnold N. May Builders v. Bruketta,* 377 N.E. 2nd 579 [1978]). Lay witness could testify soil muddy enough to show tire marks (*Gale v. Hockstra,* 375 N.E. 2d 456 [1978]).

INDIANA: Expert opinion as to speed, point of impact and mechanical failure are admissible, though it may "invade the province of the jury" (*Rosenbalm v. Winski,* 332 N.E. 2d 249 [1975]).

KANSAS: Expert cannot tell what action caused accident (*Lolliss v. Superior Sales,* 580 P. 2d 423 [1978]).

KENTUCKY: Opinion should not be limited by ultimate issue test (see *Commonwealth, Dept. of Highways v. Widner,* 388 S.W. 2d 583 [1965]).

LOUISIANA: With proper foundation, expert could testify as to defendant's "psychological capacity to commit a particular crime" (*State v. Carey,* 392 So. 2d 445 [1980]).

MASSACHUSETTS: Witness cannot give opinion as to credibility of his testimony or other testimony (*Commonwealth v. Dickinson,* 477 N.E. 2d 381 [1985]).

MARYLAND: Court not in error in refusing expert testimony as to whether defendant acted voluntarily (*Finke v. State,* 468 A. 2d 353 [1983]).

MISSOURI: Expert can testify if "jurors themselves are not capable, for want of experience or knowledge on the subject, to draw correct conclusions" (*Benjamin v. Metropolitan St. Ry Co,* 34 S.W. 590 [1896]). Question must be "hypothesized" unless expert knows all pertinent facts, and the basis "must appear in the evidence" (*State v. Johnson*, 504 S.W. 2d 334 [1973]). Expert cannot decide ultimate issue (*Trowbridge v. Fleming*, 269 S.W. 610 [1925]).

NEW JERSEY: Hypothetical not required (Rule 58 New Jersey Rules of Evidence). "Battered-woman's syndrome" proper subject of expert testimony (*State v. Kelly*, 478 A. 2d 364 [1984]).

NEW YORK: X rays and reports found in file of deceased's physician admitted as business record without expert opinion (*Stein v. Lebowitz Pine View Hotel, Inc.*, 489 N.Y.S. 2d 635 [1985]).

PENNSYLVANIA: Rule 704 is "best approach" (*Lewis v. Meller*, 393 A. 2d 941 [1978]). Officer cannot give opinion as to fault (*Gatling v. Rothman*, 407 A. 2d 387 [1979]). "Reasonable degree of medical certainty" (*Gradl v. Inouye*, 421 A. 2d 674 [1980]).

SOUTH CAROLINA: Experiments cannot be used in court unless it is shown the conditions are comparable (see *Beasley v. Ford Motor Co.*, 117 S.E. 2d 863 [1961]).

TENNESSEE: Liberal view given re no longer excluding opinion evidence that goes to ultimate issue (*National Life & A. Ins. Co. v. Follett*, 80 S.W. 2d 92 [1935]).

VIRGINIA: Experts must deal in "probabilities" not "possibilities" (*Spruill v. Commonwealth*, 271 S.E. 2d 419 [1980]).

Sec. 12.06 Non-FRE States—Hearsay   Long before the Federal Rules of Evidence were adopted, states were taking a hard look at the hearsay rule, and its exceptions. Since the adoption of FRE, the change has continued, in non-FRE states as well as in the states adopting the Federal Rules.

A review of a few cases in non-FRE states shows this trend:

ALABAMA: Spontaneous exclamations can be admitted (*Harris v. State*, 394 So. 2nd 96 [1981]). Mental hospital records admitted under Business Records Act (*Seay v. State*, 390 So. 2d 11 [1981]).

CALIFORNIA: Court talks of TRUSTWORTHINESS of an admission against penal interest (*People v. Chapman*, 50 CA App. 2d 872 [1975]). Deceased donor's statement admitted to show state of mind, but not that certain event occurred (*Estate of Truckenmiller*, 97 CA App. 3d 326 [1985]). Poems of defendant should have been admitted during penalty phase of murder trial, as non-hearsay for purpose of showing he was "sensitive individual who expressed himself in poetry," or as "mental state" exception (*People v. Harris*, 679 P. 2d 433 [1984]). Victim's fear of accused admitted only if victim's conduct conformed to that fear (*People v. Armendariz*, 693 P. 2d 243 [1984]).

Declarant's statement he intended to burn down house admitted to show he did burn down house (*People v. Earnest*, 53 CA App. 3d 747 [1975]).

CONNECTICUT: Report from Health Department showing substance was heroin was admitted as public record (*State v. Johnson*, 352 A. 2d 294 [1974]). Business records could have been prepared by others (*State v. Cosgrove*, 436 A. 2d 33 [1980]). Declaration must be made under circumstances that are "impartial and disinterested" (*Dimaggio v. Cannon*, 327 A. 2d 561 [1973]).

GEORGIA: Three-year-old girl's statement admitted as parts of res gestae, since "free from device or afterthought" (*Kilgore v. State*, 340 S.E. 2d 640 [1986]).

ILLINOIS: Where original witness and interpreter are both under oath, no hearsay problem (*People v. DeJesus*, 389 N.E. 2d 260 [1979]). Testator's statement admitted to prove agreement not to revoke will (*Schwebel v. Sheets*, 479 N.E. 2d 500 [1985]).

INDIANA: Evidence of reputation cannot be used to prove guilt (*Sumpter v. State*, 306 N.E. 2d 95 [1974]). Excited utterance of bystander admissible as long as "level of excitement which prevents the witness from fabricating testimony" (*Holmes v. State*, 480 N.E. 2d 916 [1985]).

KANSAS: Statute uses FRE test as to unavailability of witness (*Kansas Stat. Sec. 60-459(g)* [1988]). Journalism textbook admitted under statute where identified as authoritative in field of journalism (*Gobin v. Globe Publishing Co.*, 620 P. 2d 1163 [1980]). See also, "A Proposal For The Use of Otherwise Inadmissible Hearsay In Kansas Preliminary Examinations" (Tonkovich, 32 *U. Kansas Law Review* 837, Summer 1984).

KENTUCKY: "Fundamental test of cross-examination" still very important (*Kinder v. Commonwealth*, 306 S.W. 2d 265 [1957]). Evidence as to pedigree of animal not hearsay *(Hagedorn v. Reiser*, 221 S.W. 2d 633 [1949]).

LOUISIANA: Admitted evidence that other person, now deceased, committed the crime (*State v. Gilmore*, 332 So. 2d 789 [1976]). Exclamations of five-year-old made ten hours later admitted, since first opportunity to speak to close member of family (*State v. Adams*, 3394 So. 2d 1204 [1981]). Doctor can testify as to past medical history obtained from patient (*State v. Andrews*, 369 So. 2d 1049 [1979]).

MASSACHUSETTS: Witness can testify he examined records and found nothing, without bringing in records (*Commonwealth v. Scanlon*, 400 N.E. 2d 1265 [1980]). Public opinion poll admitted to show community standards if no bias (*Commonwealth v. Trainer*, 374 N.E. 2d 1216 [1978]).

MARYLAND: Declaration against interest has "inherent indicium of trustworthiness" (*Harris v. State*, 387 A. 2d 1152 [1978]). Woman denied fair trial where court excluded statement of victim that she was in fear of her life because husband of accused had threatened to kill her (*Foster v. State,* 464 A. 2d 986 [1983]). Statement by third person in reaction to defamatory statement is admitted as state-of-mind exception to show publication and damages (*Embrey v. Holly,* 429 A. 2d 251 [1981]). Psychiatrist cannot testify as to what patient told him when he merely examined patient to testify (*Candella v. Subsequent Injury Fund,* 353 A. 2d 263 [1976]).

MISSOURI: Hearsay must come from a source not subject to cross-examination (*Opponents to the Petition for Formation of the Community Care Nursing Home District v. Petitioners For . . . ,* 564 S.W. 2d 552 [1978]), and must be offered as proof of the matters therein stated" (*State v. Walker,* 484 S.W. 2nd 284 [1972]). Most federal exceptions accepted in Missouri, to some degree, (no learned treatise) (*Missouri Evidence Updated*), and though Missouri has not adopted an overall exception, the courts have talked about not excepting hearsay evidence because other proof was available (*Pietrowski v. Mykins,* 498 S.W. 2d 572 [1973]).

NEW JERSEY: "Youth and naivete" postpone the time of excitement, but are not substitutes for the "stress of a nervous excitement" that must be present for hearsay exception (*In Re C. A.,* 492 A. 2d 683 [1985]). Information from National Automobile Theft Bureau could be admitted re identification of auto if proper foundation laid as to Bureau's procedures (*State v. Lungsford,* 400 A. 2d 843 [1979]).

NEW YORK: "Spontaneous exclamation" extended to bystander (*People v. Caviness,* 379 N.Y.S. 2d 695 [1975]). Statement in hospital record that patient was intoxicated admitted as pertinent to "diagnosis and treatment" (*Campbell v. Manhattan & Bronx Surface Transit Operating Auth.,* 438 N.Y.S. 2d 87 [1981]).

PENNSYLVANIA: Statement on phone by victim to her mother that her boyfriend was about to kill her was admitted as "present sense impression" (talks of "indices of reliability") (*Commonwealth v. Coleman,* 326 A. 2d 387 [1974]). Hospital record admitted as to hospitalization, treatment and symptoms, but not as to opinions, diagnoses, and conclusions (*Commonwealth v. Seville,* 405 A. 2d 1262 [1979]).

SOUTH CAROLINA: "Excited utterance" plus "present sense impression" equal "res gestae," thus admitted (*State v. Blackburn,* 247 S.E. 2d 334 [1978]).

TENNESSEE: "Excited utterance" extends to bystander who was present, observed, and made statement based on the personal observation (*Underwood v. State,* 604 S.W. 2d 875 [1979]).

VIRGINIA: Statement is only hearsay when offered as an assertion to "evidence the truth of the matter asserted" (*Manetta v. Commonwealth,* 340 S.E. 2d 828 [1986]).

Sec. 12.07 Non-FRE States—Authentication and Identification—Writings, Recordings, Photographs

The FRE concept as to Authentication and Identification is based on showing "the matter in question is what its proponent claims (examples given in rule), and self-authentication.

Special statutes and case law in the non-FRE states have brought all states closer to the federal concept:

ALABAMA: Hospital record containing diagnosis by doctor was admitted (*Bailey v. Tennessee Coal, Iron & R. Co.,* 75 So. 2d 117 [ALA 1954]).

CALIFORNIA: Foundation must be laid for admission of city ordinance (*Higbe v. LaSalle,* 303 P. 2d 65 [1956]).

CONNECTICUT: Attesting witnesses must be produced or accounted for (*Lowenberg v. Wallace,* 166 A. 2 150 [1960]).

GEORGIA: Dead Man Statute does not apply to the state and its agencies (*Anderson v. Dept. of Family and Children Services,* 163 S.E. 2d 328 [1968]).

ILLINOIS: Army records showing history of psychiatric problems should not have been admitted (*T and D Co. v. Industrial Commission,* 219 N.E. 2d 486 [1966]).

INDIANA: State Board of Accounts records "probably" admissible (*Etherton v. Wyatt,* 293 N.E. 2d 43 [1973]).

KANSAS: County real estate appraiser cannot testify as to value another appraiser put on certain property (*Love v. School District,* 391 P. 2d 152 [1964]).

KENTUCKY: Photo of "comparable" house used by appraiser admitted if it can be identified (*Robinette v. Commission of Kentucky Department of Highways,* 380 S.W. 2d 78 [1964]).

LOUISIANA: Order from city advising installation of automatic exhaust system cannot be used in suit in which such a system was issue in lawsuit (*Cupping v. Bertolino,* 245 S. 2d 735 [1971]).

MASSACHUSETTS: Statute making insurance commissioner's report admissible in suits he files, does not make it admissible in private litigation (*Commissioner of Insurance v. First National Bank of Boston,* 223 N.E. 2d 684 [1966]).

MARYLAND: Computer printout becomes "certified" when attached to certified document ordered at the same time (*Payne v. Payne,* 366 A. 2d 405 [1976]).

MISSOURI: Foundation for admitting tape recording includes (a) device was capable of taking testimony, (b) operator was competent, (c) recording authentic and correct, (d) no changes, additions or deletions made, (e) proper preservation of recording, (f) speakers identified, and (g) testimony was voluntarily elicited (*State v. Spica,* 389 S.W. 2d 35 [1965]). Business record could be identified by "custodian or other qualified witness" (*MO Rev. Stat.,* Sec. 490.680). Self-authentication only where by statute, so not as broad as federal rule. Computer printouts admitted, and are business record (*Union Station v. Mansion House Center North Development Co.,* 494 S.W. 2d 309 [1973]).

NEW JERSEY: Modified federal rule on authentication (Rules 67, 68 and 69 *New Jersey Rules of Evidence*).

NEW YORK: All right to show jury color photo of quadriplegic on Stryker frame with attachments to scalp (*Capara v. Chrysler Corp.,* 423 N.Y.S. 2d 694 [1979]).

PENNSYLVANIA: Memo by electrical inspector as to what caused fire, not admitted to show what caused fire (*Githens, Rex etc. v. Wildstein,* 236 A. 2d 792 [1968]).

SOUTH CAROLINA: The part of the letter about the doctor's treatment was admissible, but not parts dealing with his self-serving statements that he gave unnecessary treatment to patients, said statements being made in defense of himself (*Woodward v. South Carolina Family,* 282 S.E. 2d 99 [1981]).

TENNESSEE: Court has much discretion in admitting business records under Uniform Business Records Evidence Act (*Tullahoma v. Gillespi,* 405 S.W. 2d 657 [1966]).

VIRGINIA: X-ray photo admitted if authenticated (*Meade v. Belcher,* 188 S.E. 2d 211 [1972]).

Article Ten of the Federal Rules, Contents of Writings Recordings and Photographs, modernized the Best Evidence Rule, without even using the term. It deals specifically with use of duplicates and other substitutes for originals, modernizing the writing, recording, and photograph terms, admission of public records, use of summaries, use of admissions as to writings, and records of the court and jury relative to admission of writings, recordings, and photographs.

The following cases show what the non-FRE states are doing in this area of law:

ALABAMA: Where existence of insurance policy, not its contents, was being proved, policy need not be produced (*Adams v. Queen Insurance Co. of America,* 88 So. 2d 331 [1956]).

CALIFORNIA: Books need not be produced where witness was telling about "facts within his knowledge," not "contents of the books" (*Vickter v. Pan Pacific Sales Corp.,* 239 P. 2d 463 [1952]).

CONNECTICUT: Witness who heard a statement can testify as to it if witness remembers it, though verbatim transcript exists (*State v. Moynahan,* 325 A. 2d 199 [1973]).

GEORGIA: Receipts and cancelled checks would help prove payment, but the act of paying can be proven without such papers (*Hale v. Hale,* 33 S.E. 2d 441 [GA 1945]).

ILLINOIS: Secondary evidence can be used where lost best evidence can be explained (*Lueth v. Goodkneckt,* 177 N.E. 690 [ILL 1931]).

INDIANA: Court admitted oral testimony to show corporate minutes were not accurate and part of fraud (*Floyd v. Jay County Rural Electric Membership Corp.,* 405 N.E. 2d 630 [IND. App 1980]).

KANSAS: Copy of telegraphic message admitted when proved to be correct (*Western Union Teleg. Co. v. Collins,* 25 P. 187 [KA 1890]).

KENTUCKY: Witness could testify church merged, though the merger might also be proven through the document setting forth the merger (*Vogler v. Salem Primitive Baptist Church,* 415 S.W. 2d 72 [1967]).

LOUISIANA: To show document you must use first, original, then copy, and if neither available then parol evidence (*Hilton v. Hilton,* 165 So. 2d 332 [1964]).

MASSACHUSETTS: Doctor can give opinion without examining patient, and there can be no comment as to why treating physician did not testify (*Kaye v. New Halal,* 277 N.E. 2d 697 [1971]).

MARYLAND: Where company kept records of defects, such records can establish prima facie evidence of defect (*Glen Alden Corp. v. Duvall,* 215 A. 2d 155 [1965]).

MISSOURI: To prove a disputed fact contained in a written document, that document must be produced (*Straughan v. Murphy,* 484 S.W. 2d 465 [1972]). If the evidence exists in writing, and otherwise, either may be used (*Jourdan v. Gilmore,* 638 S.W. 2d 763 [1982]).

NEW JERSEY: Modified federal rule on writings (best evidence, Rule 70) (*New Jersey Rules of Evidence*).

NEW YORK: To show work was "extra" on construction job, plans and contract must be produced (*Taft v. Little,* 70 N.E. 211 [N.Y. 1904]).

PENNSYLVANIA: Prosecution of possession of numbers slips need not include the slips, since evidence must show they are slips, not contents of slips (*Commonwealth v. Gazal,* 137 A. 2d 814 [1958]).

SOUTH CAROLINA: Where claim that failure of defendant to follow its own regulation caused death, that regulation must be produced (*Price v. Richmond & DRR,* 17 S.E. 732 [1892]).

TENNESSEE: To show services of publishing advertisement in newspaper, newspaper need not be produced (*Enloe v. Hall,* 1 Humph. 303 [TENN 1939]).

VIRGINIA: The ambiguity must be apparent on the face of the document before parol evidence can be used (*Cohan v. Thurston,* 292 S.E. 2d 45 [1982]).

Table One

The following states adopted the Federal Rules of Evidence by 1989:

1. ALASKA: 1979, by Supreme Court; Alaska Rules of Evidence
2. ARIZONA: 1977, by Supreme Court; Arizona Rules of Evidence
3. ARKANSAS: 1975, by Legislature, 1976 by Supreme Court; Arkansas Rules of Evidence
4. COLORADO: 1980, Supreme Court; Colorado Rules of Evidence
5. DELAWARE: 1980, by Supreme Court; Delaware Uniform Rules of Evidence
6. FLORIDA: 1978, by Legislature, effective 1981; Florida Statutes Annotated, Sec. 90.101 et. seq.
7. HAWAII: 1979, by Legislature, effective 1981; Hawaiian Rules of Evidence; Hawaiian Revised Statutes, Title 33, Chapter 626
8. IDAHO: 1985, by Supreme Court; Idaho Rules of Evidence
9. IOWA: 1983, by Legislature; Iowa Rules of Evidence
10. MAINE: 1975, by Supreme Judicial Court of Maine, effective 1976; Maine Rules of Evidence; Revised Statutes Annotated, Vol. 8, Title 14, 1975, Supp. Pamphlet
11. MICHIGAN: 1978, by Supreme Court; Michigan Rules of Evidence, 402 Mich lxxxviii
12. MINNESOTA: 1977, by Supreme Court; Rules of Evidence
13. MISSISSIPPI: 1985, by Supreme Court, effective 1986; Mississippi Rules of Evidence
14. MONTANA: 1976, by Supreme Court, effective 1977; Montana Rules of Evidence; 7 Montana Rev. Codes (1977 Supp.)
15. NEBRASKA: 1975, by Legislature, effective 1976; Nebraska Rules of Evidence; Nebraska Revised Statutes, Sec. 1943, Chapter 27
16. NEVADA: 1971, by Legislature; Nevada Revised Statutes, Sec. 47.020 et. seq.
17. NEW HAMPSHIRE: 1985, by Supreme Court; New Hampshire Rules of Evidence

18. NEW MEXICO: 1973, amended 1976 to comply with FRE, by Supreme Court; amended further, 1983; New Mexico Rules of Evidence; 4 N.M. Statutes Annotated, Sec. 20-4-101 et. seq.

19. NORTH CAROLINA: 1983, by Legislature, effective 1984; North Carolina Rules of Evidence

20. NORTH DAKOTA: 1976, by Supreme Court, effective 1977; North Dakota Rules of Evidence

21. OHIO: 1990, by Supreme Court; Ohio Rules of Evidence (may be cited as Evidence Rule)

22. OKLAHOMA: 1978, by Legislature; Oklahoma Evidence Code; Twelve Oklahoma Statutes, Sec. 21-1-3103

23. OREGON: 1982, by Legislature; Oregon Evidence Code

24. RHODE ISLAND: 1987, by Supreme Court; Rhode Island Rules of Evidence

25. SOUTH DAKOTA: 1978, by Supreme Court, effective 1988 (except provisions re privilege); South Dakota Rules of Evidence

26. TEXAS: 1982, by Supreme Court, effective 1983, amended 1984; Texas Rules of Evidence

27. UTAH: 1983, by Supreme Court; Utah Rules of Evidence

28. WASHINGTON: 1978, by Supreme Court, effective 1979; Washington Rules of Evidence; 91 WA2d 1117, et. seq.

29. WEST VIRGINIA: 1984, by Supreme Court of Appeals, effective 1985; West Virginia Rules of Evidence

30. WISCONSIN: 1973, by Supreme Court, effective 1974; Wisconsin Rules of Evidence; 59 WI2nd; Wisconsin Statutes Annotated, Sec. 901.01 et. seq.

31. WYOMING: 1977, by Supreme Court, effective 1978; Wyoming Rules of Evidence

Table Two

The law of evidence in states that have not adopted the Federal Rules of Evidence can be found:

1. ALABAMA: Certain statutes and case decisions. (See Code of Alabama, Title 12-21-1 et. seq.)

2. CALIFORNIA: Certain statutes and case decisions. (See West Annotated California Codes: Evidence Code; Code of Civil Procedure.)

3. CONNECTICUT: Certain statutes and case decisions. (See Connecticut General Statutes Annotated, Ch. 899 Sec. 52-143 et. seq.)

4. GEORGIA: Certain statutes and case decisions. (See Georgia Statutes, Title 24: Evidence, Sec. 24-1-1 et. seq.)

5. ILLINOIS: Certain statutes and case decisions. Illinois Rules.

6. INDIANA: Certain statutes and case decisions. (See West's Annotated Indiana Code, Title 34 Article 3 Ch. 1.)

7. KANSAS: Certain statutes and case decisions. (See Code of Civil Procedure: Kansas Statutes Annotated.)

8. KENTUCKY: Certain statutes and case decisions.

9. LOUISIANA: Certain statutes and case decisions. (See Louisiana Statutes Annotated, 13-3711 et. seq.)

10. MARYLAND: Certain statutes and case decisions.

11. MASSACHUSETTS: Certain statutes and case decisions. Massachusetts had not adopted its proposed rules, similar to federal rules.

12. MISSOURI: Certain statutes and case decisions. (See *MISSOURI EVIDENCE RESTATED,* the Missouri Bar Task Force's "compilation of evidence principles written in the style and format of the Federal Rules of Evidence to reflect the evidence law of Missouri.")

13. NEW JERSEY: Certain statutes and case decisions (New Jersey Rules of Evidence). New Jersey is studying Federal Rules.

14. PENNSYLVANIA: Certain statutes and case decisions. (See Purdon's Pennsylvania Consolidated Statutes, Title 42 Ch. 61 Sec. 610 et. seq.)

15. SOUTH CAROLINA: Certain statutes and case decisions. (See Code of Ann. Statutes of South Carolina Title 19 Sec. 19-1-10 et. seq.)

16. TENNESSEE: Certain statutes and case decisions.

17. VIRGINIA: Certain statutes and case decisions.

APPENDIX

FEDERAL RULES OF EVIDENCE

Federal Rules of Evidence

As Amended To 1989

ARTICLE ONE: GENERAL PROVISIONS

Rule 101. Scope

These rules govern proceedings in the courts of the United States and before United States bankruptcy judges and United States magistrates, to the extent and with the exceptions stated in rule 1101.

Rule 102. Purpose and Construction

These rules shall be construed to secure fairness in administration, elimination of unjustifiable expense and delay, and promotion of growth and development of the law of evidence to the end that the truth may be ascertained and proceedings justly determined.

Rule 103. Rulings on Evidence

(a) **Effect of erroneous ruling.** Error may not be predicated upon a ruling which admits or excludes evidence unless a substantial right of the party is affected, and

(1) **Objection.** In case the ruling is one admitting evidence, a timely objection or motion to strike appears of record, stating the specific ground of objection, if the specific ground was not apparent from the context; or

(2) **Offer of proof.** In case the ruling is one excluding evidence, the substance of the evidence was made known to the court by offer or was apparent from the context within which questions were asked.

(b) **Record of offer and ruling.** The court may add any other or further statement which shows the character of the evidence, the form in which it was offered, the objection made, and the ruling thereon. It may direct the making of an offer in question and answer form.

(c) **Hearing of jury.** In jury cases, proceedings shall be conducted, to the extent practicable, so as to prevent inadmissible evidence from being suggested to the jury by any means, such as making statements or offers of proof or asking questions in the hearing of the jury.

(d) Plain error. Nothing in this rule precludes taking notice of plain errors affecting substantial rights although they were not brought to the attention of the court.

Rule 104. Preliminary Questions

(a) Questions of admissibility generally. Preliminary questions concerning the qualification of a person to be a witness, the existence of a privilege, or the admissibility of evidence shall be determined by the court, subject to the provisions of subdivision (b). In making its determination it is not bound by the rules of evidence except those with respect to privileges.

(b) Relevancy conditioned on fact. When the relevancy of evidence depends upon the fulfillment of a condition of fact, the court shall admit it upon, or subject to, the introduction of evidence sufficient to support a finding of the fulfillment of the condition.

(c) Hearing of Jury. Hearings on the admissibility of confessions shall in all cases be conducted out of the hearing of the jury. Hearings on other preliminary matters shall be so conducted when the interests of justice require, or when an accused is a witness and so requests.

(d) Testimony by accused. The accused does not, by testifying upon a preliminary matter, become subject to cross-examination as to other issues in the case.

(e) Weight and Credibility. This rule does not limit the right of a party to introduce before the jury evidence relevant to weight or credibility.

Rule 105. Limited Admissibility

When evidence which is admissible as to one party or for one purpose but not admissible as to another party or for another purpose is admitted, the court, upon request, shall restrict the evidence to its proper scope and instruct the jury accordingly.

Rule 106. Remainder of or Related Writings or Recorded Statements

When a writing or recorded statement or part thereof is introduced by a party, an adverse party may require the introduction at that time of any other part or any other writing or recorded statement which ought in fairness to be considered contemporaneously with it.

ARTICLE TWO: JUDICIAL NOTICE

Rule 201. Judicial Notice of Adjudicative Facts

(a) Scope of rule. This rule governs only judicial notice of adjudicative facts.

(b) Kinds of facts. A judicially noticed fact must be one not subject to reasonable dispute in that it is either (1) generally known within the territorial jurisdiction of the trial court or (2) capable of accurate and ready determination by resort to sources whose accuracy cannot reasonably be questioned.

(c) When discretionary. A court may take judicial notice, whether requested or not.

(d) When mandatory. A court shall take judicial notice if requested by a party and supplied with the necessary information.

(e) Opportunity to be heard. A party is entitled upon timely request to an opportunity to be heard as to the propriety of taking judicial notice and the tenor of the matter noticed. In the absence of prior notification, the request may be made after judicial notice has been taken.

(f) Time of taking notice. Judicial notice may be taken at any stage of the proceeding.

(g) Instructing jury. In a civil action or proceeding, the court shall instruct the jury to accept as conclusive any fact judicially noticed. In a criminal case, the court shall instruct the jury that it may, but is not required to, accept as conclusive any fact judicially noticed.

ARTICLE THREE: PRESUMPTIONS IN CIVIL ACTIONS AND PROCEEDINGS

Rule 301. Presumptions in General in Civil Actions and Proceedings

In all civil actions and proceedings not otherwise provided for by Act of Congress or by these rules, a presumption imposes on the party against whom it is directed the burden of going forward with evidence to rebut or meet the presumption, but does not shift to such party the burden of proof in the sense of the risk of nonpersuasion, which remains throughout the trial upon the party on whom it was originally cast.

Rule 302. Applicability of State Law in Civil Actions and Proceedings

In civil actions and proceedings, the effect of a presumption respecting a fact which is an element of a claim or defense as to which State law supplies the rule of decision is determined in accordance with State law.

ARTICLE FOUR: RELEVANCY AND ITS LIMITS

Rule 401. Definition of "Relevant Evidence"

"Relevant evidence" means evidence having any tendency to make the existence of any fact that is of consequence to the determination of the action more probable or less probable than it would be without the evidence.

Rule 402. Relevant Evidence Generally Admissible; Irrelevant Evidence Inadmissible

All relevant evidence is admissible, except as otherwise provided by the Constitution of the United States, by Act of Congress, by these rules, or by other rules prescribed by the Supreme Court pursuant to statutory authority. Evidence which is not relevant is not admissible.

Rule 403. Exclusion of Relevant Evidence on Grounds of Prejudice, Confusion, or Waste of Time

Although relevant, evidence may be excluded if its probative value is substantially outweighed by the danger of unfair prejudice, confusion of the issues, or misleading the jury, or by considerations of undue delay, waste of time, or needless presentation of cumulative evidence.

Rule 404. Character Evidence Not Admissible to Prove Conduct; Exceptions; Other Crimes

(a) **Character evidence generally.** Evidence of a person's character or a trait of character is not admissible for the purpose of proving action in conformity therewith on a particular occasion, except:

(1) **Character of accused.** Evidence of a pertinent trait of character offered by an accused, or by the prosecution to rebut the same;

(2) **Character of victim.** Evidence of a pertinent trait of character of the victim of the crime offered by an accused,[1] or by

the prosecution to rebut the same, or evidence of a character trait of peacefulness of the victim offered by the prosecution in a homicide case to rebut evidence that the victim was the first aggressor;

(3) **Character of witness.** Evidence of the character of a witness, as provided in rules 607, 608, and 609.

(b) **Other crimes, wrongs, or acts.** Evidence of other crimes, wrongs, or acts is not admissible to prove the character of a person in order to show action in conformity therewith. It may, however, be admissible for other purposes, such as proof of motive, opportunity, intent, preparation, plan, knowledge, identity, or absence of mistake or accident.

Rule 405. Methods of Proving Character

(a) **Reputation or opinion.** In all cases in which evidence of character or a trait of character of a person is admissible, proof may be made by testimony as to reputation or by testimony in the form of an opinion. On cross-examination, inquiry is allowable into relevant specific instances of conduct.

(b) **Specific instances of conduct.** In cases in which character or a trait of character of a person is an essential element of a charge, claim, or defense, proof may also be made of specific instances of that person's conduct.

Rule 406. Habit; Routine Practice

Evidence of the habit of a person or of the routine practice of an organization, whether corroborated or not and regardless of the presence of eyewitnesses, is relevant to prove that the conduct of the person or organization on a particular occasion was in conformity with the habit or routine practice.

Rule 407. Subsequent Remedial Measures

When, after an event, measures are taken which, if taken previously, would have made the event less likely to occur, evidence of the subsequent measures is not admissible to prove negligence or culpable conduct in connection with the event. This rule does not require the exclusion of evidence of subsequent measures when offered for another purpose, such as proving ownership, control, or feasibility of precautionary measures, if controverted, or impeachment.

Rule 408. Compromise and Offers to Compromise

Evidence of (1) furnishing or offering or promising to furnish, or (2) accepting or offering or promising to accept, a valuable consideration in compromising or attempting to compromise a claim which was disputed as to either validity or amount, is not admissible to prove liability for or invalidity of the claim or its amount. Evidence of conduct or statements made in compromise negotiations is likewise not admissible. This rule does not require the exclusion of any evidence otherwise discoverable merely because it is presented in the course of compromise negotiations. This rule also does not require exclusion when the evidence is offered for another purpose, such as proving bias or prejudice of a witness, negativing a contention of undue delay, or proving an effort to obstruct a criminal investigation or prosecution.

Rule 409. Payment of Medical and Similar Expenses

Evidence of furnishing or offering or promising to pay medical, hospital, or similar expenses occasioned by an injury is not admissible to prove liability for the injury.

Rule 410. Inadmissibility of Pleas, Plea Discussions, and Related Statements

Except as otherwise provided in this rule, evidence of the following is not, in any civil or criminal proceeding, admissible against the defendant who made the plea or was a participant in the plea discussions:

(1) a plea of guilty which was later withdrawn;

(2) a plea of nolo contendere;

(3) any statement made in the course of any proceedings under Rule 11 of the Federal Rules of Criminal Procedure or comparable state procedure regarding either of the foregoing pleas; or

(4) any statement made in the course of plea discussions with an attorney for the prosecuting authority which do not result in a plea of guilty or which result in a plea of guilty later withdrawn.

However, such a statement is admissible (i) in any proceeding wherein another statement made in the course of the same plea or plea discussions has been introduced and the statement ought in fairness be considered contemporaneously with it, or (ii) in a criminal proceeding for perjury or false statement if the statement was made by the defendant under oath, on the record and in the presence of counsel.

Rule 411. Liability Insurance

Evidence that a person was or was not insured against liability is not admissible upon the issue whether the person acted negligently or otherwise wrongfully. This rule does not require the exclusion of evidence of insurance against liability when offered for another purpose, such as proof of agency, ownership, or control, or bias or prejudice of a witness.

Rule 412. Rape Cases; Relevance of Victim's Past Behavior

(a) Notwithstanding any other provision of law, in a criminal case in which a person is accused of rape or of assault with intent to commit rape, reputation or opinion evidence of the past sexual behavior of an alleged victim of such rape or assault is not admissible.

(b) Notwithstanding any other provision of law, in a criminal case in which a person is accused of rape or of assault with intent to commit rape, evidence of a victim's past sexual behavior other than reputation or opinion evidence is also not admissible, unless such evidence other than reputation or opinion evidence is—

(1) admitted in accordance with subdivisions (c)(1) and (c)
(2) and is constitutionally required to be admitted; or

(2) admitted in accordance with subdivision (c) and is evidence of—

(A) past sexual behavior with persons other than the accused, offered by the accused upon the issue of whether the accused was or was not, with respect to the alleged victim, the source of semen or injury; or

(B) past sexual behavior with the accused and is offered by the accused upon the issue of whether the alleged victim consented to the sexual behavior with respect to which rape or assault is alleged.

(c)(1) If the person accused of committing rape or assault with intent to commit rape intends to offer under subdivision (b) evidence of specific instances of the alleged victim's past sexual behavior, the accused shall make a written motion to offer such evidence not later than fifteen days before the date on which the trial in which such evidence is to be offered is scheduled to begin, except that the court may allow the motion to be made at a later date, including during trial, if the court determines either that the evidence is newly discovered and could not have been obtained earlier through the exercise of due diligence or that the issue to which such evidence relates has newly arisen in the case. Any motion made under this paragraph shall be served on all other parties and on the alleged victim.

(2) The motion described in paragraph (1) shall be accompanied by a written offer of proof. If the court determines that the offer of proof contains evidence described in subdivision (b), the court shall order a hearing in chambers to determine if such evidence is admissible. At such hearing the parties may call witnesses, including the alleged victim, and offer relevant evidence. Notwithstanding subdivision (b) of rule 104, if the relevancy of the evidence which the accused seeks to offer in the trial depends upon the fulfillment of a condition of fact, the court, at the hearing in chambers or at a subsequent hearing in chambers scheduled for such purpose, shall accept evidence on the issue of whether such condition of fact is fulfilled and shall determine such issue.

(3) If the court determines on the basis of the hearing described in paragraph (2) that the evidence which the accused seeks to offer is relevant and that the probative value of such evidence outweighs the danger of unfair prejudice, such evidence shall be admissible in the trial to the extent an order made by the court specifies evidence which may be offered and areas with respect to which the alleged victim may be examined or cross-examined.

(d) For purposes of this rule, the term "past sexual behavior" means sexual behavior other than the sexual behavior with respect to which rape or assault with intent to commit rape is alleged.

ARTICLE FIVE: PRIVILEGES

Rule 501.   General Rule

Except as otherwise required by the Constitution of the United States or provided by Act of Congress or in rules prescribed by the Supreme Court pursuant to statutory authority, the privilege of a witness, person, government, State, or political subdivision thereof shall be governed by the principles of the common law as they may be interpreted by the courts of the United States in the light of reason and experience. However, in civil actions and proceedings, with respect to an element of a claim or defense as to which State law supplies the rule of decision, the privilege of a witness, person, government, State, or political subdivision thereof shall be determined in accordance with State law.

ARTICLE SIX: WITNESSES

Rule 601. General Rule of Competency

Every person is competent to be a witness except as otherwise provided in these rules. However, in civil actions and proceedings, with respect to an element of a claim or defense as to which State law supplies the rule of decision, the competency of a witness shall be determined in accordance with State law.

Rule 602. Lack of Personal Knowledge

A witness may not testify to a matter unless evidence is introduced sufficient to support a finding that the witness has personal knowledge of the matter. Evidence to prove personal knowledge may, but need not, consist of the witness' own testimony. This rule is subject to the provisions of rule 703, relating to opinion testimony by expert witnesses.

Rule 603. Oath or Affirmation

Before testifying, every witness shall be required to declare that the witness will testify truthfully, by oath or affirmation administered in a form calculated to awaken the witness' conscience and impress the witness' mind with the duty to do so.

Rule 604. Interpreters

An interpreter is subject to the provisions of these rules relating to qualification as an expert and the administration of an oath or affirmation to make a true translation.

Rule 605. Competency of Judge as Witness

The judge presiding at the trial may not testify in that trial as a witness. No objection need be made in order to preserve the point.

Rule 606. Competency of Juror as Witness

(a) **At the trial.** A member of the jury may not testify as a witness before that jury in the trial of the case in which the juror is sitting. If the juror is called so to testify, the opposing party shall be afforded an opportunity to object out of the presence of the jury.

(b) Inquiry into validity of verdict or indictment. Upon an inquiry into the validity of a verdict or indictment, a juror may not testify as to any matter or statement occurring during the course of the jury's deliberations or to the effect of anything upon that or any other juror's mind or emotions as influencing the juror to assent to or dissent from the verdict or indictment or concerning the juror's mental processes in connection therewith, except that a juror may testify on the question whether extraneous prejudicial information was improperly brought to the jury's attention or whether any outside influence was improperly brought to bear upon any juror. Nor may a juror's affidavit or evidence of any statement by the juror concerning a matter about which the juror would be precluded from testifying be received for these purposes.

Rule 607. Who May Impeach

The credibility of a witness may be attacked by any party, including the party calling the witness.

Rule 608. Evidence of Character and Conduct of Witness

(a) Opinion and reputation evidence of character. The credibility of a witness may be attacked or supported by evidence in the form of opinion or reputation, but subject to these limitations: (1) the evidence may refer only to character for truthfulness or untruthfulness, and (2) evidence of truthful character is admissible only after the character of the witness for truthfulness has been attacked by opinion or reputation evidence or otherwise.

(b) Specific instances of conduct. Specific instances of the conduct of a witness, for the purpose of attacking or supporting the witness' credibility, other than conviction of crime as provided in rule 609, may not be proved by extrinsic evidence. They may, however, in the discretion of the court, if probative of truthfulness or untruthfulness, be inquired into on cross-examination of the witness (1) concerning the witness' character for truthfulness or untruthfulness, or (2) concerning the character for truthfulness or untruthfulness of another witness as to which character the witness being cross-examined has testified.

The giving of testimony, whether by an accused or by any other witness, does not operate as a waiver of the accused's or the witness' privilege against self-incrimination when examined with respect to matters which relate only to credibility.

Rule 609. Impeachment by Evidence of Conviction of Crime

(a) **General rule.** For the purpose of attacking the credibility of a witness, evidence that the witness has been convicted of a crime shall be admitted if elicited from the witness or established by public record during cross-examination but only if the crime (1) was punishable by death or imprisonment in excess of one year under the law under which the witness was convicted, and the court determines that the probative value of admitting this evidence outweighs its prejudicial effect to the defendant, or (2) involved dishonesty or false statement, regardless of the punishment.

(b) **Time limit.** Evidence of a conviction under this rule is not admissible if a period of more than ten years has elapsed since the date of the conviction or of the release of the witness from the confinement imposed for that conviction, whichever is the later date, unless the court determines, in the interests of justice, that the probative value of the conviction supported by specific facts and circumstances substantially outweighs its prejudicial effect. However, evidence of a conviction more than 10 years old as calculated herein, is not admissible unless the proponent gives to the adverse party sufficient advance written notice of intent to use such evidence to provide the adverse party with a fair opportunity to contest the use of such evidence.

(c) **Effect of pardon, annulment, or certificate of rehabilitation.** Evidence of a conviction is not admissible under this rule if (1) the conviction has been the subject of a pardon, annulment, certificate of rehabilitation, or other equivalent procedure based on a finding of the rehabilitation of the person convicted, and that person has not been convicted of a subsequent crime which was punishable by death or imprisonment in excess of one year, or (2) the conviction has been the subject of a pardon, annulment, or other equivalent procedure based on a finding of innocence.

(d) **Juvenile adjudications.** Evidence of juvenile adjudications is generally not admissible under this rule. The court may, however, in a criminal case allow evidence of a juvenile adjudication of a witness other than the accused if conviction of the offense would be admissible to attack the credibility of an adult and the court is satisfied that admission in evidence is necessary for a fair determination of the issue of guilt or innocence.

(e) **Pendency of appeal.** The pendency of an appeal therefrom does not render evidence of a conviction inadmissible. Evidence of the pendency of an appeal is admissible.

Rule 610.   Religious Beliefs or Opinions

Evidence of the beliefs or opinions of a witness on matters of religion is not admissible for the purpose of showing that by reason of their nature the witness' credibility is impaired or enhanced.

Rule 611.   Mode and Order of Interrogation and Presentation

(a) **Control by court.** The court shall exercise reasonable control over the mode and order of interrogating witnesses and presenting evidence so as to (1) make the interrogation and presentation effective for the ascertainment of the truth, (2) avoid needless consumption of time, and (3) protect witnesses from harassment or undue embarrassment.

(b) **Scope of cross-examination.** Cross-examination should be limited to the subject matter of the direct examination and matters affecting the credibility of the witness. The court may, in the exercise of discretion, permit inquiry into additional matters as if on direct examination.

(c) **Leading questions.** Leading questions should not be used on the direct examination of a witness except as may be necessary to develop the witness' testimony. Ordinarily leading questions should be permitted on cross-examination. When a party calls a hostile witness, an adverse party, or a witness identified with an adverse party, interrogation may be by leading questions.

Rule 612.   Writing Used to Refresh Memory

Except as otherwise provided in criminal proceedings by section 3500 of title 18, United States Code, if a witness uses a writing to refresh memory for the purpose of testifying, either—

(1) while testifying, or

(2) before testifying, if the court in its discretion determines it is necessary in the interests of justice,

an adverse party is entitled to have the writing produced at the hearing, to inspect it, to cross-examine the witness thereon, and to introduce in evidence those portions which relate to the testimony of the witness. If it is claimed that the writing contains matters not related to the subject matter of the testimony the court shall examine the writing in camera, excise any portions not so related, and order delivery of the remainder to the party entitled thereto. Any portion withheld over objections shall be preserved and made available to the appellate court in the event of an appeal. If a writing is not produced or delivered pursuant to order under this rule, the court shall make any order justice requires, except that in criminal cases when the prosecution elects not to comply, the order shall be one striking the testimony or, if the court in its discretion determines that the interests of justice so require, declaring a mistrial.

Rule 613. Prior Statements of Witnesses

(a) **Examining witness concerning prior statement.** In examining a witness concerning a prior statement made by the witness, whether written or not, the statement need not be shown nor its contents disclosed to the witness at that time, but on request the same shall be shown or disclosed to opposing counsel.

(b) **Extrinsic evidence of prior inconsistent statement of witness.** Extrinsic evidence of a prior inconsistent statement by a witness is not admissible unless the witness is afforded an opportunity to explain or deny the same and the opposite party is afforded an opportunity to interrogate the witness thereon, or the interests of justice otherwise require. This provision does not apply to admissions of a party-opponent as defined in rule 801(d)(2).

Rule 614. Calling and Interrogation of Witnesses by Court

(a) **Calling by court.** The court may, on its own motion or at the suggestion of a party, call witnesses, and all parties are entitled to cross-examine witnesses thus called.

(b) **Interrogation by court.** The court may interrogate witnesses, whether called by itself or by a party.

(c) **Objections.** Objections to the calling of witnesses by the court or to interrogation by it may be made at the time or at the next available opportunity when the jury is not present.

Rule 615. Exclusion of Witnesses

At the request of a party the court shall order witnesses excluded so that they cannot hear the testimony of other witnesses and it may make the order of its own motion. This rule does not authorize exclusion of (1) a party who is a natural person, or (2) an officer or employee of a party which is not a natural person designated as its representative by its attorney, or (3) a person whose presence is shown by a party to be essential to the presentation of the party's cause.

ARTICLE SEVEN: OPINIONS AND EXPERT TESTIMONY

Rule 701. Opinion Testimony by Lay Witnesses

If the witness is not testifying as an expert, the witness' testimony in the form of opinions or inferences is limited to those opinions or inferences which are (a) rationally based on the perception of the witness and (b) helpful to a clear understanding of the witness' testimony or the determination of a fact in issue.

Rule 702. Testimony by Experts

If scientific, technical, or other specialized knowledge will assist the trier of fact to understand the evidence or to determine a fact in issue, a witness qualified as an expert by knowledge, skill, experience, training, or education, may testify thereto in the form of an opinion or otherwise.

Rule 703. Bases of Opinion Testimony by Experts

The facts or data in the particular case upon which an expert bases an opinion or inference may be those perceived by or made known to the expert at or before the hearing. If of a type reasonably relied upon by experts in the particular field in forming opinions or inferences upon the subject, the facts or data need not be admissible in evidence.

Rule 704. Opinion on Ultimate Issue

(a) Except as provided in subdivision (b), testimony in the form of an opinion or inference otherwise admissible is not objectionable because it embraces an ultimate issue to be decided by the trier of fact.

(b) No expert witness testifying with respect to the mental state or condition of a defendant in a criminal case may state an opinion or inference as to whether the defendant did or did not have the mental state or condition constituting an element of the crime charged or of a defense thereto. Such ultimate issues are matters for the trier of fact alone.

Rule 705. Disclosure of Facts or Data Underlying Expert Opinion

The expert may testify in terms of opinion or inference and give reasons therefor without prior disclosure of the underlying facts or data, unless the court requires otherwise. The expert may in any event be required to disclose the underlying facts or data on cross-examination.

Rule 706. Court Appointed Experts

(a) **Appointment.** The court may on its own motion or on the motion of any party enter an order to show cause why expert witnesses should not be appointed, and may request the parties to submit nominations. The court may appoint any expert witnesses agreed upon by the parties, and may appoint expert witnesses of its own selection. An expert witness shall not be appointed by the court unless the witness consents to act. A witness so appointed shall be informed of the witness' duties by the court in writing, a copy of which shall be filed with the clerk, or at a conference in which the parties shall have opportunity to participate. A witness so appointed shall advise the parties of the witness' findings, if any; the witness' deposition may be taken by any party; and the witness may be called to testify by the court or any party. The witness shall be subject to cross-examination by each party, including a party calling the witness.

(b) **Compensation.** Expert witnesses so appointed are entitled to reasonable compensation in whatever sum the court may allow. The compensation thus fixed is payable from funds which may be provided by law in criminal cases and civil actions and proceedings involving just compensation under the fifth amendment. In other civil actions and proceedings the compensation shall be paid by the parties in such proportion and at such time as the court directs, and thereafter charged in like manner as other costs.

(c) **Disclosure of appointment.** In the exercise of its discretion, the court may authorize disclosure to the jury of the fact that the court appointed the expert witness.

(d) **Parties' experts of own selection.** Nothing in this rule limits the parties in calling expert witnesses of their own selection.

ARTICLE EIGHT: HEARSAY

Rule 801. Definitions

The following definitions apply under this article:

(a) **Statement.** A "statement" is (1) an oral or written assertion or (2) nonverbal conduct of a person, if it is intended by the person as an assertion.

(b) Declarant. A "declarant" is a person who makes a statement.

(c) Hearsay. "Hearsay" is a statement, other than one made by the declarant while testifying at the trial or hearing, offered in evidence to prove the truth of the matter asserted.

(d) Statements which are not hearsay. A statement is not hearsay if—

(1) Prior statement by witness. The declarant testifies at the trial or hearing and is subject to cross-examination concerning the statement, and the statement is (A) inconsistent with the declarant's testimony, and was given under oath subject to the penalty of perjury at a trial, hearing, or other proceeding, or in a deposition, or (B) consistent with the declarant's testimony and is offered to rebut an express or implied charge against the declarant of recent fabrication or improper influence or motive, or (C) one of identification of a person made after perceiving the person; or

(2) Admission by party-opponent. The statement is offered against a party and is (A) the party's own statement, in either an individual or a representative capacity or (B) a statement of which the party has manifested an adoption or belief in its truth, or (C) a statement by a person authorized by the party to make a statement concerning the subject, or (D) a statement by the party's agent or servant concerning a matter within the scope of the agency or employment, made during the existence of the relationship, or (E) a statement by a coconspirator of a party during the course and in furtherance of the conspiracy.

Rule 802. Hearsay Rule

Hearsay is not admissible except as provided by these rules or by other rules prescribed by the Supreme Court pursuant to statutory authority or by Act of Congress.

Rule 803. Hearsay Exceptions; Availability of Declarant Immaterial

The following are not excluded by the hearsay rule, even though the declarant is available as a witness:

(1) Present sense impression. A statement describing or explaining an event or condition made while the declarant was perceiving the event or condition, or immediately thereafter.

(2) Excited utterance. A statement relating to a startling event or condition made while the declarant was under the stress of excitement caused by the event or condition.

(3) **Then existing mental, emotional, or physical condition.** A statement of the declarant's then existing state of mind, emotion, sensation, or physical condition (such as intent, plan, motive, design, mental feeling, pain, and bodily health), but not including a statement of memory or belief to prove the fact remembered or believed unless it relates to the execution, revocation, identification, or terms of declarant's will.

(4) **Statements for purposes of medical diagnosis or treatment.** Statements made for purposes of medical diagnosis or treatment and describing medical history, or past or present symptoms, pain, or sensations, or the inception or general character of the cause or external source thereof insofar as reasonably pertinent to diagnosis or treatment.

(5) **Recorded recollection.** A memorandum or record concerning a matter about which a witness once had knowledge but now has insufficient recollection to enable the witness to testify fully and accurately, shown to have been made or adopted by the witness when the matter was fresh in the witness' memory and to reflect that knowledge correctly. If admitted, the memorandum or record may be read into evidence but may not itself be received as an exhibit unless offered by an adverse party.

(6) **Records of regularly conducted activity.** A memorandum, report, record, or data compilation, in any form, of acts, events, conditions, opinions, or diagnoses, made at or near the time by, or from information transmitted by, a person with knowledge, if kept in the course of a regularly conducted business activity, and if it was the regular practice of that business activity to make the memorandum, report, record, or data compilation, all as shown by the testimony of the custodian or other qualified witness, unless the source of information or the method or circumstances of preparation indicate lack of trustworthiness. The term "business" as used in this paragraph includes business, institution, association, profession, occupation, and calling of every kind, whether or not conducted for profit.

(7) **Absence of entry in records kept in accordance with the provisions of paragraph (6).** Evidence that a matter is not included in the memoranda, reports, records, or data compilations, in any form, kept in accordance with the provisions of paragraph (6), to prove the nonoccurrence or nonexistence of the matter, if the matter was of a kind of which a memorandum, report, record, or data compilation was regularly made and preserved, unless the sources of information or other circumstances indicate lack of trustworthiness.

(8) Public records and reports. Records, reports, statements, or data compilations, in any form, of public offices or agencies, setting forth (A) the activities of the office or agency, or (B) matters observed pursuant to duty imposed by law as to which matters there was a duty to report, excluding, however, in criminal cases matters observed by police officers and other law enforcement personnel, or (C) in civil actions and proceedings and against the Government in criminal cases, factual findings resulting from an investigation made pursuant to authority granted by law, unless the sources of information or other circumstances indicate lack of trustworthiness.

(9) Records of vital statistics. Records or data compilations, in any form, of births, fetal deaths, deaths, or marriages, if the report thereof was made to a public office pursuant to requirements of law.

(10) Absence of public record or entry. To prove the absence of a record, report, statement, or data compilation, in any form, or the nonoccurrence or nonexistence of a matter of which a record, report, statement, or data compilation, in any form, was regularly made and preserved by a public office or agency, evidence in the form of a certification in accordance with rule 902, or testimony, that diligent search failed to disclose the record, report, statement, or data compilation, or entry.

(11) Records of religious organizations. Statements of births, marriages, divorces, deaths, legitimacy, ancestry, relationship by blood or marriage, or other similar facts of personal or family history, contained in a regularly kept record of a religious organization.

(12) Marriage, baptismal, and similar certificates. Statements of fact contained in a certificate that the maker performed a marriage or other ceremony or administered a sacrament, made by a clergyman, public official, or other person authorized by the rules or practices of a religious organization or by law to perform the act certified, and purporting to have been issued at the time of the act or within a reasonable time thereafter.

(13) Family records. Statements of fact concerning personal or family history contained in family Bibles, genealogies, charts, engravings on rings, inscriptions on family portraits, engravings on urns, crypts, or tombstones, or the like.

(14) Records of documents affecting an interest in property. The record of a document purporting to establish or affect an interest in property, as proof of the content of the original recorded document and its execution and delivery by each person by whom it purports to have been executed, if the record is a record of a public office and an applicable statute authorizes the recording of documents of that kind in that office.

(15) Statements in documents affecting an interest in property. A statement contained in a document purporting to establish or affect an interest in property if the matter stated was relevant to the purpose of the document, unless dealings with the property since the document was made have been inconsistent with the truth of the statement or the purport of the document.

(16) Statements in ancient documents. Statements in a document in existence twenty years or more the authenticity of which is established.

(17) Market reports, commercial publications. Market quotations, tabulations, lists, directories, or other published compilations, generally used and relied upon by the public or by persons in particular occupations.

(18) Learned treatises. To the extent called to the attention of an expert witness upon cross-examination or relied upon by the expert witness in direct examination, statements contained in published treatises, periodicals, or pamphlets on a subject of history, medicine, or other science or art, established as a reliable authority by the testimony or admission of the witness or by other expert testimony or by judicial notice. If admitted, the statements may be read into evidence but may not be received as exhibits.

(19) Reputation concerning personal or family history. Reputation among members of a person's family by blood, adoption, or marriage, or among a person's associates, or in the community, concerning a person's birth, adoption, marriage, divorce, death, legitimacy, relationship by blood, adoption, or marriage, ancestry, or other similar fact of his personal or family history.

(20) Reputation concerning boundaries or general history. Reputation in a community, arising before the controversy, as to boundaries of or customs affecting lands in the community, and reputation as to events of general history important to the community or State or nation in which located.

(21) Reputation as to character. Reputation of a person's character among associates or in the community.

(22) **Judgment of previous conviction.** Evidence of a final judgment, entered after a trial or upon a plea of guilty (but not upon a plea of nolo contendere), adjudging a person guilty of a crime punishable by death or imprisonment in excess of one year, to prove any fact essential to sustain the judgment, but not including, when offered by the Government in a criminal prosecution for purposes other than impeachment, judgments against persons other than the accused. The pendency of an appeal may be shown but does not affect admissibility.

(23) **Judgment as to personal, family, or general history, or boundaries.** Judgments as proof of matters of personal family or general history, or boundaries, essential to the judgment, if the same would be provable by evidence of reputation.

(24) **Other exceptions.** A statement not specifically covered by any of the foregoing exceptions but having equivalent circumstantial guarantees of trustworthiness, if the court determines that (A) the statement is offered as evidence of a material fact; (B) the statement is more probative on the point for which it is offered than any other evidence which the proponent can procure through reasonable efforts; and (C) the general purposes of these rules and the interests of justice will best be served by admission of the statement into evidence. However, a statement may not be admitted under this exception unless the proponent of it makes known to the adverse party sufficiently in advance of the trial or hearing to provide the adverse party with a fair opportunity to prepare to meet it, the proponent's intention to offer the statement and the particulars of it, including the name and address of the declarant.

Rule 804. Hearsay Exceptions; Declarant Unavailable

(a) **Definition of unavailability.** "Unavailability as a witness" includes situations in which the declarant—

(1) is exempted by ruling of the court on the ground of privilege from testifying concerning the subject matter of the declarant's statement; or

(2) persists in refusing to testify concerning the subject matter of the declarant's statement despite an order of the court to do so; or

(3) testifies to a lack of memory of the subject matter of the declarant's statement; or

(4) is unable to be present or to testify at the hearing because of death or then existing physical or mental illness or infirmity; or

(5) is absent from the hearing and the proponent of statement has been unable to procure the declarant's attendance (or in the case of a hearsay exception under subdivision (b)(2), (3), or (4), the declarant's attendance or testimony) by process or other reasonable means.

A declarant is not unavailable as a witness if exemption, refusal. claim of lack of memory, inability, or absence is due to the procurement or wrongdoing of the proponent of a statement for the purpose of preventing the witness from attending or testifying.

(b) Hearsay exceptions. The following are not excluded by the hearsay rule if the declarant is unavailable as a witness:

(1) Former testimony. Testimony given as a witness at another hearing of the same or a different proceeding, or in a deposition taken in compliance with law in the course of the same or another proceeding, if the party against whom the testimony is now offered, or, in a civil action or proceeding, a predecessor in interest, had an opportunity and similar motive to develop the testimony by direct, cross, or redirect examination.

(2) Statement under belief of impending death. In a prosecution for homicide or in a civil action or proceeding, a statement made by a declarant while believing that the declarant's death was imminent, concerning the cause or circumstances of what the declarant believed to be his impending death.

(3) Statement against interest. A statement which was at the time of its making so far contrary to the declarant's pecuniary or proprietary interest, or so far tended to subject the declarant to civil or criminal liability, or to render invalid a claim by the declarant against another, that a reasonable person in the declarant's position would not have made the statement unless believing it to be true. A statement tending to expose the declarant to criminal liability and offered to exculpate the accused is not admissible unless corroborating circumstances clearly indicate the trustworthiness of the statement.

(4) Statement of personal or family history. (A) A statement concerning the declarant's own birth, adoption, marriage, divorce, legitimacy, relationship by blood, adoption, or marriage, ancestry, or other similar fact of personal or family history, even though declarant had no means of acquiring personal knowledge of the matter stated; or (B) a statement concerning the foregoing matters, and death also, of another person, if the declarant was related to the other by blood, adoption, or marriage or was so intimately associated with the other's family as to be likely to have accurate information concerning the matter declared.

(5) Other exceptions. A statement not specifically covered by any of the foregoing exceptions but having equivalent circumstantial guarantees of trustworthiness, if the court determines that (A) the statement is offered as evidence of a material fact; (B) the statement is more probative on the point for which it is offered than any other evidence which the proponent can procure through reasonable efforts; and (C) the general purposes of these rules and the interests of justice will best be served by admission of the statement into evidence. However, a statement may not be admitted under this exception unless the proponent of it makes known to the adverse party sufficiently in advance of the trial or hearing to provide the adverse party with a fair opportunity to prepare to meet it, the proponent's intention to offer the statement and the particulars of it, including the name and address of the declarant.

Rule 805.   Hearsay Within Hearsay

Hearsay included within hearsay is not excluded under the hearsay rule if each part of the combined statements conforms with an exception to the hearsay rule provided in these rules.

Rule 806.   Attacking and Supporting Credibility of Declarant

When a hearsay statement, or a statement defined in Rule 801(d)(2), (C), (D), or (E), has been admitted in evidence, the credibility of the declarant may be attacked, and if attacked may be supported, by any evidence which would be admissible for those purposes if declarant had testified as a witness. Evidence of a statement or conduct by the declarant at any time, inconsistent with the declarant's hearsay statement, is not subject to any requirement that the declarant may have been afforded an opportunity to deny or explain. If the party against whom a hearsay statement has been admitted calls the declarant as a witness, the party is entitled to examine the declarant on the statement as if under cross-examination.

ARTICLE NINE: AUTHENTICATION AND
IDENTIFICATION

Rule 901.   Requirement of Authentication or Identification

(a) General provision. The requirement of authentication or identification as a condition precedent to admissibility is satisfied by evidence sufficient to support a finding that the matter in question is what its proponent claims.

(b) Illustrations. By way of illustration only, and not by way of limitation, the following are examples of authentication or identification conforming with the requirements of this rule:

(1) Testimony of witness with knowledge. Testimony that a matter is what it is claimed to be.

(2) Nonexpert opinion on handwriting. Nonexpert opinion as to the genuineness of handwriting, based upon familiarity not acquired for purposes of the litigation.

(3) Comparison by trier or expert witness. Comparison by the trier of fact or by expert witnesses with specimens which have been authenticated.

(4) Distinctive characteristics and the like. Appearance, contents, substance, internal patterns, or other distinctive characteristics, taken in conjunction with circumstances.

(5) Voice identification. Identification of a voice, whether heard firsthand or through mechanical or electronic transmission or recording, by opinion based upon hearing the voice at any time under circumstances connecting it with the alleged speaker.

(6) Telephone conversations. Telephone conversations, by evidence that a call was made to the number assigned at the time by the telephone company to a particular person or business, if (A) in the case of a person, circumstances, including self-identification, show the person answering to be the one called, or (B) in the case of a business, the call was made to a place of business and the conversation related to business reasonably transacted over the telephone.

(7) Public records or reports. Evidence that a writing authorized by law to be recorded or filed and in fact recorded or filed in a public office, or a purported public record, report, statement, or data compilation, in any form, is from the public office where items of this nature are kept.

(8) Ancient documents or data compilation. Evidence that a document or data compilation, in any form, (A) is in such condition as to create no suspicion concerning its authenticity, (B) was in a place where it, if authentic, would likely be, and (C) has been in existence 20 years or more at the time it is offered.

(9) Process or system. Evidence describing a process or system used to produce a result and showing that the process or system produces an accurate result.

(10) Methods provided by statute or rule. Any method of authentication or identification provided by Act of Congress or by other rules prescribed by the Supreme Court pursuant to statutory authority.

Rule 902.   Self-Authentication

Extrinsic evidence of authenticity as a condition precedent to admissibility is not required with respect to the following:

(1) Domestic public documents under seal. A document bearing a seal purporting to be that of the United States, or of any State, district, Commonwealth, territory, or insular possession thereof, or the Panama Canal Zone, or the Trust Territory of the Pacific Islands, or of a political subdivision, department, officer, or agency thereof, and a signature purporting to be an attestation or execution.

(2) Domestic public documents not under seal. A document purporting to bear the signature in the official capacity of an officer or employee of any entity included in paragraph (1) hereof, having no seal, if a public officer having a seal and having official duties in the district or political subdivision of the officer or employee certifies under seal that the signer has the official capacity and that the signature is genuine.

(3) Foreign public documents. A document purporting to be executed or attested in an official capacity by a person authorized by the laws of a foreign country to make the execution or attestation, and accompanied by a final certification as to the genuineness of the signature and official position (A) of the executing or attesting person, or (B) of any foreign official whose certificate of genuineness of signature and official position relates to the execution or attestation or is in a chain of certificates of genuineness of signature and official position relating to the execution or attestation. A final certification may be made by a secretary of embassy or legation, consul general, consul, vice consul, or consular agent of the United States, or a diplomatic or consular official of the foreign country assigned or accredited to the United States. If reasonable opportunity has been given to all parties to investigate the authenticity and accuracy of official documents, the court may, for good cause shown, order that they be treated as presumptively authentic without final certification or permit them to be evidenced by an attested summary with or without final certification.

(4) Certified copies of public records. A copy of an official record or report or entry therein, or of a document authorized by law to be recorded or filed and actually recorded or filed in a public office, including data compilations in any form, certified as correct by the custodian or other person authorized to make the certification, by certificate complying with paragraph (1), (2), or (3) of this rule or complying with any Act of Congress or rule prescribed by the Supreme Court pursuant to statutory authority.

(5) Official publications. Books, pamphlets, or other publications purporting to be issued by public authority.

(6) Newspapers and periodicals. Printed materials purporting to be newspapers or periodicals.

(7) Trade inscriptions and the like. Inscriptions, signs, tags, or labels purporting to have been affixed in the course of business and indicating ownership, control, or origin.

(8) Acknowledged documents. Documents accompanied by a certificate of acknowledgment executed in the manner provided by law by a notary public or other officer authorized by law to take acknowledgments.

(9) Commercial paper and related documents. Commercial paper, signatures thereon, and documents relating thereto to the extent provided by general commercial law.

(10) Presumptions under Acts of Congress. Any signature, document, or other matter declared by Act of Congress to be presumptively or prima facie genuine or authentic.

Rule 903. Subscribing Witness' Testimony Unnecessary

The testimony of a subscribing witness is not necessary to authenticate a writing unless required by the laws of the jurisdiction whose laws govern the validity of the writing.

ARTICLE TEN: CONTENTS OF WRITINGS, RECORDINGS, AND PHOTOGRAPHS

Rule 1001. Definitions

For purposes of this article the following definitions are applicable:

(1) Writings and recordings. "Writings" and "recordings" consist of letters, words, or numbers, or their equivalent, set down by handwriting, typewriting, printing, photostating, photographing, magnetic impulse, mechanical or electronic recording, or other form of data compilation.

(2) **Photographs.** "Photographs" include still photographs, X-ray films, video tapes, and motion pictures.

(3) **Original.** An "original" of a writing or recording is the writing or recording itself or any counterpart intended to have the same effect by a person executing or issuing it. An "original" of a photograph includes the negative or any print therefrom. If data are stored in a computer or similar device, any printout or other output readable by sight, shown to reflect the data accurately, is an "original".

(4) **Duplicate.** A "duplicate" is a counterpart produced by the same impression as the original, or from the same matrix, or by means of photography, including enlargements and miniatures, or by mechanical or electronic re-recording, or by chemical reproduction, or by other equivalent technique which accurately reproduces the original.

Rule 1002. Requirement of Original

To prove the content of a writing, recording, or photograph, the original writing, recording, or photograph is required, except as otherwise provided in these rules or by Act of Congress.

Rule 1003. Admissibility of Duplicates

A duplicate is admissible to the same extent as an original unless (1) a genuine question is raised as to the authenticity of the original or (2) in the circumstances it would be unfair to admit the duplicate in lieu of the original.

Rule 1004. Admissibility of Other Evidence of Contents

The original is not required, and other evidence of the contents of a writing, recording, or photograph is admissible if—

(1) **Originals lost or destroyed.** All originals are lost or have been destroyed, unless the proponent lost or destroyed them in bad faith; or

(2) **Original not obtainable.** No original can he obtained by any available judicial process or procedure; or

(3) **Original in possession of opponent.** At a time when an original was under the control of the party against whom offered, that party was put on notice, by the pleadings or otherwise, that the contents would be a subject of proof at the hearing, and that party does not produce the original at the hearing; or

(4) Collateral matters. The writing, recording, or photograph is not closely related to a controlling issue.

Rule 1005. Public Records

The contents of an official record, or of a document authorized to be recorded or filed and actually recorded or filed, including data compilations in any form, if otherwise admissible, may be proved by copy, certified as correct in accordance with rule 902 or testified to be correct by a witness who has compared it with the original. If a copy which complies with the foregoing cannot be obtained by the exercise of reasonable diligence, then other evidence of the contents may be given.

Rule 1006. Summaries

The contents of voluminous writings, recordings, or photographs which cannot conveniently be examined in court may be presented in the form of a chart, summary, or calculation. The originals, or duplicates, shall be made available for examination or copying, or both, by other parties at reasonable time and place. The court may order that they be produced in court.

Rule 1007. Testimony or Written Admission of Party

Contents of writings, recordings, or photographs may be proved by the testimony or deposition of the party against whom offered or by that party's written admission, without accounting for the nonproduction of the original.

Rule 1008. Functions of Court and Jury

When the admissibility of other evidence of contents of writings, recordings, or photographs under these rules depends upon the fulfillment of a condition of fact, the question whether the condition has been fulfilled is ordinarily for the court to determine in accordance with the provisions of rule 104. However, when an issue is raised (a) whether the asserted writing ever existed, or (b) whether another writing, recording, or photograph produced at the trial is the original, or (c) whether other evidence of contents correctly reflects the contents, the issue is for the trier of fact to determine as in the case of other issues of fact.

ARTICLE ELEVEN: MISCELLANEOUS RULES

Rule 1101. Applicability of Rules

(a) **Courts and magistrates.** These rules apply to the United States district courts, the United States bankruptcy courts, the

District Court of Guam, the District Court of the Virgin Islands, the District Court for the Northern Mariana Islands, the United States courts of appeals, the United States Claims Court, and to United States bankruptcy judges and United States magistrates, in the actions, cases, and proceedings and to the extent hereinafter set forth. The terms "judge" and "court" in these rules include United States bankruptcy judges and United States magistrates.

(b) Proceedings generally. These rules apply generally to civil actions and proceedings, including admiralty and maritime cases, to criminal cases and proceedings, to contempt proceedings except those in which the court may act summarily, and to proceedings and cases under title 11, United States Code.

(c) Rule of privilege. The rule with respect to privileges applies at all stages of all actions, cases, and proceedings.

(d) Rules inapplicable. The rules (other than with respect to privileges) do not apply in the following situations:

(1) Preliminary questions of fact. The determination of questions of fact preliminary to admissibility of evidence when the issue is to be determined by the court under rule 104.

(2) Grand jury. Proceedings before grand juries.

(3) Miscellaneous proceedings. Proceedings for extradition or rendition; preliminary examinations in criminal cases; sentencing, or granting or revoking probation; issuance of warrants for arrest, criminal summonses, and search warrants; and proceedings with respect to release on bail or otherwise.

(e) Rules applicable in part. In the following proceedings these rules apply to the extent that matters of evidence are not provided for in the statutes which govern procedure therein or in other rules prescribed by the Supreme Court pursuant to statutory authority: the trial of minor and petty offenses by United States magistrates; review of agency actions when the facts are subject to trial de novo under section 706(2)(F) of title 5, United States Code; review of orders of the Secretary of Agriculture under section 2 of the Act entitled "An Act to authorize association of producers of agricultural products" approved February 18, 1922 (7 U.S.C. 292), and under sections 6 and 7(c) of the Perishable Agricultural Commodities Act, 1930 (7 U.S.C. 499f, 499g(c)); naturalization and revocation of naturalization under sections 310–318 of the Immigration and Nationality Act (8 U.S.C. 1421–1429); prize proceedings in admiralty under sections 7651–7681 of title 10, United States

Code; review of orders of the Secretary of the Interior under section 2 of the Act entitled "An Act authorizing associations of producers of aquatic products" approved June 25, 1934 (15 U.S.C. 522); review of orders of petroleum control boards under section 5 of the Act entitled "An Act to regulate interstate and foreign commerce in petroleum and its products by prohibiting the shipment in such commerce of petroleum and its products produced in violation of State law, and for other purposes", approved February 22, 1935 (15 U.S.C. 715d); actions for fines, penalties, or forfeitures under part V of title IV of the Tariff Act of 1930 (19 U.S.C. 1581–1624), or under the Anti-Smuggling Act (19 U.S.C. 1701–1711); criminal libel for condemnation, exclusion of imports, or other proceedings under the Federal Food, Drug, and Cosmetic Act (21 U.S.C. 301–392); disputes between seamen under sections 4079, 4080, and 4081 of the Revised Statutes (22 U.S.C. 256–258); habeas corpus under sections 2241–2254 of title 28, United States Code; motions to vacate, set aside or correct sentence under section 2255 of title 28, United States Code; actions for penalties for refusal to transport destitute seamen under section 4578 of the Revised Statutes (46 U.S.C. 679); actions against the United States under the Act entitled "An Act authorizing suits against the United States in admiralty for damage caused by and salvage service rendered to public vessels belonging to the United States, and for other purposes", approved March 3, 1925 (46 U.S.C. 781–790), as implemented by section 7730 of title 10, United States Code.

Rule 1102. Amendments

Amendments to the Federal Rules of Evidence may be made as provided in section 2076 of title 28 of the United States Code.

Rule 1103. Title

These rules may be known and cited as the Federal Rules of Evidence.

INDEX

Q

R

S

T

WHERE TO FIND FEDERAL RULES OF EVIDENCE IN THIS BOOK

Federal Rule No.	Subject of Rule	Section of This Book
803	Hearsay Exceptions; Availability of Declarant Immaterial	8.09
	1. Present Sense Impression	8.10
	2. Excited Utterance	8.10
	3. Then-Existing Mental, Emotional, or Physical Condition	8.11
	4. Statement for Purposes of Medical Diagnosis or Treatment	8.11
	5. Recorded Recollection	8.12
	6. Records of Regularly Conducted Activity	8.12
	7. Absence of Entry in Records Kept in Accordance with Provisions of Paragraph (6)	8.12
	8. Public Records and Reports	8.13
	9. Records of Vital Statistics	8.13
	10. Absence of Public Record or Entry	8.13
	11. Records of Religious Organizations	8.14
	12. Marriage, Baptismal, and Similar Certificates	8.14
	13. Family Records	8.14
	14. Records of Documents Affecting an Interest in Property	8.15
	15. Statements in Documents Affecting an Interest in Property	8.15
	16. Statements in Ancient Documents	8.15
	17. Market Reports; Commercial Publications	8.16
	18. Learned Treatises	8.16
	19. Reputation Concerning Personal or Family History	8.17
	20. Reputation Concerning Boundaries or General History	8.17
	21. Reputation as to Character	8.17
	22. Judgment of Previous Conviction	8.18
	23. Judgment as to Personal, Family, or General History, or Boundaries	8.18